RAYMOND KLIBANSKY

RAYMOND KLIBANSKY

A LIFE IN PHILOSOPHY

CONVERSATIONS WITH

GEORGES LEROUX

TRANSLATED BY PETER FELDSTEIN

McGILL-QUEEN'S UNIVERSITY PRESS

Montreal & Kingston | London | Chicago

First published in French as *Le Philosophe et la Mémoire du siècle* by Raymond Klibansky

ISBN 978-0-2280-1437-9 (cloth)
ISBN 978-0-2280-1541-3 (ePDF)
ISBN 978-0-2280-2653-2 (ePUB)

Legal deposit third quarter 2025
Bibliothèque et Archives nationales du Québec

Printed in Canada on acid-free paper that is 100% ancient-forest-free, containing 100% sustainable, recycled fibre, and processed chlorine-free.

We acknowledge the support of the Canada Council for the Arts.
Nous remercions le Conseil des arts du Canada de son soutien.

McGill-Queen's University Press in Montreal is on land which long served as a site of meeting and exchange amongst Indigenous Peoples, including the Haudenosaunee and Anishinabeg nations. In Kingston it is situated on the territory of the Haudenosaunee and Anishinaabek. We acknowledge and thank the diverse Indigenous Peoples whose footsteps have marked these territories on which peoples of the world now gather.

LIBRARY AND ARCHIVES CANADA CATALOGUING IN PUBLICATION

Title: Raymond Klibansky: a life in philosophy / conversations with Georges Leroux; translated by Peter Feldstein.
Other titles: Philosophe et la mémoire du siècle. English
Names: Klibansky, Raymond, 1905–2005, interviewee | Leroux, Georges, interviewer | Feldstein, Peter, 1962– translator
Description: Translation of: Le philosophe et la mémoire du siècle. | Includes bibliographical references and index.
Identifiers: Canadiana (print) 20250170310 | Canadiana (ebook) 20250173697 | ISBN 9780228014379 (hardcover) | ISBN 9780228015413 (PDF) | ISBN 9780228026532 (EPUB)
Subjects: LCSH: Klibansky, Raymond, 1905-2005—Interviews. | LCSH: Jewish philosophers—Québec (Province)—Montréal—Interviews. | LCSH: Philosophy, Modern—20th century. | LCSH: Liberty. | LCSH: Toleration. | LCSH: Europe—History—20th century. | LCGFT: Interviews.
Classification: LCC B995.K547 A513 2025 | DDC 191—dc23

This book was designed and typeset by Lara Minja in 11 pt Adobe Jenson Pro.
Copyediting by Jane McWhinney.

McGill-Queen's University Press
Suite 1720, 1010 Sherbrooke St West, Montreal, QC, H3A 2R7

Authorized safety representative in the EU: Mare Nostrum Group BV, Mauritskade 21D, 1091 GC Amsterdam, the Netherlands, gpsr@mare-nostrum.co.uk

CONTENTS

AN OUTSIDER'S FOREWORD *vii*
Alberto Manguel

ACKNOWLEDGMENTS *xi*

Raymond Klibansky:
Outline of an Intellectual Biography *3*
Georges Leroux

1 From Paris to Heidelberg: A Studious Youth *39*

2 Literary Heidelberg *69*

3 The German Masters: Eckhart and Cusanus *88*

4 Leaving Germany: From Heidelberg to Oxford *100*

5 London and the Fight against Nazism *112*

6 The Children of Saturn *139*

7 From Oxford to Montreal *151*

8 The Neoplatonic Tradition *169*

9 The English Masters and the Question of Tolerance *178*

10 The International Institute of Philosophy *195*

11 Jan Patočka *216*

Epilogue
Tolerance, Liberty, Philosophy *224*

NOTES *233*

WORKS BY AND ABOUT RAYMOND KLIBANSKY *267*

INDEX *277*

AN OUTSIDER'S FOREWORD

Alberto Manguel

It is a strange fact that, from the vantage point of the end of a person's life, that life seems to have traced a coherent and logical pattern. Upon looking back from the last page of any biography, its stepping-stones and chance happenings seem to form a well-plotted story in which personal and historical events as well as circumstantial meetings and strange occurrences acquire something of the nature of foreshadowing, and coalesce in a portrait of a protagonist who was never (nor could ever have been) quite aware of the adventurous path he or she was undertaking. Every moment of a person's life is passed at the end through a capricious sieve, and certain circumstances are discarded and forgotten, others rescued and set up as fundamental, in order to single out the three or four that give most meaning to a life lived. It seems to me that the case of Raymond Klibansky is in this sense exemplary, and that those essential circumstances are to be found in his books.

Spanning a good part of the twentieth century – as Klibansky witnessed the rise of the Third Reich and the catastrophic consequences of the Second World War, acquiring in the process the cumulative identities of academic intellectual, persecuted Jew, exiled European, and foreign resident in Canada, and finally being recognized as a luminary of the history of philosophy and philology – this intellectual biography (so clearly organized in the following dialogues by his student, and later colleague and friend Georges Leroux) serves as a model for the intelligent pursuit of truth.

There is something exhilarating about reading conversations between two intelligent people, or rather, conversations in which one intelligent person leads and structures the intelligent thoughts of another. As is shown in these pages, Raymond Klibansky possessed a superb mind: keen, precise, always curious, constantly probing in unexpected corners of the universal library for connections between ancient wisdom and modern tribulations. His curiosity seems to have been something of a system of thought in itself, akin to the Socratic method or Simone Weil's "education of attention." Through Klibansky's observations and recollections, the ordinary reader can discern an impartial encouragement of doubt and a series of cumulative epiphanies, directed both at the mazes of abstract ideas and at the evidence of moments lived. As a learned traveller through most of his century, Klibansky navigated the turbulent events of European politics, at times an active partisan, at times an enlightened observer, always a rational investigator of causes and effects. He concentrated on his intellectual talents, following the methods of his beloved Nicholas of Cusa, making use of conjectures and surmises as rational instruments in an attempt to reach an understanding of what is true. Klibansky concludes his conversations with an appeal against falsity or wilful misunderstanding. "Make no mistake," he tells Leroux. "We need what Nietzsche calls *Wahrhaftigkeit*, veracity, the power to become aware of the state of things."

Klibansky's *peregrinatio academica*, as aptly termed by Leroux, reveals a life of scholarship in constant counterpoint with political awareness. From his student days and early career in Germany to his years as an academic refugee in England and postwar appointments in Canada, his *Wahrhaftigkeit* would not allow him to be blind to political reality. "I saw so many terrible things I could do nothing about," he acknowledged in his last conversation with Leroux. "There was no act of will or intelligence on my part that could effect the slightest change." But, he adds, "I could observe." Perhaps in this attitude of critical observation Klibansky was echoing Nicholas of Cusa's notion, expressed in *De concordantia catholica*, of collective responsibility in relation to the conduct of those in positions of authority, *quando inutiliter administraret*, both as practical and ideological, *propter utilitatem*, expanding on the idea that governance stems from the "harmony and consent of the subjects" and hoping that they will elect authorities who will carry out the rule of law. "I could in some cases suggest an action or appeal to the authorities, during the war. But the power of each individual is so limited!" Faced with the atrocities of our time, Klibansky asks: "Why all this? If we identify with the search for the good, why is that search so impotent? We wonder how, in an orderly world, so much suffering can be possible."

One manifestation of this suffering is the state of the soul that the ancients, beginning with a fragment wrongly attributed to Aristotle, defined as melancholia, an innate humour evoked by the fifteenth-century Catalan poet Ausiàs March in his words: *"d'un ventre trist eixir m'ha fet Natura,"*[1] "Nature brought me forth from a melancholy womb." Much about melancholia is discussed in these conversations, and very appropriately, since the subject runs through most of Klibansky's work and finds its clearest expression in his collaboration with Fritz Saxl and Erwin Panofsky on their *Saturn* book. It was evident to Klibansky that melancholia did not refer to a single psychological or intellectual state, and that both positive and negative qualities were attributed to it. In Klibansky's own case, though he never says this in so many words, the state of melancholia was evinced by a reflective and creative interrogation, an introverted questioning of matters related to the (admittedly limited) possibilities of human understanding. "What meaning can melancholy still have after Auschwitz and Hiroshima," Klibansky asks, "after the systematic application of the most advanced techniques of mass destruction of human beings?"

The existence of evil in the world (as Leibniz maintained, likely following Nicholas of Cusa) stems from these limitations, and is the cause both of our unhappiness and of our optimistic belief that it can be overcome. And, as Klibansky asserts in these conversations, quoting Kant: "The melancholy condition is the one that appears to harmonize best with 'true and principled virtue.' To the melancholy person, 'all shackles, from the golden ones worn at court to the heavy irons of the galley-slave, are abominable.'" But Klibansky was far from condoning a refusal of all constraint, or assigning virtue to all those who feel constrained. His belief in intellectual freedom was matched by his confidence in dialogue and the importance of autocritical and thoughtful self-restraint. As he tells Leroux, it is in Nicholas of Cusa's notion of self-possession, as expressed in *De visione dei*, that he finds "the kernel of the doctrine of liberty."

George Steiner believed that an intelligent person thinks in quotations. The mind of a scholar is like his or her library, and Klibansky had an excellent collection, which Leroux says his students often wished to explore. "If only he had taken a phone call," Leroux wistfully muses, "I might have had the great pleasure of wandering the library's many aisles. That never happened, at least not to me." But Klibansky's readings spilled into his lessons, which Leroux describes as "slow and careful," comparing Klibansky's teaching to that of a lucid Platonic philosopher in the quest for *sophia*. "Lucidity, yes," Klibansky admits. "But it must not lead to nihilism. Just because the result of our efforts is often minimal, or even non-existent, that does not mean we should not make them."

I cannot think of a better rallying cry for our troubled times.

ALBERTO MANGUEL
Lisbon

ACKNOWLEDGMENTS

The starting point for these conversations was provided by a series of three radio broadcasts that I prepared in 1991 for Radio-Canada at the request of producer Jean-Charles Déziel, who was hosting a series titled "Sur les traces d'un maître." Later, with Radio-Canada cultural channel producer François Ismert (1946–2021), we did several radio interviews on the life of Raymond Klibansky, which were followed by a two-hour broadcast in 1995, sponsored by the Communauté des radios publiques de langue française and titled "Jan Patočka: la vie en vérité." The latter was produced with the participation of Paul Ricoeur and other philosophers as well as friends, family members, translators, and members of the Patočka community in Paris and Prague. We produced some additional broadcasts when Klibansky was awarded the Lessing Prize in Germany and the Nonino Prize in Italy.

Dr Ethel Groffier, Raymond Klibansky's wife, and I transcribed these interviews, and Raymond Klibansky reread the text; but he was reluctant to transform the result into an autobiography. So many things had been left unsaid! He was much more interested in others' experience than his own. In the end, he agreed to enrich the interviews by answering questions from some of his good friends, who took turns doing genial injury to his modesty. I am indebted in particular to Michèle Le Doeuff, professor of philosophy at the Université de Genève, for raising a number of questions on the theme of tolerance, and to Michel Bitbol, a theoretical physicist and research director at the Centre national de la recherche scientifique in Paris, for expanding the scope of our discussions on Klibansky's involvement in the Political Warfare Executive. Désirée Park, a good friend and professor of philosophy at Montreal's Concordia University, reminded me of certain noteworthy aspects of Klibansky's life in Montreal. There was also Nikolaus Halmer of the Austrian Broadcasting Corporation (ORF), who came to Montreal to meet Klibansky in connection with the German translation of these conversations, and with whom we discussed the importance of Patočka's thought and testimony. Lastly, I would like to pay tribute to my dear friend, the late Alain-Philippe Segonds (1942–2011), a specialist in the Platonic tradition and a seasoned editor of Proclus, who in 1998 hosted the first edition of our conversations at the offices of the Paris publisher Les Belles Lettres, of which he was then general manager. Segonds was intimately familiar with Klibansky's work and greatly admired him.

I would also like to thank François Ismert, a close friend and active participant in several memorable conversations with Raymond Klibansky. Since the initial publication of these conversations in French in 1998, I have had the opportunity to collaborate with the distinguished comparatist and Germanist Philippe Despoix of the Université de Montréal. Together, we oversaw a reprint of the 1964 English edition of *Saturn and Melancholy*, published in 2019 with considerable new material. I am grateful for all he taught me about Warburg's circle and many other subjects related to Klibansky's intellectual biography. In 2016 we collaborated on a French-language anthology of his major studies titled *Tradition antique et tolérance moderne*. In 2018, with Jillian Tomm and Éric Méchoulan, we published a collection of studies under the title *Raymond Klibansky and the Warburg Library Network*. Tomm has become a specialist in Raymond Klibansky's library over the years; I am very grateful for her help with all things Klibansky, in particular the bibliography included here. I also wish to express my gratitude to Petra Willim, who translated these conversations into German;[1] I learned a great deal from her scholarly notes.

In sum, these interviews relied on the friendly involvement of many people in gathering from Klibansky the material for this book. However, the book would not have been possible without the generous collaboration of Dr Ethel Groffier, emeritus researcher at the Paul-André Crépeau Centre for Private and Comparative Law (McGill University), who endorsed our project from the start. Herself the editor, with McGill University professor Michel Paradis, of a book of essays in honour of her late husband,[2] she spared no effort in ensuring that these interviews faithfully encapsulate the life and work of Raymond Klibansky. My deepest gratitude goes to her.

RAYMOND KLIBANSKY

RAYMOND KLIBANSKY

OUTLINE OF AN INTELLECTUAL BIOGRAPHY

Georges Leroux

In the conversations with Raymond Klibansky presented in this book, we sought to reconstruct his long *peregrinatio academica*, to use the phrase of the Renaissance humanists: the road that led him from one cultural capital to another – from Paris to Heidelberg to Hamburg, from Hamburg to Paris and London, from Oxford to Montreal – and also the side roads he followed into activities and engagements that are not the ordinary lot of intellectuals and scholars. We are here in the presence of an exceptionally full, well-lived life, in terms of the diversity of his research and the authenticity of his endeavours. Klibansky's whole oeuvre finds its source in the battles of his era, in which he was the furthest thing from a bystander; it of course reflects a deep groundedness not only in twentieth-century philosophy but also in the history of a century wracked by unspeakable violence, and in a striving for peace and tolerance in the midst of that violence. Klibansky remained unswerving in his belief that philosophy could make a contribution to this endeavour.

Were we to grasp how this groundedness was the source of Klibansky's international commitments, we might be better prepared to take on the intellectual tasks incumbent on us today. I had the privilege of being his student at the Université de Montréal's Institut d'études médiévales in the late 1960s, but much terrain had already been travelled by then. It was only later, as I read his works or conversed with him in his impressive library at McGill University, that I came to understand just who had been standing before us on those splendid late afternoons in autumn explaining Plato's *Timaeus*. When I myself embarked on studies in Greek philology and opted to specialize in Neoplatonism, I gained a renewed appreciation for his work, for on the path leading from Plotinus to Proclus, and from there to Meister Eckhart and Nicholas Cusanus, it was he who had placed the waymarks. Later still, when he asked me to contribute to the bibliographic work of the International Institute of Philosophy (IIP), I came to appreciate the extent of his commitment to fostering dialogue among traditions and cultures.

Thus, for example, I found myself standing with him, alongside Charles Taylor and Vianney Décarie, at the door of the Czechoslovakian consulate one winter morning in 1977. We had come on behalf of the philosophers of Canada to demand the release of the philosopher Jan Patočka, imprisoned for the third time in Prague for having endorsed Charter 77, a civic initiative for the defence of human rights. It was only one of many causes that Klibansky took up in an era when philosophers frequently found themselves on the front lines of struggles for freedom. His investment in the dialogue promoted by the IIP, of which he was president for several years, took him to where this struggle was waged.

A man of study as much as of action, and a man who combined the two in the numerous works on toleration that he published in the latter half of his life, Klibansky agreed to retrace with me, in these conversations, a life lived in a turbulent century. This was why, when choosing a subtitle for this book, I decided to present it as a testimonial to the philosophical fight for freedom and reason that had best characterized his life.

Klibansky's intellectual biography represents a complex itinerary, but several major segments can be discerned: early education in Heidelberg, with immersion in Weimar culture; study of the works of Nicholas Cusanus and Meister Eckhart; research into medieval Platonism and publication of the *Corpus Platonicum Medii Aevi* at the Warburg Institute in London; the literary and philosophical tradition of melancholy; the modern ideal of toleration, particularly in the work of John Locke; and finally, international engagement in the service of philosophy. This account leaves aside various complementary interests that readers can find in his ample bibliography.[1]

Born in Paris into a Jewish family from Frankfurt on 15 October 1905, Raymond Klibansky attended primary school in French in the 9th arrondissement. His father, Hermann, was a wine merchant who had settled in France. In 1914 the First World War forced the family to return to Germany, and Raymond was enrolled in the Goethe-Gymnasium in Frankfurt. In 1920, at the age of fifteen, he received his father's permission to attend Paul Geheeb's pioneering Odenwald School. The school was committed to a liberal, open-ended pedagogy and was held in high esteem by intellectuals such as Thomas Mann and Ernst Cassirer, who sent their children there. Klibansky was fond of quoting its motto, Pindar's "Become who you are." One of his report cards, found in the school archives and bearing Geheeb's personal remarks, reveals a disciplined, talented student. Culture was instilled by having the pupils read the great German authors, notably the poets Hölderlin and Goethe, but also the Greek and Roman poets and philosophers. In our conversations Klibansky pays tribute to this pedagogy of freedom, which he contrasted with the authoritarian tradition of Wilhelminian Germany.

From the early years of his university education, he found himself turning toward the humanities. After a short stay in Kiel, where he had the privilege of assisting the pioneering sociologist Ferdinand Tönnies, he moved to Heidelberg at the height of the Weimar era, and the city became his lifelong intellectual and spiritual home. Notable among his friends during this formative period were Walter Solmitz, whom he met again later at the home of Ernst Cassirer in Hamburg, and Lotte Labowsky, with whom he worked on the Neoplatonic corpus. He was not, however – apart from friendships with the literary scholar Friedrich Gundolf and the poet Karl Wolfskehl – close to the circle gathered around the poet Stefan George, whose influence was then reaching its zenith. He did acknowledge the literary importance of George's poetico-philosophical project, but its ideas also aroused deep resistance in him by contrast with those of the democratization and modernization movements then developing in Germany. Still, he could recite some of George's poems by heart. George wanted to bring about a new *Reich* founded on spiritual values; he expressed this ambition in flights of lyricism that gave rise to much ambiguity when Nazism took hold. Who was this charismatic poet whom George tasked with leading the people? Surely George himself, thought Klibansky.

In Heidelberg, close contact with masters such as the philosophers Heinrich Rickert and Karl Jaspers instilled profound republican convictions in Klibansky; by the same token, it distanced him from the pessimism that nurtured the fascism already pervading German culture.[2] His personal philosophical path seems beholden neither to Rickert's Kantian orientation nor to Jaspers's existential psychology, which was indebted to German *Lebensphilosophie*. Yet Klibansky remained close to Jaspers; he was often to acknowledge his deep debt to the older man's philosophy of existence and to his humanistic reflections on communication and freedom. Heidelberg was also the home of Max Weber, and Klibansky had the privilege of frequenting the circle of friends who would gather at the home of his widow, Marianne. As Klibansky wrote in an autobiographical account in 1991, Marianne warmly welcomed the young scholar and did much to speed his integration into Heidelberg literary society.

It was there that he became aware of Max Weber's interpretation of modernity and his critique of contemporary irrationalism. Heidelberg was one of the main centres of the German cultural revival, its intellectuals finding themselves obliged to choose their political camp.[3] There was no avoiding the debates about democracy and support for republican principles, or the question of whether the new social science was destined to replace philosophy. Very quickly, within the space of a generation, the Weberian ideal of "objectivity" had won out: sociology was not to reproduce the aporias of the speculative philosophy of history and culture by attempting to supplant it, and it *was* to pursue a scientific ideal subjected to the rigour of an established method. Most intellectuals thought the speculative tradition, once the glory of German intellectual life, was doomed. Weber's critique of subjectivity and his quest for a scientific ideal shorn of personal convictions left indelible traces in the mind of the young Klibansky, who often paid tribute to Weber later on.

The era also saw the publication of Martin Heidegger's *Being and Time*, its first part appearing in 1927. Indifferent to sociologists' debates over modernity, Heidegger had embarked on a critical enterprise founded on the new premises of phenomenology, whose development was in full swing. It may come as a surprise that, while many philosophers considered phenomenology a good match for the suffering of the postwar years, Klibansky never showed the slightest interest in it – nor in Husserl or Heidegger, whose writings he must have known. This silence may have been explainable, at least after 1934 when Klibansky was already in Britain, by the pervasive antisemitism to be found in the latter's writings. This formative period was instead dominated by his admiration for Jaspers, itself partaking of a philosophical choice largely conditioned by the theme of free will. As with many young people beginning their studies as the war ended and finding themselves immersed in Weimar culture, Klibansky's primary concern had to do with the extent to which people could intervene in history and slow the development of irrational forces.

Perhaps the most steadfastly expressed of Klibansky's lifelong convictions was the certainty that individuals are not in fact powerless; that not everything is determined by the structure of an epoch, by social and economic conditions. Marxism never had any hold over him. Nor did Oswald Spengler's *The Decline of the West*, written before the First World War and published in two volumes in 1918 and 1922. The book was strongly influenced by Nietzsche, from whom it derived its historical critique of democracy. To Klibansky, cultural pessimism of that sort was not an option. Spengler's book posited a meta-historical interpretation of civilizations, warning Germany of the dangers of the irrational. The book's doctrine of Faustian man became highly influential; with Germany defeated, its heroic tone took on an air of prophesy. Its worldview was centrally aligned with everything Klibansky disapproved of: the power of fate; intellectual prophetism; the putative mission of Prussian Germanism; authoritarian elitism; and a form of historicism utterly at odds with a quest for freedom.

In short, Klibansky's philosophical trajectory must above all be understood in terms of the decisive influence of Jaspers. In his existential philosophy (which he saw as surpassing the Neo-Kantians' attempts to renew the theory of knowledge), Klibansky perceived the values of freedom that were essential to him. Jaspers believed that the Hegelian enterprise of a history of mind was no longer relevant but that theoretical sociology would not replace it. His first major work, *Philosophy*, published in three volumes, dates from 1932, but there was also *Man in the Modern Age*, an essay written in 1929 when Klibansky was close to Jaspers at Heidelberg. Taking up the Hegelian concept of forms of consciousness, Jaspers stresses the importance of experience as the soil from which the mind grows and denounces the illusions of the Enlightenment.

He interprets the crisis of German culture as a spiritual crisis and does not entirely succeed in avoiding the temptation of an authoritarian critique of democracy – a position he would subsequently revise.

Klibansky was a constant and studious audience for Jaspers's teaching, alongside Hannah Arendt and Jeanne Hersch, disciples of the philosopher who came up briefly during our conversations. Above all, Klibansky appears to have retained his insistence on the concreteness of individual freedom. The Nazi regime, notoriously, deprived Jaspers of his university chair because of his marriage to Gertrud Mayer, a woman of Jewish heritage. This situation fostered enduring bonds between him and his Jewish students – bonds that would deepen as the regime's antisemitism made discrimination a feature of people's daily lives. Jaspers's ideas on the freedom of *Dasein*, on the necessity of conceptualizing existence (*Existenz*) as a fundamental concept, greatly influenced Klibansky at a critical moment in his life, as he confronted the consequences of the racial laws for himself and his family. One can only imagine the discussions that took place between him and Jaspers in the summer of 1933 as the newly appointed *Privatdozent* weighed his decision to leave Germany.[4]

Jaspers was also an admirable historian of ideas, one who wished to recapitulate the history of philosophy as a genealogy within which the present could be situated. In his research into the philosophical sources of concrete freedom, he had begun by turning to Nietzsche and Kierkegaard, whom he saw as thinkers of boundary situations, extremes. In his search for the foundations of individual liberty, he was then led to Eckhart and Cusanus, in many respects precursors of German idealism and bearers of a view of the individual as someone who carries on an authentic dialogue with the transcendent.[5] Jaspers supervised Arendt's 1929 thesis on the concept of love in St Augustine (submitted the same year as Klibansky's on Proclus, supervised by Ernst Hoffmann), and in his published correspondence with her, he discusses the need to strive for balance between the work of illuminating existence (*Existenzerhellung*) and that of searching for orientation (*Orientierung*). On this point, Eckhart's thought provided a strong foundation upon which to reconstruct a concept of subjectivity freed from the purely critical concerns of Neo-Kantianism. It was this position that attracted Klibansky, and no doubt also Arendt, whose thinking was close to that of Heidegger.

At Heidelberg, Klibansky embarked on his doctoral research with the Hellenist and historian of philosophy Ernst Hoffmann. What led him to choose Hoffmann? Undoubtedly – indeed certainly – his initial interest in Cusanus, whom Hoffmann had undertaken to publish after his stay with Cassirer in Hamburg. The publication of Cassirer's *Individuum und Kosmos in der Philosophie der Renaissance,* a book that concentrated on the ideas of Cusanus, was the main influence leading to this research program. Klibansky became closely associated with Hoffmann, as his earliest published work indicates. Together, starting in 1932, they produced editions of Cusanus, notably the treatise *De docta ignorantia,* which constituted the first volume of the *Opera omnia.* Here can be found the fundamental elements that were later to lead Klibansky to Eckhart. In particular, his work on Eckhart – and subsequently on the medieval Neoplatonic tradition that gave renascent humanism its model of humanity – flowed from his interest in Cusanus's mysticism and negative thinking, a central theme of the research undertaken with Hoffmann. What Klibansky was mainly searching for in these great texts were the pillars of a doctrine of freedom that could be pitted against the irrationalism of the interwar period. He soon became convinced of the need for an edition of Eckhart's Latin works, over and above the German sermons that had become popular and were often manipulated by the prevailing nationalist ideology. He garnered the support of the Heidelberg Academy and embarked on a collaboration with the Dominicans in Rome, who also wanted to produce such an edition. These projects, however, were hindered by the Nazi government, which was then attempting to co-opt Eckhart's thought on behalf of a totalitarian Germanic mysticism expressed in the post-Nietzschean ideal of the divine superman (*Übermensch*). The work was interrupted and Klibansky narrowly escaped the political police, soon going into exile like so many other Jewish scholars.

But before returning to his doctoral research in Heidelberg under Hoffmann's supervision, I wish to comment briefly on what seems to have been the most important academic year in the education of Raymond Klibansky, which was 1926–27. Ernst Cassirer, then on the faculty at Hamburg University, heard of him from his son Heinrich, a fellow student at Heidelberg, and invited him to undertake a research fellowship at the new university.

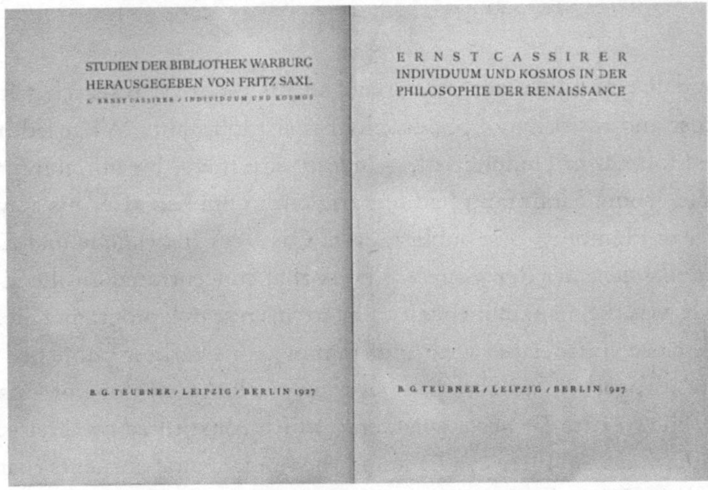
STUDIEN DER BIBLIOTHEK WARBURG
HERAUSGEGEBEN VON FRITZ SAXL
ERNST CASSIRER / INDIVIDUUM UND KOSMOS

B. G. TEUBNER / LEIPZIG / BERLIN 1927

ERNST CASSIRER
INDIVIDUUM UND KOSMOS IN DER
PHILOSOPHIE DER RENAISSANCE

B. G. TEUBNER / LEIPZIG / BERLIN 1927

I.1 / Ernst Cassirer, *Individuum und Kosmos in der Philosophie der Renaissance*, 1927. This book contains the edition of *De sapiente* by Charles de Bovelles prepared by Raymond Klibansky.

Klibansky went there in May 1926 and stayed until March 1927. Course registration sheets in his personal archives show that, among other courses, he took Cassirer's seminars on Kant and Greek philosophy. This trip had a very important consequence for his subsequent work: despite his youth, he was asked by Cassirer to prepare the first modern edition of the *Book of the Wise* (*Liber de sapiente*), a treatise by the philosopher Charles de Bovelles (1479–1566), upon which he had presumably already begun working with Hoffmann at Heidelberg. This edition appeared as an appendix to Cassirer's *Individuum und Kosmos in der Philosophie der Renaissance*, published in 1927 in honour of Aby Warburg (and in English translation in 1963 as *The Individual and the Cosmos in Renaissance Philosophy*). Principally devoted to Cusanus, this superlative book attests to Cassirer's decisive influence on Klibansky's research and to a rare intellectual and spiritual convergence between master and disciple, as evidenced by the memories recalled by Klibansky in an interview published in 1999, in the final years of his life.

Cassirer's interest in the pivotal period of the early Renaissance is worth dwelling on for a moment.[6] To certain thinkers and historians, the great Hegelian thesis concerning the role of philosophy as a recapitulative synthesis of culture finds a refutation of sorts in the Renaissance; Renaissance philosophy is argued to have remained in thrall to medieval scholastic schemes of thought and not to have attained its own philosophical synthesis. As an example of this position, Cassirer cites Petrarch's attack on scholastic philosophy as being symptomatic of the philosophical sclerosis of the era. As productive a time as it was for arts and literature, the Renaissance was said to have been a disappointment for philosophy. Jacob Burckhardt, considered a canonical interpreter of the Italian Renaissance as judged from his magnum opus of 1860, *The Civilization of the Renaissance in Italy*, ignored it entirely! Cassirer took a contrary position and proposed to give all the witnesses a new hearing. How, he asked, did the universality adumbrated by the Renaissance lead to the creation of a new galaxy of thought?

In coming up with his answer, he appealed forthrightly to Cusanus: first, as the disseminator of a theology of intellectual union with God that demanded a reconciliation with the intellectual effort of philosophy; and second as a theorist of history. For Cusanus, there was no way to grasp the divine essence other than through the *visio intellectualis*. His magisterial *De docta ignorantia* (1440) revived for modern readers the late medieval debate around the place of love in the union with principle. Cusanus espoused an asceticism rooted in mathematical and ontological ideas (the coincidence of opposites and the doctrine of the infinite), but nonetheless hesitated to renounce the logic of Aristotle. In Cassirer's view, Cusanus had been the first Western thinker wholeheartedly to take on the mantle of Platonism and to strive for a speculative synthesis with Aristotelian metaphysics. This synthesis undoubtedly flowed from the in-depth knowledge of the Greek texts that he had acquired at Padua; it would not have been possible, however, without his friendly relationship with Cardinal Bessarion, whose magnificent library, amassed while he served as the patriarch of Constantinople, was bequeathed to the Republic of Venice in 1468 and ultimately became the Biblioteca Marciana.

Through its breadth and richness, Cassirer's exposition attests to the importance of Cusanus's interpretation for the Neo-Kantians, who sought to recast the history of German thought within the framework of a synthesis of culture. Cassirer did not lay out the reasoning that had led him to this reading, but it may be summarized as follows. To him, Cusanus put forward the fullest synthesis of a realm in which, as he saw it, everything making up

NICOLAI DE CUSA
OPERA OMNIA
IUSSU ET AUCTORITATE
ACADEMIAE LITTERARUM
HEIDELBERGENSIS
AD CODICUM FIDEM EDITA
I
DE DOCTA IGNORANTIA
EDIDERUNT
ERNESTUS HOFFMANN
ET
RAYMUNDUS KLIBANSKY

LIPSIAE
IN AEDIBUS FELICIS MEINER
MCMXXXII

I.2 / Nicholas of Cusa, *De docta ignorantia*, *Opera Omnia*, vol. I, Leipzig, Meiner, 1932, edited by Ernst Hoffmann and Raymond Klibansky.

the world of symbolic forms came together. He believed this synthesis made it possible to bring a new philosophy of culture to fruition. From physics and cosmology to theodicy, Cusanus's work had striven for this synthesis. Given Cassirer's aim of developing a philosophy of symbolic forms, it thus became essential to study the Cusanian synthesis as a condensation of Renaissance ideas and to scrutinize its every nuance. Cassirer proposed summarizing this synthesis as a tension between individual and cosmos: what, fundamentally, was the Renaissance individual's new place within the machinery of the cosmos and before the forces of historical inevitability? Cassirer presents several facets of this question in his wide-ranging study, working from Cusanus to the latter's relationship with Italian thinkers, notably Leonardo da Vinci, Pico della Mirandola, and Giordano Bruno. One discerns in the work of these scholars an increasing secularization of medieval themes in the face of new knowledge of the physical world. Cassirer accords great importance to the theme of the readability of the world (depicted as God's book), a theme restated in Galileo and Kepler, who contrasted it with a mathematical system of meaning. Knowledge of nature must be unburdened of religious prejudices. The relationship between liberty and necessity and the dialectic between subject and object constituted the other components of Cassirer's enterprise. One can hardly fail to notice the importance that this philosophical narrative took on for the young Klibansky.

The publisher Felix Meiner took on the project of a modern critical edition of Cusanus's works to be edited by Ernst Hoffmann, who had been Cassirer's colleague and close friend, and had in 1930 published a book on Cusanus. Between 1916 and 1920, while in Berlin, Hoffmann had been an auditor of Cassirer's lectures and in 1922 had come as a professor (*Ordinarius*) to Heidelberg, where he occupied a chair in philosophy and pedagogy. He was an ardent student of ancient Platonism and the Platonic tradition, as attested by the Warburg Library's 1926 edition of his lecture "Platonism and the Middle Ages," given in 1924. Klibansky attended his seminar in 1927 and was assigned the task of presenting a report on the research; a description of Hoffmann's plan to publish Cusanus's works is found in a program submitted to the Heidelberg Academy in which he stresses the importance of making reliable scientific editions available. The academy accepted his work plan and put Hoffmann in charge of a scientific committee in which Klibansky participated as a collaborator (*Mitarbeiter*). It should be recalled that Klibansky was then only twenty-two and already showed exceptional talent for philology and paleography. Meiner's personal notes contain repeated praise for Klibansky's talents and his role in reconstructing the manuscript tradition. Klibansky's personal archives contain many traces of this multi-year collaboration.[7]

As mentioned above, Klibansky's first publication was an edition of Charles de Bovelles's *Book of the Wise*. Bovelles had been well versed in Cusanus and drew upon his work in writing this comprehensive text on the place of man in the world. Taking up the theme of microcosm *versus* macrocosm prominent in Renaissance art and particularly prevalent in depictions of the planetary system and discussions of geocentrism, Bovelles presents, in chapter 26 of his work, an image of man as mirror of the universe: "riddled beyond imagining with the arrows and emanations of the specific forms of the whole world, raining down on him from all sides." Bovelles's work is heir to the doctrine of astrological influences and a hymn to the perfect, sublime human creature, "convergence and end of all discernible things."[8] How Klibansky came to work on this then little-known text lacking a critical edition, it is hard to say; one imagines that he had discovered it at Heidelberg in Hoffmann's seminar or while doing preliminary work for the Cusanus edition. In any case, it seems unlikely that he accomplished this substantial work exclusively during his stay at the Kulturwissenschaftliche Bibliothek Warburg founded by Aby Warburg in Hamburg.

Cassirer's invitation thus takes on fundamental importance, for he gave impetus to the project of publishing a critical edition of Cusanus that would occupy Klibansky for the next ten years. An essential task here would be to clarify the relationship between Cassirer and Hoffmann, given that, when Klibansky left Hamburg to return to Heidelberg, where he finished his thesis on Proclus, he was to become enduringly involved in Hoffmann's research on Cusanus. The proof can be found in the précis of the curriculum vitae (*Lebenslauf*) that he produced later as part of his application for *Habilitation*. Interest in Cusanus, present in German culture since the eighteenth century, had subsequently been taken up by three eminent philosophers linked to Neo-Kantianism: Hermann Cohen, Heinrich Rickert, and Ernst Cassirer. The *Opera omnia* publication project can be considered a direct heir to this tradition.

In the research program that he submitted to the Warburg Institute and published in 1939, Klibansky demonstrated the continuity of the humanist Platonic tradition from the great figure of the philosopher Proclus (412–485), among the last scholarchs of the Academy of Athens, to whom he had devoted his thesis in 1929, all the way through the Middle Ages. Klibansky had, as it happens, found in Cusanus's library the Latin translation of one of the most important texts of late antiquity: Proclus's voluminous commentary on Plato's *Parmenides*. Prior to this discovery, it had been unclear whether this text had been known in its entirety during the Middle Ages. This Latin translation, due to William of Moerbeke (1215–1286), the famous Flemish translator and correspondent of Thomas Aquinas, was preserved in a fifteenth-century manuscript by Cusanus (Codex Cusanus 186) and contains a more complete text than the one found in the Greek manuscripts. In particular, it contains the final part of book VII, the conclusion to the commentary, which had been presumed lost. Klibansky's exceptional discovery filled out the scholarly picture of Proclus's commentary, forming an essential link in the chain along which Greek Platonism was transmitted.

And so Klibansky turned to Proclus from the earliest days of his research on Cusanus, who had identified the Greek master as the source of the doctrine of negative theology. His thesis was published in 1929 as part of a series titled "Cusanus Studien," and the study of Proclus is only a part of it, as he made a point of specifying in his application for *Habilitation*. The Latin manuscript that had belonged to Cusanus is annotated in the margin with a large number of the cardinal's comments, indicating that he worked on the text continually over the years. As his own philosophy illustrates, he had derived from this text various aspects of his thinking on the infinite One and the fundaments of negative theology as interpreted from Plato. In short, not only had Klibansky discovered an essential source of Cusanus's thought: he had also helped clarify the continuity between Neoplatonism and German idealism, thus reconstructing what Hegel, a great reader of Proclus, called a "history of the mind." He brought to light a deeply significant and fundamental link between these two bodies of thought.

This work led Klibansky to the major project of the *Corpus platonicum*, presented later at the Warburg Institute in London in an attempt to restore the entire chain leading from Platonism to Hegel. The corpus was divided into two series, *Plato Latinus* and *Plato Arabus*, thus accounting for the entire known medieval Neoplatonic tradition. In seeking to show that the Aristotelian tradition was neither the only tradition nor even the dominant one, Klibansky's first task was to shed light on the persistence of Platonism from the end of the imperial philosophical schools to the first Renaissance thinkers. The breadth of this program mandated the collaboration of a large number of scholars. As he embarked on it, and while pursuing research on Apuleius at the Vatican Library, he discovered in a manuscript (Reg. Lat. 1572) an anonymous summary of Neoplatonic philosophy to which he gave the title *Summarium librorum platonicorum*. He prepared it for publication, including an introduction, an index of sources, and a wealth of notes, but the work remains unpublished.

The year 1929 saw the publication, in collaboration with Hoffman, of the first volume of Cusanus's sermons. In 1932, again with Hoffman, Klibansky prepared an initial volume of Cusanus's works which contained his celebrated treatise on learned ignorance, *De docta ignorantia*. In a prospectus distributed in 1932 by Felix Meiner, the publication plan for the complete works in fourteen volumes was presented to subscribers as being slated for completion in 1939, the five-hundredth anniversary of the treatise. This immense project was to demand many years of work. The first two volumes of the Latin works were published, with Latin commentary by Klibansky, in 1932 and 1934. This work was hailed by critics, including the great medievalist Kurt Flasch, who wrote: "Working from hundreds of precise indications, Raymond Klibansky has shown how Nicolaus Cusanus was an heir to the tradition and how his work was then disseminated in the modern period, leading to many productive developments … Klibansky had previously brought to light the link between the thought of Cusanus and that of Eckhart. No one before him has contributed as much to knowledge of these two philosophers."[9] This monumental edition, begun in 1927 under the general direction of Hoffmann, was finally completed by the Heidelberg Academy of Sciences and Humanities in 2007; it can be considered the most direct legacy of Klibansky's efforts in the service of Cusanian thought.[10]

The edition of Meister Eckhart's works met a different fate, finding itself ensnared in politics. Alfred Rosenberg, the theoretician of Nazism, in his *The Myth of the Twentieth Century*, had presented the great master of Rhenish mysticism as a precursor to a flamboyant German mystic tradition. Yet one could, by referring to the Latin works of Cusanus rediscovered in Germany in 1886, show that medieval Jewish sources such as the philosopher Maimonides had also influenced him. Eckhart had taken from Maimonides a desire to reconcile philosophy with religion through a philosophical interpretation of *Revelation*; to wit, by positing that the discoveries of science and philosophy could not contradict the verities of the faith and then interpreting the biblical texts with adherence to this principle. Klibansky's project of publishing scholarly editions of these texts and, in particular, identifying their sources was seen as a political act in that it flatly contradicted the Nazi conception of Eckhart's ideas. The edition, already in progress, was interrupted because a group of party-aligned scholars led by Erich Seeberg had undertaken a separate edition. Seeberg, a Protestant theologian committed to promoting Nazism, had been appointed director of the Eckhart Commission of the Emergency Association of German Science (*Notgemeinschaft der deutschen Wissenschaft*) and put multiple obstacles in the way of Klibansky's research.

In July 1932, after giving his inaugural lecture (*Antrittsvorlesung*), Klibansky received his *Habilitation* (*Venia legendi*) from Heidelberg University. His unpublished thesis consisted of a study of Bernard and

Thierry of Chartres, accompanied by a substantial compendium of texts. This study demonstrated both his knowledge of twelfth-century thought and his desire to highlight the tradition of the *Timaeus* in the period of the first schools. The full importance of the connections between this research on medieval Platonism and the Proclean tradition is revealed when one recalls that the two most important thinkers in the medieval development of "Neoplatonism" were Eckhart and Cusanus, both heirs to Proclus's philosophical theology. Both also figure among the scholars who clearly influenced Hegel – Eckhart directly, Cusanus indirectly, via Giordano Bruno and Johann Georg Hamann. As of this period of Klibansky's early works, spanning 1927 to 1939, the importance of tradition and heritage impressed itself on him as the central concept in historical and philosophical study. With deep loyalty to Cassirer, Klibansky devoted himself to tradition for the hope it held out and for its resistance to the dominant tendency of 1930s German culture to turn a blind eye to inconvenient truths. As to asking which of the three great masters with whom Raymond Klibansky had the good fortune and privilege to study during his formative years – Karl Jaspers, Ernst Hoffmann, and Ernst Cassirer – had the greatest influence on him, the answer would have to emphasize the particular philosophical influence of each. Jaspers certainly made a deep imprint on Klibansky's lifelong belief in the paramount value of liberty; Hoffmann, the master historian, instilled in him ideals of philological rigour that were to remain central to his research into the Platonic tradition; but it was Cassirer, I would suggest, whose influence was the most decisive, for it was Cassirer's synthesis that showed how philosophy could encompass history and find meaning in the evolution of culture.

~

Klibansky's year in Hamburg was certainly the most decisive year in the formative period of his life. Notably, his encounter with Cassirer was an opportunity to immerse himself in Kant, on whom Cassirer taught a full-year course. It was also a chance for an unexpected collaboration on the metaphysical themes of Renaissance philosophy with which he was already occupied. Most important, it was an opportunity to enter the circle of Aby Warburg. Thanks to the friendship of Cassirer, a pillar of the group,

Klibansky was introduced into the community of scholars associated with the work of the Kulturwissenchaftliche Bibliothek that Warburg, a historian specializing in Renaissance art and culture, had founded several years earlier in Hamburg. Under the aegis of Mnemosyne, the Greek muse of memory, this rich library functioned as a haven for multidisciplinary work on art, literature, and history. Klibansky was invited to collaborate with the librarian Gertrud Bing on organizing the philosophy and classics sections.[11] It was here that he made the acquaintance of Fritz Saxl, who succeeded Warburg as director of the institution in 1929.

Saxl was a respected historian of medieval art and a specialist in astrological manuscripts who had co-authored, with Erwin Panofsky, a study of Dürer's engraving *Melencolia I* in 1923. Saxl was influenced by Warburg's method and devoted himself to the work that Panofsky had begun. Klibansky was invited to work with them, and their collaboration ultimately resulted in the co-authored volume *Saturn and Melancholy*. Klibansky's contribution to a reworking of the first edition soon proved essential, and the work then continued on a much broader basis. With this book, the creative and transformative aspects of tradition in his research came to the fore, and the results of his collaboration can be seen in the book's new philosophical sections, which gave the iconographic studies the historical context they had hitherto lacked. The tradition that had been the bearer of the ancient theme showed itself to be inseparably iconographic and philosophical.

Warburg's method is well known and has been the subject of extensive research. Like Cassirer a devotee of the Renaissance, Warburg sought to understand the resurgence of images and themes inherited from Greek paganism, viewing them as rooted in a collective unconscious composed of primitive, emotionally charged tropes that he called *Pathosformeln*. Warburg came to base his explanation of symbol formation on the conflict between individuals and a hostile nature, an idea also found in Cassirer's work on myth. Like Cassirer, Warburg believed that the development of human culture went hand in hand with liberation from the perceptible, with a form of detachment – and Cusanus's work emphasizing mathematical knowledge of the universe and God signalled the importance of the Renaissance as a crucial station along this path of intellectualization. Number, Warburg asserted, is the defeat of superstition: "In the transitional age of the early Renaissance, pagan-cosmological causality was defined in classicizing terms by means of the symbols of the gods; and these were approached in due proportion to their degree of saturation with human quality: from a religious daemon-worship at one extreme to a purely artistic and intellectual reinterpretation at the other."[12] This, he felt, was the meaning of Dürer's engraving *Melencolia I*, which was given pride of place in *Saturn and Melancholy*. He saw it above all as the bulwark that humanism offered against the fear inspired by Saturn – the instruments afforded by this intellectual tradition as a means of acquiring scientific and rational knowledge of the world. Panofsky later altered this interpretation to emphasize a sense of doubt and discouragement.

The common theme of Cassirer's and Warburg's research was thus that of a philosophy of culture, which they regarded as a purposive developmental process in which each epochal acquisition of knowledge rendered previous symbolic forms obsolete. Might one perhaps criticize their enterprise for falling prey to the idiosyncrasy of historicism? Cassirer remained sensitive to the diversity and multiplicity of meanings arising in history, but his fundamental concern was the search for an essential motif that manifested itself in each symbolic form, through each particular element of culture in history, and allowed for its identification. Did Warburg adopt Cassirer's Kantian premises? Nothing could be less certain: while Cassirer sought both a reconciliation and a unification, Warburg seems to have been most interested in the construction of constitutive, irreducible polarities such as the opposition between magic and science. When one considers Cassirer's epistemological program, its univocality appears to contradict Warburg's methodology, with its abiding sensitivity to diversity. In this sense, *The Individual and the Cosmos* offers an almost unilinear, teleological approach to modernity that diverges from Warburg's principles.

While Warburg sees in the Renaissance a conflict of unconscious forces, Cassirer posits it as an epoch of resolution and speculative synthesis. The Renaissance, he believed, offered the new language of modern knowledge that would triumph over these conflicts (finite/infinite, sensible/intelligible). In this it constituted the long-awaited successor to Neoplatonism and a return to strict dualism, which favoured mathematics. This speculative, ontological dualism is particularly evident in the work of Charles de Bovelles, in whom the young Klibansky took such a keen interest. Cassirer, in his chapter on magic and astrology, relies heavily on Warburg, conceding that the development was not perfectly linear but proceeded instead by fits and starts. Evoking the immanent progressive movement of thought, he shows that its empirical, temporal course corresponded only very imperfectly to this evolution of symbolic forms.

Cassirer, who had authored a thesis on Leibniz, postulates a progression leading to the author of the *Monadology* and to Hegel. Attentive to symbols in myth and religion, he arrives at the contention that symbols are the form in which thought fundamentally crystallizes; that they can only gravitate toward their own explanation by means of mediation. This is how Cassirer interprets the transition from the Middle Ages to the Renaissance; it is a theme that would fascinate Klibansky throughout his life, so much so that it inspired his research program on the history of Platonism. The relationship between this historical perspective and the particular form of Neo-Kantianism professed by Cassirer emerges when one examines the latter's theory of symbolic forms – a doctrine that would not, however, reappear in the work of Klibansky, who was to become a more traditional historian of ideas. Although primarily concerned with producing critical editions of texts that could serve to validate a rigorous interpretation of the history of culture, he nonetheless derived from Cassirer the importance of philology pursuing a *telos*, a purposeful end. Within this academic culture fascinated by the richness of the symbolic world, Klibansky was to acknowledge the overarching continuity through which the Platonic heritage of antiquity was transformed into a new cosmological and spiritual synthesis. In a passage that Klibansky liked to quote, Cassirer cites Warburg's evocation of a movement away from Alexandria and toward Athens, the source of his own rationalist program:

> In his work on Luther, Warburg gives this summary of the astrological ideas in the Renaissance: "We are in the age of Faust. The modern scientist tries to carve out an intellectual realm for reflection between himself and the object – a realm located somewhere between magical practice and cosmological mathematics. Athens once again wants to be liberated from Alexandria." This "liberation of Athens from Alexandria" was the common objective of the Renaissance theory of art and the theory of science. The "intellectual realm for reflection" was won back by recalling the Platonic *logos* and the Socratic-Platonic requirement of λόγον διδόναι.[13]

In 1936, with his friend the Scottish philosopher H.J. Paton (1887–1969), Klibansky published a magnificent *Festschrift* titled *Philosophy and History* on the occasion of Cassirer's sixtieth birthday. It is a paean to Weimar culture, and in particular to the striving of European intellectuals toward a theory of culture undergirded by this universal culture. It contains essays not only by the Warburg Library masters – Saxl and Panofsky, who contributed some of their best work, along with Edgar Wind – but also by great European scholars and philosophers such as Émile Bréhier, Étienne Gilson, Bernard Groethuysen, Giovanni Gentile, and Johann Huizinga. A particularly moving, posthumous contribution by Friedrich Gundolf (1880–1931) reminds us of the friendship that had marked Klibansky's youth and of the great writer's premature demise. Klibansky's deep bonds with Walter Solmitz are evoked in a closing bibliographical tribute to Cassirer, a superb piece of erudition and academic devotion. In an essay on the philosophical character of history, one of the few speculative philosophical texts that Klibansky ever published – most of his effort was devoted to the history of ideas and to advocating for freedom of conscience and tolerance – he pays tribute to Cassirer's Kantian ideal and his attempts to devise a logic of symbolic forms. The understanding of history, writes Klibansky, must rest upon the attribution of meaning. His criticism of Karl Mannheim's project of a sociology of knowledge shows that he was capable of taking sides,[14] but the most important point is his plea for an undying quest for objectivity and for relegating the symbolic forms of myth and magic to the past. This shows his profound fidelity to Cassirer, for surely no Warburgian would have expressed himself in this way.

It was on this horizon that Klibansky was subsequently to play a critical role. Tirelessly studying and elucidating each moment in the intellectual tradition leading from German idealism back to the Neoplatonism of late antiquity, he developed new methods to clarify this tradition and to restore to it, in art as in literature, the power to speak to the postwar era. How indeed were intolerance and the forces of the irrational that had appeared within Weimar culture to be fought? This was the question that gave rise, after Klibansky settled in Montreal, to his great projects on freedom and tolerance.

Forced to leave Hitler's Germany on account of their Jewish heritage, Panofsky, Saxl, and Klibansky carried on their research into the history of melancholy elsewhere. The German edition of what was to become *Saturn and Melancholy* was completed in London in 1939 but did not see publication because of the war, finally appearing in English in 1964, in London and New York.[15] Meanwhile, in 1948, Saxl had died in England, his place of refuge since 1933, while Panofsky had settled in the United States. Thanks to the support of Aby Warburg's younger brother Max, director of an important Hamburg bank,[16] the library was saved and transferred to London, where Klibansky too had sought asylum in 1933. As Saxl was later to confirm, the idea for this transfer had been Klibansky's.

Saturn and Melancholy is unanimously considered a masterpiece in the history of ideas, in terms of the originality of its methods and the staggering erudition to which it attests. Briefly summarized, what interested Panofsky, Saxl, and Klibansky in the history and interpretation of melancholy – even though they were working within an atmosphere pervaded by the post-romantic ethos of the Weimar era as it coalesced in the circle of Stefan George – was actually more closely related to Cassirer's investment in symbolic thought. His belief that the ideas of an epoch inhere not only in its philosophy but also in its myth and art was seminal for the project. This position, which now seems self-evident, was uncommon at the time when Panofsky was developing his methodology. From this standpoint, *Saturn and Melancholy* reveals itself as a far-reaching effort to give a historical basis to the conception of genius and individual destiny. In its analysis of Dürer's engraving, what the book reconstructs is the entire history, both medical and philosophical, of the concept of genius.

Interested by the symbols depicted in the engraving, Panofsky and Saxl had produced in their 1923 study an interpretation based on the evolution of the iconographic motif; for variations on the theme of the angel saddened by the vanity of knowledge, disheartened by the passage of time, have indeed arisen since antiquity. Klibansky, newly arrived in Hamburg, was critical of this approach, proposing instead a literary and philosophical approach that would fill out the scholarly understanding of this symbolic form. Klibansky made the text of Pseudo-Aristotle's *Problema* XXX.1 on genius – which begins, "Why is it that all those who have become eminent in philosophy or politics or poetry or the arts are clearly of an atrabilious temperament?"[17] – central to the analysis. In so doing, he sought to reconstruct the tradition undergirding this iconographic representation. He thus shed light on the conceptual content, *sensu* Cassirer, of the symbolic figure. In Warburg's model, this figure embodies the conflict between the mind and the turbulence of the world; whenever this conflict resurfaces in culture, as when it does so in philosophy, for example, the motif is reconfigured. Moreover, the function of the symbol is not to resolve the polarity from which it arises; all it can do is express the conflict and thereby make it apprehensible. Klibansky must certainly have recognized the fecundity of Warburg's approach, both for the history of ideas and for the philosophy of culture in general. How is one to think of the connections between art and philosophy if not by linking the history of the images with the conceptualizations used in expounding on them? These connections are not always visible; indeed, they are often unconscious, as are the connections between the demonology inherited from Plato's *Symposium* and the Renaissance ideas of magic, in Marsilio Ficino especially.

The historical conceptualization of melancholy begins with the ancient doctrine of the humours. Melancholy was first known as black bile, associated since high antiquity with death and gloom. However, the Hippocratic doctrines only take on their contour of meaning in Pseudo-Aristotle's *Problema* XXX.1, the most important document of the ancient period. This text, as we know, was the first to associate melancholy with uncommon beings, persons of genius, beings touched by greatness, philosophers, tragic heroes. The conjunction of genius and melancholy was to traverse the history of ideas and coalesce in Dürer's engraving. To follow its evolution, one must revisit the physiological literature of antiquity and the Middle Ages. Melancholy is one of the four humours associated with the cosmic elements and the divisions of time. That the humours held sway over human life and individual character was one of the beliefs most strongly rooted in ancient thought. In the system of temperaments, melancholy is linked to autumn, the earth, maturity. The system incorporates Pythagorean foundations by virtue of its veneration of the number four. The fourfold division of time (the seasons) and the elements (earth, water, fire, air) formed the framework in which the theory of humours could be developed.

The historical details are complex, inasmuch as it was difficult to distinguish the natural melancholic temperament from sickly melancholy. Here we see the applicability of *Problema* XXX.1, a text basing some of its argument on the importance of madness in tragedy and on Plato's concept of frenzy. These elements militated in favour of an idealization of the melancholic disposition, with the black humour (*melan-cholia*) being conceived of as the source of the noblest spiritual exaltation – Plato had, after all, considered it a divine gift. The connection was made in the natural philosophy of Aristotle's school, in which not only tragic heroes but all uncommon individuals, artists, philosophers, and poets, were melancholic. The spiritual singularity of this elect group stemmed from the influence of black bile over the disposition of their souls. Where Plato had offered only a myth of genius, Aristotle's natural philosophy provided a scientific explanation. Genius was to be identified with natural characteristics of human beings, their capacity for suffering and exaltation.

The second part of the book is devoted to representations of Saturn, which Arabic authors first associated with the theme of melancholy around the ninth century. The colour of the orb, its coldness, its bitterness: these attributes predisposed it to this association. Likewise, its attributes in ancient mythology and astrology dictated that it be connected with the theory of temperaments. Saturn's children had a dire fate in store, characterized by the most extreme possibilities of good and evil, not merely by the relationship between their predisposition to despondency and solitude and the planet of tears. Strongly influenced by Neoplatonic hierarchies, this representation was handed down through medieval mythography. The iconographic repertoire is notably rich, and one can trace in it the representation of the god/planet up until the remarkable painting of Saturn by the Venetian painter Girolamo da Santacroce (c. 1480/85–c. 1556), in which one feels the same inspiration as in Dürer: it is as if the whole weight of time seeks expression in the face of the melancholic, in its weary solitude.

The third part of *Saturn and Melancholy*, albeit the shortest, is central, for it makes the transition to the notion of "sadness without cause." Robert Burton (1577–1640), in his great compendium *The Anatomy of Melancholy* (1621), situates himself within this tradition. The distinction between dispositional melancholy and melancholy that is transitory, linked to a fleeting state, is an important one, for upon it rests the fate of modern subjectivity, the ability to either give in to melancholy or reject it. An intensification of self-awareness linked to the sadness of music, melancholy reinforces the ideal of a meditative retreat from the world. "My joy is melancholy," wrote Michelangelo.

This whole poetics was developed over a trajectory that found in melancholy the condition of genius and creativity, at a point where it becomes a force and not merely a subjective state. The slow elaboration of Renaissance thinking, and in particular the philosophy of Ficino, had gradually led to an understanding of the unique, divine gift of Saturn, a gesture that Ficino made with full loyalty to Plato. It was the sway of Saturn, he believed, that had raised the intellectual elite toward higher, secret things while at the same time plunging them into their accustomed depths of anguish and suffering. Permeated with Neoplatonism, and particularly with a hierarchy of life forms and the eminence of the spiritual life, Ficino's writing seeks to reconcile a spiritual ethics with the influence of the planets. This synthesis was not without risk, and Ficino's genius was to have endowed the immanent contradiction of Saturn with redemptive power: through contemplation and creation, the melancholic turns toward the very power that both discourages and redeems him.

The fourth and final part of the work is devoted to Dürer's engraving. The artist had engraved the temperaments for the frontispiece of a book by Conrad Celtes in 1502, but he had merely reproduced the traditional schema in which the melancholic is represented. Yet what is expressed in *Melencolia I* is the influence of Florentine Neoplatonism, as can be seen in the figure's inclined head, its clenched fist and sombre visage. These motifs, associated with the *typus acediae*, the popular image of melancholic paralysis, are conjoined here with the *typus geometriae*, identified by the authors in a woodcut from Gregor Reisch's *Margarita Philosophica* (1504). In the confluence of Florentine Neoplatonism with the themes of traditional astrophysiology, the sorrow of the human soul and its redemption through knowledge come together in the image of the wingèd genius. The iconological elements in this part of the book, bearing the signature of Panofsky's theoretical approach, would reveal the notional and allegorical content of the details filling out the scene, but the essence of the meaning is found in the posture and gaze of the figure. Beyond the prodigious erudition that Panofsky, Saxl, and Klibansky applied to this interpretive endeavour, we find here an answer to the question asked at the outset, for the whole book is suffused with a sensibility in which pathological melancholy is transformed into something central to the essence of human beings. What Dürer gives us in his engraving, as in his youthful self-portrait, is his own melancholy – an expression of the gulf separating metaphysical revelation from all other forms of human knowledge. The gaze of this figure reflects the intolerably limited character of what the human mind can claim as its own. *Melencolia I* is, in short, a melancholy acknowledgment of all bounds.

Here at last is the meaning of "I," that enigmatic numbered clue in the title of the engraving: it denotes the first stage of an ascension leading to a melancholy both rational and spiritual. In remaining at the first stage, that of imaginative or intuitive melancholy, whose literary sources can be traced in the Neoplatonic tradition up to the *De occulta philosophia* of the hermetic philosopher Cornelius Agrippa, Dürer chose to remain within the domain of the visible arts and to express a sombre awareness of the limits of knowledge acquired through the senses, before it is processed by reason and the mind. This first-degree knowledge is the cause of despondency. Melancholy as it appears here is neither disease nor temperament, but an admission of our insurmountable finitude. In Saturn's staring face, we recognize both Dürer's features and the face of modern worry. Klibansky often returned to the genesis of this great work and to his collaboration with the Warburg Library scholars, and it was always to pay tribute to the cultural milieu in which he had been formed and that had made this new reading possible.

After Hitler's catastrophic reign, this configuration went dormant for many years. It stood aside for the critique of culture that materialized as a critique of alienation in the Frankfurt School, with which, notably, Klibansky had no relationship. He knew it only from afar. When asked about this intellectual realm that was not his own, he responded by evoking nothing more and nothing less than the pessimism of Berlin that pervaded the thought of Walter Benjamin and Theodor W. Adorno. His attachment to Weimar culture remained an attachment to the radiant figures of his youth: especially his friends and teachers Friedrich Gundolf, Karl Wolfskehl, and Ernst Cassirer in particular, as he recalls in his commemorative interview with Thomas Göller, published in 1999.

Klibansky had perceived the danger represented by Hitler early on, and when the Nazis took power, he was quick to realize that he could not stay in Germany. After a short sojourn in Belgium and France, where he was disappointed by a spirit of compromise portending surrender, he exiled himself to England in 1933. The racial laws passed in 1935 had been preceded by a series of discriminatory measures that left no doubt as to what would follow. Moreover, the obstacles placed in the way of his research on Meister Eckhart, whom the Nazi regime then considered a forerunner of Aryan thought, confirmed him in his intention to leave. As he recounts here, he obtained a diplomatic passport and found refuge in England, where he was supported by the Academic Assistance Council, an agency founded in 1933 to assist academic refugees. Albert Einstein had helped fund this organization from its inception.[18] Klibansky was first received in London (King's College, 1934–36), then at Oxford (Oriel College, 1936–48), where he briefly re-encountered Cassirer, who had sought asylum with his son Heinz. He made the acquaintance of Albert Einstein, with whom he discussed the idea of founding an institute for exiled academics in Jerusalem. A memorandum written by Klibansky, followed by an exchange of correspondence beginning on 7 October 1933, attests to their shared decision not to pursue this project and instead to work on the settlement of academic refugees in the diaspora. Einstein wrote from Princeton explaining his position and encouraging Klibansky to follow his example by emigrating to North America.[19]

Klibansky became a British citizen in 1938. In 1942 he was recruited into the newly created Political Warfare Executive (PWE), a secret counter-propaganda agency directed by the Foreign Office. The exact nature of Klibansky's work can be deduced from certain memoranda that he wrote during the war on propaganda intelligence and on knowledge of the German mind. These documents are in his private archives. An examination of his passports shows a number of trips to Germany after the war to study the denazification process and observe the trials. This responsibility compelled him to leave Oxford and take a hiatus from the research he had been carrying out since arriving in England. In these conversations he gives us a striking portrait of activities atypical for scholars of his generation. His first-hand account of counter-propaganda efforts tells us much about the

British war effort and the importance of academic cooperation with it, particularly on the part of German Jewish scholars. His commitment was total, and although he does not dwell on the minute details of the work, one can imagine the considerable challenge it must have been for a young scholar accustomed to the quiet of libraries and manuscript cabinets to be in charge of such operations and maintain such contacts.

Despite these commitments, Klibansky did manage, as early as 1934–35 following discussions with Fritz Saxl, to pursue at Oxford the critical work dedicated to publishing the *Corpus Platonicum Medii Aevi*, which was divided into the medieval Latin and Arabic editions of the Platonic texts. It must have been quite a feat, considering the circumstances, for the Warburg Institute to publish the Latin version of the *Meno*, prepared by Lotte Labowsky, in 1940. A study of Klibansky's ample correspondence, with his publishers in particular, might serve to confirm his exceptional integration into British scholarly circles. His most important accomplishment in this phase of his career was the critical edition of the Latin *Parmenides* with commentary by Proclus, published in 1953 in collaboration with Labowsky. To this must be added the nine volumes of *Medieval and Renaissance Studies*, the first of them published at the start of the war in 1941, the last in 1968. Klibansky fondly recalled his friendship with Richard Hunt, who welcomed him with such generosity.

In 1946 Klibansky was invited to Montreal's McGill University, with which he was to remain associated for the rest of his life. In the first two years, perhaps because he had yet to make a final decision, he divided his time between Montreal and London, where he had been offered a position as director of research at the Warburg Institute. In 1948 he became Frothingham Professor of Logic and Metaphysics at McGill, where he taught until his retirement in 1975. He also taught at the Université de Montréal, and his collaboration with the Institut d'études médiévales, directed by a group of Dominican fathers, dates to his early years in Montreal. He was active there, building enduring friendships, until his retirement. And it was during this period that I made his acquaintance, a matter on which I would like to dwell momentarily.

This institute offered a multidisciplinary program that provided an excellent education in Greek and Latin as well as an introduction to the subtle techniques involved in producing critical editions of texts. How did it come to pass that Klibansky should join what was, on its face, a Christian institute? The answer is that it had a strong ecumenical bent. The Christian tradition was accorded great importance, of course, but we also took courses in medieval Jewish thought with Rabbi Chaim Denburg, and in Islamic thought with Jean Jolivet and other members of the Institute of Islamic Studies. This ecumenical character was a perfect fit for Klibansky, who was introduced to us as a specialist in late Platonism with an interest in the Jewish, Christian, and Islamic traditions. I took several seminars with him focusing on that theme. He never missed an opportunity to stress the importance of the mutual influences of these traditions on one another.

I was then ruminating upon a decision to study ancient Greek philosophy and it was Professor Klibansky and my supervisor, the patrologist Georges-Mathieu de Durand, who finally persuaded me that the Neoplatonic tradition was a rich and fruitful subject. Following their advice, I embarked on a study of Plotinus.

The first course I took with Klibansky consisted of a series of readings about the version of Platonism found in Augustine's *Confessions, Academica,* and *The City of God*. The second was devoted to the reception of the *Timaeus,* from Calcidius's translation to the School of Chartres. Only later did I discover that Klibansky had written his 1931 *Habilitation* dissertation – a text referenced in his 1939 book *The Continuity of the Platonic Tradition* – on Bernard and Thierry of Chartres. The third course was an introduction to Renaissance philosophy of science, from Cusanus on the infinite to the commentaries of Francis Bacon on Aristotle's *Physics* and Bacon's *Novum Organum,* which were included in a multi-year seminar on the history and philosophy of science.

In those days, the immense prestige enjoyed by some of our teachers was such that they had less in common with the average university professor of today than with masterly figures like Hegel or Humboldt: they embodied for us the ideal of European scholarship. Their lofty status ultimately came down, I think, to their philological precision and their love of books. Klibansky, like many others, often had a new book to recommend; however, when we met him in his office in McGill's Stephen Leacock Building, he always reached for his copy of the 1514 edition of Cusanus, undoubtedly the most precious book he owned.

As a man of Jewish heritage, Klibansky greatly valued the philosophical ecumenism practised at the institute. Sadly, he never gave a course on the German mystics. He encouraged us to learn Hebrew and Arabic, but I have no memory of any student in my cohort following that path. Later, when we paid homage to him, I came to understand the importance that he accorded to the Dominicans' welcome, first in Paris, then here in Montreal. The Dominicans, he liked to repeat, had been there at every decisive stage of his life. A prime example was father Gabriel Théry (1891–1959), director of the Dominican Historical Institute of Santa Sabina in Rome, whom he had met in 1934 and who had supported his research for the edition of Eckhart's Latin works. When I made Klibansky's acquaintance in 1964, I quickly understood that the importance of this friendship with the Dominican had never faded.

One day during a class on a text by the medieval philosopher Peter Abelard, Klibansky went on a long digression about medieval Islamic thought, which he followed by a comment on Peter the Venerable (making sure, *en passant,* that we didn't confuse the two Peters), and then by some reminiscences about his own personal hero, the medieval Catalonian philosopher Ramon Llull, an interesting interdisciplinary thinker. I recall all this because I kept every one of my notebooks from his courses and our meetings. Yet I was then unaware of the world-historical importance of Klibansky's work.

Of course, we all knew about his personal library – how could anyone avoid glancing at it while seated in his office?[20] If only he had taken a phone call, I might have had the great pleasure of wandering the library's many aisles. That never happened, at least not to me. But if asked about a given topic, he would invariably stand up and take a book off the shelf as a suggestion for my reading. Anne-Marie Tougas's film about him[21] shows a large table in the library covered with papers, letters, and prospectuses from publishers and antiquarian dealers around the world. He also collected stamps – not for himself but for friends – and would sometimes ask if we did so as well. He spoke often of the European libraries that he had worked in, most notably the Bodleian at Oxford, but also several Italian and German libraries that he knew intimately. These were beyond comparison with ours, though it can be said that the Dominicans of Saint-Albert-le-Grand kept a very good collection; I can still recall Klibansky searching for a book in the big wooden cabinet that housed the card catalogue in the centre of the main reading room. Some of us students even had a key to this library, as well as a personal desk on the second floor where we could keep our books and discuss our work in the evening. We frequently found Klibansky there after hours, carrying on a discussion with a white-robed medievalist. He was also a regular visitor to McGill University's splendid libraries, especially the Osler Library of the History of Medicine, which housed the university's books on the history of melancholy and depression.[22]

Klibansky's scholarship was awe-inspiring, his lectures filled with a profound love of knowledge, which he presented to us as a goal worthy of lifelong devotion. And he was himself the model of a Platonic philosopher whose life is devoted to the quest of *sophia*. First and foremost, however, he was the philomath described by Plato in the *Republic*: a lover of learning and study as a path to wisdom. He loved nothing more than to search the past for new meanings relevant to our historical experience.

His teaching consisted mainly of a slow and careful reading of great texts, giving special attention to their style and rhetoric. If works such as Plato's *Timaeus* are to convey meaning to us, he insisted, we should strive to experience them as if they were addressed directly to us. Needless to say, all his students deeply admired him. He would sit quietly before us, surrounded by his papers and books, and speak in a calm, almost intimate voice – one that his dear friend Father Benoît Lacroix loved to imitate.

He would continually ask important questions about his preferred topics. Why is history able to produce both good and evil simultaneously? Why do religions seem unable to produce peace? Why does the claim of the oneness of truth appear to be incompatible with dialogue and tolerance? And most important: Why have the demands of philosophical reason for dialogue and respect historically met with refusal? These were the central questions to which this great scholar devoted his life. Raymond Klibansky had found them in Nicholas Cusanus's Renaissance masterwork *On the Peace of Faith* (*De pace fidei*) along with the question central to all his intellectual endeavours: What is the point of striving for knowledge unless it brings goodness and peace?

Convinced by his experience of war that it takes action by courageous and determined individuals to have any influence over the advent of peace, Klibansky became a philosopher of a new type: an ambassador whose initiatives cannot be contained by national borders. The Cold War had made him a witness to the disastrous consequences of totalitarianism and an apostle of philosophical dialogue rooted in tradition. He returned to the principal representatives of this tradition of dialogue, from the *De pace fidei* by his cherished Cusanus to John Locke's *Letter Concerning Toleration*, sparing no effort to disseminate the texts embodying this ideal of peace and tolerance. The most important of these was Locke's letter, for which he arranged publication in several editions and translations. His ample bibliography bears witness to the scope of his commitment on this front, as do his countless international interventions to protect freedom of thought and promote philosophical dialogue.

This period saw the appearance in his work of the great figures Locke and Hume as the emblems of his engagement. He saw these early modern thinkers as models of tolerance, which became, in those years, the central subject of his thinking and publication as well as the inspiration for his action. This philosophical ideal was his lodestar throughout his international involvement in institutions such as the International Institute of Philosophy. He was deeply attached to it, serving from 1966 to 1969 as its president (and subsequently as its honorary president), and dedicated to it his final book, a plea for international dialogue titled *Idées sans frontières*, published in 2005. His hope for these editions was that they would contribute to philosophical and political rapprochements conducive to peace. Klibansky's oeuvre was, in this regard, an engagement in the service of communication among peoples and cultures. This commitment led him to foster exchanges between intellectuals of East and West at a time when doing so was a real challenge. Key venues for this work were the congresses of the IIP, and a notable example was his action in defence of the Czech philosopher Jan Patočka, the initiator of Charter 77. Readers will find his vibrant eulogy to Patočka in these conversations, and I shall return to it in closing.

Throughout his life, Klibansky showed himself to be an attentive interlocutor of international philosophy. His bibliography during these years shows that he stepped up the pace of his publication of syntheses, bibliographies, and encyclopedic volumes in an effort to cross the constricting borders of ideologies and initiate authentic philosophical dialogue. He chaired the bibliographical committee of the IIP until his death,[23] overseeing the annual publication of the *Bibliography of Philosophy* and faithfully supporting the organization's annual congress. Another exemplary illustration of his dedication is *La philosophie en Europe* (1993), a survey co-edited with his friend David Pears and published with the support of UNESCO. The internationalism characteristic of his work forms a counterpoint in which modernity interrogates history and derives from it lessons of openness and continuity. The oeuvre is vast and multifaceted, but its fundamental unity can be seen in this reciprocal interrogation of history and modernity.

Klibansky was a member of numerous academies, scholarly associations, and institutes. He proved himself an indefatigable voyager during these years, driven by an unshakable belief in the value of dialogue. For him, the Cold War was not only a political ordeal but also a personal and profoundly philosophical one: its very existence demonstrated the importance of friendship and hospitality across party lines. The primary characteristic of such friendship, experienced as part of a striving for justice, was its focus on peace: unlike those who had chosen entrenched positions and, in practice, called for a separation between friends and enemies, Klibansky was a paragon of openness. The principle of his action could be expressed as follows: recognize as a friend anyone who seeks peace and justice, regardless of the ideologies to which he subscribes, regardless of the institutions supporting him; be a witness to his sincerity. Academic life and research were not mere pieties for him; he was an institution man, in that he believed that institutions are the guarantors of justice and democracy.

He repeatedly mentioned the names of friends, people who had joined this shared quest for justice in a world divided into blocs, in which philosophy, he felt, was failing at its task of bringing people together around rational ideals. His friends among philosophers were numerous: Paul Ricoeur, Max Black, Guido Calogero, Leszek Kołakowski, Hans-Georg Gadamer, to name just a few of those he mentions here and with whom he made common cause. With them he sought to found a world community of intellectuals committed to peace, organizing many gatherings to that end. His Philosophy and World Community series, published under the auspices of the IIP, is ample testimony to his efforts in favour of universal dialogue; one of its volumes reminds us of the Buddhist emperor Asoka's ideals of tolerance. The year after the American invasion of Afghanistan in 2001, Klibansky published a short piece titled "Le trésor de Kandahar," reminding us that the emperor's edicts could still be found in Kandahar, engraved in stone.[24]

The importance of Klibansky's contribution to the development of contemporary philosophical discussion was underscored by numerous awards and distinctions, including the Ordre du Québec in 1999 and the Order of Canada in 2000, not to mention the many honorary doctorates that he received around the world. But no distinction touched him more than those he received in Germany in his final years. This recognition was most clearly manifested in Heidelberg, in 1991, with his appointment to the university's hall of honour, and in Hamburg, in 1993, with his receipt of the Lessing Prize.[25] In 1994 he was awarded the Great Cross of the Order of Merit, the German government's highest distinction.

Raymond Klibansky liked nothing more than to be able to say of someone that she or he was a person of good will. He meant: here is someone sincere, who seeks to do good and on whom one can rely. He had sufficient authority to say that of someone but, more important, he had the special gift of being able to speak of others benevolently. I would say that he knew how to recognize the brave, the *spoudaioi*, and to do everything he could to help them. How often did he come to the aid of young people in difficulty? I could testify to specific cases in which I saw him take a personal interest in people whom he knew relatively little, but who were involved in enterprises he admired and believed to be just.

Good will is first and foremost a will to good, a form of benevolence, as Kant and his friends Emmanuel Levinas and Hans-Georg Gadamer remind us; and political friendship is the destiny of those who, awakened to the perils of a violent world, join forces on the basis of a shared ideal of tolerant welcome and dialogue. Klibansky detested ideologues, self-proclaimed authorities (that tendency was, he said, the visceral failing of German culture), and his appreciation of good will was as keen as his ability to recognize it. The political friendship of which he was an exemplar throughout his life was enriched by this spirit of welcome and tolerance, for him the most fundamental virtues of democracy. He liked to cite Lessing's parable of the ring and had similarly made of Cusanus's maxim *Una veritas in variis signis varie resplendet* ("the one truth shines in various forms") almost a personal credo.[26] The opening prayer of *De pace fidei,* with its plea for unity in religious diversity, is one that he could have written himself. Philosophers are the keepers of truth for the universal community and must unceasingly pursue it with respect for differences. In this sense, his life bespeaks a rigorous and constant effort in the striving for peace.

As I mentioned at the outset, Jan Patočka was one of those on whose behalf Klibansky intervened repeatedly, energetically, insistently, and, in the philosophical sense, justly; that is, with a striving for justice. He had met Patočka in Vienna in 1968 and again in Bulgaria in 1973, at the international congresses of philosophy. He had every reason to understand him, beginning with Patočka's concept of negative Platonism, on which they saw eye to eye within the Cusanian tradition. But even more trenchantly, there was a basic bond, an affinity that might at first sight appear primarily, or merely, political. This friendship went beyond the demand for justice against totalitarianism: it constituted a form of testimony.

Klibansky had read *Heretical Essays in the Philosophy of History* in French translation (published in 1981); he understood the "solidarity of the shaken" of which his friend spoke, and knew that within every person whose life has been disrupted by violence lies a just individual wanting nothing more than to testify to it, awaiting nothing more than the opportunity or the courage to do so. Such friendship, experienced in solitude, away from public demands for justice, constitutes an eternal bond between those who have undergone oppression, whether of the Nazi or Stalinist totalitarian variety. The mere fact of having continued to read and write, to keep alive the ideal of "a life of truth," in Patočka's phrase, in the face of what they have known, gives their life the value, the true value, of silent testimony.

Over the years, I had the privilege of speaking with Raymond Klibansky, of listening and asking questions, and I would like to say one thing about this notion of testimony: never did I hear him complain about the crater opened up by Nazism in his youth, about what had happened to him personally or to his family; it had been the fate of so many people, after all, many of them much more impoverished than himself. I heard what I perhaps wished to hear only obliquely, in his homage to Patočka. What he saw in the Czech philosopher was what he hoped others would recognize in himself: the courage, within absolute adversity, to persevere, to carry on, and hence to act. His testimony did not take the form of words alone, a decision that differentiated him from other witnesses (such as the poet Paul Celan, whom he read reverently): it took the form of action. What he saw with his own eyes, in Nazi Germany, in Germany at war, in Germany defeated, no one saw as he did, and what he heard and knew under totalitarian oppression, no one heard as he did. He never harked back to any of it, except as it arose along the ethical path he walked.

His silent testimony is that of an act purified by philosophy and borne in generous silence. I never knew anyone as disinclined to dramatize his own experiences as he was: a ghost of a smile, a flash in those bright blue eyes, said everything. He was never self-satisfied or sentimental. Only that friendship among witnesses, the friendship that binds those who have known the worst, can evoke those things of which their testimony is the irrefutable proof. The wise person remains standing, without complaining, in the face of evil or turbulence. Patočka died of exhaustion after being forced to remain standing during a seventy-two-hour interrogation. Klibansky admired his friend's courage and, though he mourned him, refused to succumb to hopelessness, just as he wouldn't have wanted anyone to lose hope over his own death. I never met that immense strength in anyone else. It took me much time to understand that to be a "very dear friend" of Raymond Klibansky, if it was to go beyond the community of writing and the political community, was inevitably to be a friend in this deepest and most silent way: to be joined in the friendship of witness. Like Patočka, he was a witness to our era, our society, and also to Canada, the country where he chose to live the latter half of his life. He was a witness to the infinite value of our freedom. But above all, he bore witness to the fact that freedom is primarily safeguarded by those who, having known danger and peril, having been shaken to their very core, continue to write and act under the gaze of their essential and most substantial friends, those whom a community of experience has led to the same understanding of the world.

When reading these conversations, a question arises for which an answer is not easily found. Not the question of divinity, for he never stopped being deeply Cusanian – that is, fascinated by the threshold of the infinite, and respectful of religious diversity. I speak, rather, of the question of melancholy. While I had been his student, it was neither Proclus nor even Plato that made his conversation so indispensable to me. How many hours did I spend listening to him on the subject of Plato's *Timaeus* and its medieval interpreters? How many days exploring the shelves of the library at the Institut d'études médiévales or the Osler Library, whose holdings he knew by heart, to say nothing of the collection of Hoffmann, his teacher at Heidelberg, which he had arranged for the Université de Montréal to acquire? Who could fail to love such a generous, devoted, just teacher?

But the question remains: How could someone take an interest in melancholy – in that sad, serene gaze of Dürer's seated angel, wearily contemplating the efforts of the arts and sciences, their symbols and writings – without *ipso facto* turning it into an ethic? Yet I never saw that gaze in his eyes, never found him weary or depressed. The distress of poets and artists seemed to him an indulgence that the philosopher could not allow himself. Klibansky often quoted Baudelaire, whose urbane depth he admired, but could not identify with the stance of Walter Benjamin, the poet's most melancholy reader; nor with that of Sigmund Freud. The romanticism of Heidelberg was his world, the pessimism of Berlin a foreign place. Even psychoanalysis, he felt, was the pursuit of a truth useless to the wise. So I would ask him: Why should anyone immerse himself in the world of melancholy, knowing in advance that it has the power to weaken or even paralyze us? Why not stick to the world of reason, to Eckhart, Cusanus, Locke, and Hume?

There is no answer to this question, because that answer is surely to be found in the way he lived his life. Raymond Klibansky, that polymathic and indefatigable scholar, was joyous and often ironic: his company was tonic, his friendship fortifying; both led one to read and to write ever more. To be politically connected with him was to join the company of those who remain on their feet. When he exclaimed, "Mais allons donc!" (meaning roughly, "Come on, we can do something!"), you understood that the time had come for courage. Perhaps ultimately, beyond the scholarship and the political action – deep in that silent place of testimony where that young Jewish scholar foresaw, as did the Mann family with whom he had been friendly, the darkness that was to descend on Europe – he was a man not only drawn implacably to an image that illustrated the powerlessness and vanity of thought, but also one resolved to resist any such resignation.

I would venture that if melancholy – the mental state that overcame Schelling, exhausted Hölderlin and Celan, drove Benjamin to despair – was perhaps the temptation of his youth, the miracle of Raymond Klibansky's life was how he tamed it with such passion and knowledge, through writing and research; how he encircled, subdued, and ultimately submerged it within a deep well where it had to contend with the friendship of poets, the testimony of the shaken, the anxiety of philosophers, and the music of Mozart, which he loved above all else.

1

FROM PARIS TO HEIDELBERG

A STUDIOUS YOUTH

Mr Klibansky, you were born in Paris but the political situation prevented you from staying long in France. Where were your parents and your family from?

The early years of my childhood were indeed spent happily in the 9th arrondissement of Paris. My family had settled in Paris a few years before I was born. As a child I attended a private school on the rue de Rochechouart, just steps away from home. I still have my notebooks; each week, the good students received a blue ribbon, or better still a gold one.

My father was a businessman in the wine export sector.[1] He loved France but had kept his German citizenship. He was born in Frankfurt where his parents had settled. My paternal grandfather came from Lithuania, near the Russian border. There was a famous Talmudic school there, at Kaunas.

It was said that the family was descended from the Vilna Gaon, who was, in the eighteenth century, a strict interpreter of the law. He was an adversary of the Hasidim and condemned their claim to a special relationship with God.

So your father was given a very religious education?

Very orthodox, yes. As was I when I was young. At my paternal grandmother's home in Frankfurt, not only did we celebrate the Sabbath every Friday night but we also took in young foreign Jews, some of them poor and hungry. One, Lazarus Goldschmidt, was to gain fame for his German translation of the Babylonian Talmud.[2] My grandmother lived right near the place where the Rothschilds had first settled. She was no longer in the *Judengasse*, of course, but quite close to it, in the *Schöne Aussicht*, where the Schopenhauerhaus was also situated.

The people on my mother's side had been living in Germany for centuries, in Bavaria – not the Bavaria of Munich, but in Franconia, near Würzburg. I always wondered about the origins of these Jewish families that settled in Germany and Lithuania. The answer – perhaps speculative, but by far the most plausible – is that these people, who were certainly not of Germanic origin, had come with the Romans. It is probable that *caupones*, hostlers, had accompanied the legions and settled in the Rheinland. Which is by no means to assert that all these Jewish families arrived with the legions! Many of them quite likely came via Gaul.

By contrast, the history of Jewish settlement in Poland and Lithuania is known. These were fourteenth-century immigrants who came from Germany at a time of grave persecution after the Black Plague, for which the Jews were scapegoated. The king of Poland, Casimir III the Great, encouraged immigration because Poland had no middle class. There were nobles and peasants, but not much capital; the Jews arrived in numbers because they were invited. And their language was Yiddish, which retains many of the root words of fourteenth-century German. So we can surmise that these populations originally came from Germany, and before that from the Roman Empire. The largest proportion of Vilna Jews – of whom the painter Marc Chagall and the philosopher Emmanuel Levinas are examples – were probably of German and Roman origin.

And did your own childhood take place in a highly religious atmosphere?

Yes, but not obsessively so – especially not on my mother's part. It was more a way of life. Friday evening was a holiday; we celebrated the holidays, especially Hanukkah with all the little lights. We observed the fast days. Religious practice was less visible in France because French Jews were more integrated, less isolated, especially after 1870. We did of course go to synagogue on Friday nights and Saturdays as well as for the High Holidays, but that strong sense of community that existed in Germany, as I witnessed it later in Frankfurt, was lacking.

What language did you speak at home?

1.1 / Raymond Klibansky with his mother and sister, Sonia, Frankfurt, November 1921. Private collection.

We spoke both: German among ourselves, French with customers, suppliers, and most friends. My parents had many French friends and had been close to friends of Raymond Poincaré.[3] So they named me Raymond – although, as it happened, I went on to become an admirer not of him but of his cousin Henri. I should say that the plan was for me to live in France and go to the Collège Rollin on avenue Trudaine. My governess was German; the maids were French. To my little black cat, Mephisto, who meant a lot to me, I spoke French. The first tragedy of my youth was being told when I came home for the holidays that he had died.

We spent our holidays at Le Touquet or at Bad Homburg near Frankfurt, where we shared a house with my mother's sister and her children. It was there, as a small boy, that I gave free rein to a perhaps regrettable instance of French patriotism. The city was a holiday spot for the emperor and one of our pastimes as vacationers was to go out and greet him when he passed by. One day I obstinately refused to doff my hat. To show such respect to a sovereign whom I considered a foreigner seemed misplaced to me, and the only effect of my mother's exhortations to be polite was that I left my hat at home on the following days.

At what age did you leave France?

We were at Paris-Plage (Le Touquet) in July 1914 when my father arrived in a hurry to arrange our departure. It was just before war was declared and there were still trains to Belgium, but we had to cross the Belgian-German border on foot. We left with two suitcases, leaving everything else behind in Paris. The French confiscated everything.

So, at the age of eight I found myself in Germany. I was still an only child; my sister, Sonia, wasn't born yet. It was wartime, with the inevitable shortages and privations, but compared to the horrors of the Second World War, the situation was fairly easy and there was little cause to complain. Shortly after our arrival in Frankfurt, I was sent to board with one of my father's brothers, my uncle Pinkus, the principal of an excellent school, well known in the east, where the Polish in particular sent their sons.[4] I had to start high school and I had not done the three-year preparatory *Vorschule* because I'd been at school in France. I spoke German but did not write it well.

After this rather arduous period of catch-up, I was admitted to the celebrated Goethe-Gymnasium in Frankfurt, where Latin and Greek were taught. The quality of the education was very high, with a special emphasis on ancient and modern languages. Some of my fellow students went on to renown – the physicist Hans Bethe, for example, known for the discovery of the carbon cycle that bears his name.[5] He directed the Theoretical Division of the Manhattan Project during the Second World War and received the Nobel Prize in 1967.

Did the Greek classes play a decisive role in your career path?

Certainly, as well as the classes in Latin and in history and literature. My Greek professor was a great scholar, Felix Bölte, who had written the article on Sparta in the Pauly-Wissowa encyclopedia.[6] He came from the Bonn school of classical philology and had been a student of Hermann Usener's. Through him, I am an *Enkelschüler* of Usener. There's no good

English equivalent – spiritual grandchild, maybe? The other major school of German philology was the Berlin school, founded by Ulrich von Wilamowitz-Moellendorf and Hermann Diels, who had taught Otto Regenbogen, my professor at Heidelberg University.

Bölte was more than a mere scholar. Those of his former students who have written about him – and they are many – speak of his elegant attire, which went hand in hand with a great moral elegance. He dressed like a fashion model and treated his students with politeness and respect, as young adults.

Half the students in my class were Jewish, but I was the only one who did not write on Saturdays. My family was fairly orthodox and my classmates respected this. I was never bullied for it, even indirectly. A child can sense disapproval, even when it is expressed silently.

Did your father stay close to home during the war?

No, he became an army interpreter in a large POW camp. Since he was fluent in French, he had to work as a censor with a man who became his close friend, Wilhelm Uhde, a well-known art critic and collector in his day who counted Picasso, Braque, Juan Gris, Marie Laurencin, and especially Henri Rousseau among his friends. He had written on Van Gogh and the impressionists. He too was from Paris and, like my father, had kept his German citizenship. They were there together, reading prisoners' letters and serving as interpreters.

You then left your excellent high school for a very different learning environment.

Although my father strongly opposed the move at first – he was very attached to traditional forms of education – I persuaded him to let me change schools. I was fifteen when I left the Goethe-Gymnasium for a very different school, a new kind of school developed in reaction to state-sponsored education, where an effort was made to avoid imposing that discipline so dear to Germans in the form of grades and report cards. I had heard of it from friends and was very interested. To be a student at this school, one needed self-discipline. No grades were given out at the end of the year; students had to be self-motivated, driven by a desire to understand the world around them. It was a very distinctive system, deeper than the parallel public system. It really helped me. The school motto was Pindar's *genoio hoios essi*, "Become who you are." But while for Pindar it meant that the well-born were expected to grow into their elevated station in life, students at this school were expected to realize their personal potential.

We never learned anything by rote; instead, we were asked to interpret an author by trying to get inside his mind. It was the Odenwald School and it was known the world over.[7] Writers and intellectuals such as Thomas Mann, Ernst Cassirer, and Franz Wedekind, as well as artists and nonconformists, enrolled their children. I was there as a young man when Indian poet Rabindranath Tagore paid a visit, and for the visits of many others who came from all over to learn about this new pedagogy.

Then as now, German states had relative independence in the field of education. Odenwald was founded in 1910 by Paul Geheeb as part of the movement of schools known as *Landerziehungsheime*, which encouraged education close to nature, the formation of the "complete man." Before that, Gustav Wyneken, a well-known name in the history of pedagogy, had founded the Wickersdorf School with the young Geheeb in the state of Saxe-Meiningen, a small duchy famous in the history of theatre. (It was there that historical costumes were introduced on stage.)

The Wickersdorf School was the first co-educational school, revolutionary in its day. But the personality of Wyneken – an autocrat with homosexual tendencies – created a tense atmosphere at the school. This situation is described in a renowned book, *The Diary of Otto Braun*, published by his mother after his death during the First World War.[8] The ensuing tensions ultimately provoked the departure of Paul Geheeb and his future wife, Edith Cassirer, Ernst Cassirer's niece. One can imagine how shocked the family must have been at her marriage to a Protestant reformist theologian. Nevertheless, Edith Geheeb's father, Max Cassirer, the *Stadtrat* of Berlin and a great patron of the arts, put up the money to create the new Odenwald School, in Hesse, where the grand duke had a much more open mind than the emperor and other sovereigns.

Paul Geheeb was an extraordinary man, a pacifist. He loved birds. He built a huge aviary where he went each day and the birds perched on his shoulders, a tawny owl in particular. Later, when the Nazis closed the

1.2 / Paul Geheeb surrounded by students, *Odenwaldschule*. Undated postcard. Private collection.

school, he emigrated to Switzerland and founded the École d'Humanité in the Bernese Oberland. The early years were very hard. He took in orphaned, penniless children whose parents had been interned in concentration camps. Success eventually came and the school's reputation spread throughout the world. Nehru, among other prominent figures, sent his daughter there.

What was the typical teaching method?

It was totally different from the one used in the state schools and I adopted it later for my own courses. The first task is to *read*. For example, when we read Goethe or Schiller, we began by summarizing the essence of what the author was saying. The second task is to ask questions about things that could be interpreted in different ways. Third, and third only, to present a critique or judgment. The key is understanding: making an effort to understand what the author means and learning to restate it.

Which authors had the greatest influence on you?

Schiller, Goethe, Kleist, Lessing, and Herder, whom we read a great deal. I especially liked Hölderlin. It was not a very broad curriculum, but what we did, we did very intensely. It was good work.

What about the classical disciplines, Latin and Greek?

The study of ancient languages came after that of modern languages. Unfortunately, the professors were not very good. So my friend Walter Solmitz and I read Homer and Plato on our own.[9] Fortunately, I had been given a solid foundation at the Goethe-Gymnasium. We had to prepare for the *Abitur* exam to be admitted to university – it was the equivalent of a high-school diploma, the A levels. I passed this exam without too much difficulty six months earlier than I could have done in a regular school.

Manual labour was an equally important part of the Odenwald curriculum. I chose carpentry. Alas, I had no gift for it. We had to build "forms" for safe storage of skis. I never succeeded in planing those huge blocks of wood. Gardening was also compulsory. We had to plant vegetables. I hated that stuff!

Sports, on the other hand, didn't bother me at all. Every morning at seven we went out for a run, even in the rain or snow. And we did gymnastics.

A bit Spartan, wouldn't you say?

Yes, but it was fine. In really rough weather we stayed in, but that was rare. We led healthy lives. And there were sports and games. I invented night games. We went into the forest; the boys were pages, the girls had to be protected; there were two camps; the goal was to capture a ribbon. The students who took part were left with good memories.

What did you take away from this alternative pedagogy? Did it influence you?

I think it was the right approach for me. They did take things very far. They wanted the children to decide what they wanted to do. Yet children need to be given models. Choices impose extra difficulties and should be reserved for children of a certain age.

1.3 / Odenwaldschule. Undated postcard. Private collection.

The experience of this alternative pedagogy was very positive for me. The school functioned like a democratic community in which decisions concerning daily life were put to a vote. In accordance with the principle of *Selbstverwaltung*, self-administration, the elected leader of the school community, the *Schulgemeinde*, was always a student. Tasks were distributed democratically. I was often in charge of organizing table service. Each meal began with a recitation by a student: a few verses of Goethe or a philosopher's remarks.

The thing to note about this pedagogy was that the emphasis was placed on both the community and the individual. Students weren't forced into any kind of a mould – English gentleman, officer, that sort of thing. All we had was older students serving as role models for younger ones.

The students were divided into houses, each led by a teacher. There weren't very many of us, about 220 in the school and twenty or so in each house. I found myself in the house of an extraordinary woman, Alwine von Keller,[10] who was conversant not only with the English poets but also with French mystic literature, Madame Guyon for example, and even the Hindu religion. The houses bore the names of the school's heroes: Plato, Goethe, Schiller, and Fichte – Herder especially – and Humboldt, whose importance is increasingly being recognized today for his contributions to the study of language, to problems of linguistics and the humanities. Humboldt represented German humanism. He wanted to found a university based on true humanism. His ideas affected me, and when I entered university, it had to measure up in my eyes to Odenwald's humanist ideals.

The school was situated in the woods on a height of land; there were several pretty houses overlooking a valley. You could see the Rhine in the distance like a silver ribbon. The job I liked most was making the evening rounds to check that all the houses were closed up. I did this with my friend Walter Solmitz. We walked the school grounds at 10:30 in the cool of the night, taking in the delicious scent of the pines.

Was it at the Odenwald school that you met Klaus Mann?

Yes, but I wasn't particularly close to him. He wasn't athletic at all, didn't like the games I organized. He was already beginning to write at that time. It was not until much later that I came to appreciate him. After 1933 he went into exile in Zürich and with his sister Erika opened a cabaret, the Pfeffermühle (Pepper Mill), where he heaped ridicule upon the Nazis. I greatly admired him when, in Moscow, at a congress of writers invited by the Soviets, he took sharp exception to the thesis according to which art must reflect the social situation in accordance with party ideology. He stressed that beyond social situations, writers must express the tensions and tragedies of the individual, which are irreducible to social relations. He was very gifted. He produced a great deal of writing, not all of it stellar. His book on Gide and Europe greatly displeased the man himself. His destiny was tragic, for he died by suicide.[11]

I was closer to his brother Golo, with whom I struck up a friendship in Heidelberg, where he was studying history and philosophy.[12] He took Jaspers's courses. I saw him nearly every day. He had not attended Odenwald but a rival school, Salem, the school of discipline – not Prussian militarist discipline, but the discipline of stoicism and perseverance. One had to practise courage – save people from drowning, for example – and keep up a constant outward mien of discipline. Salem was a famous school, attended by the aristocracy. Golo Mann writes of it in his memoirs. He became a renowned historian. I lost touch with him after I left Germany. One day in London at the start of the war, I was on my way to my office and had reached the place where Whitehall meets Trafalgar Square when

I saw a man in an American soldier's uniform walking unsteadily, visibly drunk – not an unusual spectacle. Suddenly I recognized him: it was Golo, who had seen me first and decided to play a trick on me! I saw him again a few times during the war while he was doing a brilliant stint on American radio responding to Goebbels's propaganda, first in Britain and later, as the Allies advanced, in France and Luxembourg.

Did you know Thomas Mann?

"Know" is a stretch. I admired his work but had little sympathy for him as a person. The Mann family was extraordinary, but Thomas Mann had chilly relations with his sons; he preferred to send them to boarding school.

While you were attending this school, did you already have a feeling that you would devote your life to the history of ideas, the history of philosophy? Did you have a plan to do so?

Yes. What concerned me was the problem of humanity, and to know the true nature of humanity, one had to be conversant with ideas about humanity and one needed to know philosophy, starting with Greek philosophy. To enter the world of Greek philosophy – and this was my firm conviction – it was not enough to read the works of the philosophers. One had to become fluent in the *language* of the philosophers, the Greek language. It was also necessary to study Greek poetry. At school, the curriculum was flexible; you could go from one field to another and that is what I did. When I left Odenwald for university, I began by taking seminars in *Klassische Philologie* – Greek and Latin – and then took philosophy. And I believed that it was not enough to approach philosophy, and civilization in general, through writing alone, to the exclusion of art. So I decided to take archaeology courses as well.

1.4 / Raymond Klibansky, student, Bernkastel-Kues, 1927. Private collection.

What was the first university you attended and why?

Heidelberg, for the tradition of that university, to which the heretic Spinoza had been invited (he declined the invitation); where Hegel and other great scholars had taught, most notably Max Weber, whose three nephews and one niece, adopted after his sister's suicide, had gone to Odenwald with me. The youngest in particular, Hermann and Max, had become my close friends.

Also for the beauty of the city, overlooked by the great ruin of the castle and still imbued with the memory of the romantic poets who had chosen to live there.

I arrived in 1921 at the age of seventeen and I still treasure an unforgettable memory. Hölderlin wrote:

Long have I loved you and for my own delight
Would call you Mother, give you an artless song,
You, of all towns in our country
The loveliest that I ever saw.[13]

Did you often go for walks along the Philosophenweg, *the Philosophers' Walk?*

Yes, often. There wasn't much traffic at the time. Motor vehicles skirted the city. It was the old civilization. Café life was conducive to discussion. I remember Café Krall, where an old sage by the name of Wildhagen was a regular; he had been Hermann Cohen's student at Marburg. He held court amid students such as the philosopher Ioannis Theodorakopoulos, who wrote an ode to Heidelberg in Greek. We talked, we argued; I recall thought-provoking conversations.[14]

Who were your first professors at Heidelberg?

I started with classics and philosophy and, as luck would have it, became well acquainted with Karl Jaspers. As an elective, I registered for a seminar given by Ludwig Curtius,[15] one of the century's most important archaeologists, which was attended by a group of very advanced scholars and researchers. In that era, teaching was offered in two very different

1.5 / Heidelberg, ca. 1937. Photographer unknown. Archives of the University of Heidelberg.

forms. There were what was called *Vorlesungen*, formal lectures given before audiences that were sometimes very large. When the professor entered, the custom was for audience members to applaud with their feet! We listened religiously, asking no questions. And there were the *Seminaren*, in which students sat around a long table and gave presentations, which were followed by a question-and-answer period. Having been admitted to Curtius's seminar despite my lack of experience, I was astonished to be chosen for the first presentation. My assignment was to interpret a text by Pausanias, fraught with difficulties, on the works of art he had seen during his travels. I was told: "You're a graduate of the Arcadia School, are you not? We shall see what you are capable of!"

The presentation that I gave went on for four weeks. My conclusion was that certain contradictory theses could be defended with good arguments, and that the choice of interpretation was not always to be grounded in the reasons of Reason, but often on a decision mediated by the interpreter's own sentiments. In presenting this conclusion, I believed that this scholarly assembly would find what I was proposing heretical. On the contrary, a lively discussion followed. My argument had pleased the philosopher Karl Jaspers, who was in attendance. He invited me to his home, which I had the privilege of visiting often that semester.

I also met his adversary, Heinrich Rickert. I knew them both personally and they were both very friendly, I can even say kind to me. So, when defending my *Habilitation* to become a *Privatdozent*, I spoke of the concept of freedom and history in a manner that could possibly have been interpreted as anti-Jaspers. He argued, but did not oppose me just because I disagreed with him.

What form did the rivalry between Rickert and Jaspers take, in terms of ideas?

Rickert was the great master of the old school.[16] The successor to Windelband and famous since the end of the nineteenth century, he represented the Kantian school, the Southwest German school of Neo-Kantianism. He taught a philosophy of values, a *Wertphilosophie*, and in the work of that title he sought to establish a difference between the world of values and the world of the real, a difference overcome by the act of the valuing subject, who strives in this way to reconcile the objectivity of values with the subjectivity of the act of valuing. He was one of the last authors of a universal system of philosophy whose schematic nature allowed it to be condensed, for the reader's immediate comprehension, into diagrams reproduced on foldout sheets inserted at the end of the work. He fought the natural sciences' claims to superiority over the humanities on the grounds of the latter's putative lack of rigour. In fact, Rickert showed the limits of concept-formation in the natural sciences and delineated the various forms of concepts, in some sense freeing the humanities and defending them from criticism on the grounds of being unscientific. He showed that they were scientific, that the humanities constituted sciences, but "sciences" in another sense. He had at one point taught the young Heidegger. When I was studying in Heidelberg, Rickert was considered a demigod by a host of researchers who arrived from Japan and other countries every year. He was a man of great merit but, as the leader of a school, had no patience for the new tendencies that he called *Lebensphilosophie*, philosophy of life, and later philosophy of existence. Anything connected to existence was taboo to him.

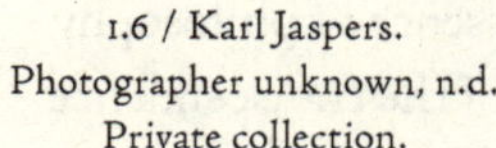
1.6 / Karl Jaspers.
Photographer unknown, n.d.
Private collection.

And that was precisely the field of Karl Jaspers,[17] whose first book was *General Psychopathology*, an introduction to the philosophical concepts implicit in any psychopathology. It was followed by *Psychologie der Weltanschauungen* ("Psychology of Worldviews").[18] He proceeded to work on modernity and developed his three-volume *Philosophy*, an outstanding enterprise, a philosophy based on reasoning but showing that one had to go beyond reasoning. For him, philosophy engaged the complete man, and indeed consisted in this very commitment itself; it was a commitment to truth, a free and absolute commitment of one's existence. *Existenzerhellung*, the illumination of existence, was a term familiar to all his listeners. People become engaged and actualize their existence through their decisions and it was only in so-called limit situations that they become conscious of their existence. Human beings, he said, find themselves only by being with each other, never through knowledge alone. Whence the importance he attached to *Kommunikation*. For him, this term did not denote exchange of information but the possibility of entering the mind of another, partaking of his intellectual life, establishing a highly personal connection as the basis for all understanding. This thesis became central in the philosophy of existence and played a major role in the development of contemporary hermeneutics.[19] For Jaspers, science is a necessary condition of all philosophical effort. He stresses, as did Kant, that it imposes standards of evidence with which philosophy must reckon, but he also insists that the essence of philosophy cannot be reduced to the clarity of reason. He writes of the transcendence that goes beyond all rational thought; the failure of reason is a "cipher" that one must know how to read, a sign giving evidence of transcendence. Consequently, when Jaspers spoke of an "absolute whole," that which encompasses without being encompassed, he did not venture to understand it as a concept and to explain it rationally. On the contrary, as he liked to repeat, "the idea of total philosophical knowledge is a totalitarian idea in the pejorative sense of the word."

Was the influence of Wilhelm Dilthey, considered the father of hermeneutics, palpable?

Undoubtedly, but for Jaspers, historicism was something very limited; it had to be transcended by means of personal commitment to interpretation and life choices. These categories of commitment were central, and on this point he brought to bear the thinking of Kierkegaard and important concepts such as the existential leap of faith. At a certain point, reasoning no longer avails; one must take a leap into an element that cannot be reduced to categories of pure reason.

You spent time with Max Weber's family and were able to gauge the influence of his thought. In "Science as a Vocation," Weber writes that "academic training of the kind that we are supposed to provide in keeping with the German university tradition is a matter of aristocratic spirit," and later, that religiously minded young people "are in search not just of religious experience, but of experience as such. The only surprising thing is the path they take ... the only realm that intellectualism had failed to touch until now, namely, the realm of the irrational, is what is now made conscious and subjected to intellectual scrutiny."[20] When we read this text and we hear you talk about Karl Jaspers's philosophy of existence, we can also call to mind the attention to experience and to the whole affective register that is found in Weber's work. I would like you to tell us how you experienced this development, which was present in the climate of Heidelberg at the time of your education. Was there a genuine mistrust of rationalism or, on the contrary, perhaps a desire to mark out its bounds in order to better achieve it?

There were a number of tendencies, certainly. To understand them, one always has to consider the frame of mind in which Germans found themselves after the First World War. This catastrophe of a great empire suddenly defeated for the first time was, for many, disastrous. Irrational thinking reigned as a way of helping people cope with their despair. They took refuge in all sorts of beliefs and cults. There was also the thinking of Oswald Spengler, whose book *The Decline of the West* articulated a terrifying pessimism.[21] On the one hand you had this pessimism, and on the other the nationalists, who did not want to admit that Germany really had been defeated. They held the internal enemy – the intellectual left, the Jews – responsible for the defeat. Others wanted to show that the whole system of thought had to be reformed; that a new faith in Germany was needed and that all science, all university teaching, had to accord with this new faith. The task at hand was to define the role of the university teacher. Must he be a prophet, or should he be a scholar who submits to the dictates of what reason teaches him?

Max Weber made war on false prophets. He wanted to show that all university teaching must be a service. Professors must not be advocates of any given belief or party. They must submit to the rigorous demands of scientific concepts and subject their work to the concepts of science, to its methods. His remark that academic prophecy, of all varieties of prophecy, was the only unendurable one, was often heard; it was the concept of *Wertfreiheit*, ethical neutrality – the postulate that value judgments must be excluded from all scientific discussion. The idea gave rise to lively argument with those who contended, as I did, that the very formation of theories is tied to practical reason and entails such judgments willy-nilly. Clearly, we always introduce values into the observation of phenomena, particularly social and human phenomena. We make value judgments. So, it is incumbent on us to acknowledge them as such, to try to eliminate them from our appreciation of situations and from our teaching. Professors must serve the cause of truth. This was Max Weber's ideal. Not personal truths, but the truth lying beyond those truths, beyond individuals. Truth as viewed by individuals, of course, but truth that must help us do everything in our power to eliminate value judgments and the sentimental irrationalism attached to them.

Did Jaspers demand an allegiance of sorts from his students? Was there a community of thought in which his students were necessarily included?

There was an authentic community of thought, but he did not demand that we follow him.[22] He had two female students who became quite well known: Hannah Arendt was one; and Jeanne Hersch, a philosopher from Geneva, and much more important in my view, was the other. Both, and especially Hersch, in some sense carried on his thought – and Hersch perhaps also surpassed it, while remaining faithful to it.[23] He did not ask for blind allegiance. On the contrary, he encouraged discussion. Yet he, the great psychologist, had a limited ability to understand others. It seemed a lofty ideal when he spoke during seminars of the need for such understanding but, as Hersch once told me, Jaspers in private conversation gave the impression of being absent, not a true interlocutor. Without a doubt, his conversation was unforgettable, inspired – when speaking about Humboldt for example. His health being fragile, he did not get out much, and his correspondence with Heidegger shows that he possessed an extraordinary nobility of spirit.[24] I was very close to him when I was about seventeen or eighteen. Impressed by what I told him of the Odenwald School, he recommended it to his uncle Theodor Tantzen, the prime minister of Oldenburg, for a member of his family. My last memory of Mrs Jaspers, who was Jewish, dates back to 1933 after the National Socialists took power. I met her one day on the old Heidelberg bridge and she said: "Your life is ruined." It was anything but consoling.

What are your memories of Hannah Arendt?

I knew her as a student, when she was drawn to Heidegger, and she was certainly a woman of great intelligence, but the reputation she now enjoys seems inflated to me. She had a way with words, but if you look more closely, her thought is not very profound. She is more a writer than a substantive critic.

Summing up: at that time in Heidelberg, you were in Karl Jaspers's intellectual circle. You also studied in Kiel. Was that before or after?

Jaspers recommended me for that trip to Kiel and it transformed my life, in a certain sense. In early 1924, a few years after Germany's defeat, inflation and material poverty prevailed. It was hard to buy bread in the afternoon, for its price had doubled since the morning. Students had no way to keep up with these dramatic fluctuations and were at the mercy of inflation. All of a sudden there came a proposal from a very rich German[25] who had made a lot of money during the war and wanted to do something for the country's future by striving to create what he called a new *Führerschicht*, a cohort of leaders who could revive Germany. He wanted to recruit the two hundred most gifted students in the whole country. Jaspers was to make the selection for Heidelberg and he said to me: "You must go to Kiel." And so I found myself in northern Germany on the Baltic Sea with 199 other students from all across the country. I got to know the life they led. A great many of them, not all, worked tirelessly all day. When the work was done, it was party time – a ritual that was generally accepted, although not by all.

In Kiel I had the great good fortune to be chosen as the last assistant of Ferdinand Tönnies, the true founder of German sociology, who was then in his seventies.[26] His contribution is increasingly recognized today. In 1887 he had written a masterwork, *Community and Society*, in which he contrasted the idea of community based on fellow feeling and organic bonds with that of contemporary mechanical society, and this work inspired the youth movement in Germany. The search for this lost community became something very important in that era. The youth movement had begun at the turn of the century when many saw that they had to distance themselves from society, regain community. But how was it to be done? By adopting Boy Scout dress, going tieless and in short pants, for instance; by hiking into the woods in groups to dance and sing around a bonfire; by making one- or two-week pilgrimages of sorts, in which one found oneself in a kind of spiritual communion. This was *Gemeinschaft*. The movement was very important for German youth and the Nazis figured out how to co-opt its symbolism. Weimar's historic failure was its failure to offer inspiring symbols; the Nazis understood the importance of the visible, the visible symbol.

Beneath all this sociology was a type of romanticism, an opposition between community and society. These are really ancient Germanic values. "Community" carries a connotation of instinctive bonds, bonds of affection, while "society" is calculated, contractual.

Tönnies told me how he had seen the first strikes in Hamburg as a young man and had taken an interest in the workers' circumstances. He came from patrician stock in eastern Frisia. Moved by the workers' poverty, he began to notice how their allegiance to the nation had eroded. He observed that modern society is the locus of a form of nationalism that does not correspond to community. Yet his attachment to community did not make him a man of the right. On the contrary, in studying the question, he discovered the literature of the socialist theoreticians. Another thing he did as a young man was to attempt to meet Marx, but the great man had died in 1883, so he wrote to Engels, who invited him to London. On his arrival, he went to the British Museum, where this young German, fresh off the boat in England, made an important discovery: an unpublished manuscript by Hobbes! He was particularly interested in Hobbes's theory of the state.

Tönnies told me at length about his encounters with Engels. So, to play a game that I made up to awaken my drowsy students after a difficult class, there is a handshake between Engels and me, or two between Marx and me. That means there are three between you and Marx.

Were those months in Kiel productive for you?

I learned a lot. Tönnies was very kind to me. I hold very pleasant memories of the man as someone who radiated great dignity. Count Harry Kessler[27] recounts in his journal, one of the most valuable documents of the interwar period, that in 1933, a month after Hitler took power, Tönnies called the new leader a buffoon. He initiated me to what was known as moral statistics. These concerns, echoing eighteenth-century French ideas, constituted attempts to comprehend societal movements, and the individual's role in them, in a scientific way. Tönnies had studied a statistical analysis of suicide in eighteenth-century France, and showed me how to derive from it statistics by sex, age, region, season, and so forth. And this is all incredibly robust! There are so many things that can be quantified! For me, brought up on the classics as I was, it was a new approach, one that I had occasion to apply during the war.

At that time, the humanities and social sciences were in the midst of their gestation, in formation. Were you tempted to go into sociology, that field of social philosophy whose importance was becoming evident all over Germany?

I admired the sociology of Weber and Tönnies, but mainly because these sociologists were exceptionally well versed in history. I noted that the following generation took sociology to be the ability to understand history by looking at it through the filter of certain concepts. Those who knew the terminology, who could name a concept that seemed to encompass certain phenomena, thought they had understood. The starting point was not historical individuality, or facts, but concepts. These scholars subordinated events and realities to concepts instead of starting from deep knowledge of the uniqueness of history and the experience of time. The starting point was the generality of sociological terminology and it was applied to history, and I regarded this approach as deeply flawed. To me, Max Weber's students were betraying their teacher. In short, I was highly critical of sociology as it was practised.

You took advantage of your stay in northern Germany to go to Berlin and hear Wilamowitz.

I made a special trip from Hamburg. I will never forget that vision: Wilamowitz was about eighty at the time.[28] He was like a piece of yellowing parchment. That day, he was to give a talk on Pericles.

I had been given numerous warnings about him. He had been denounced in the journal founded by Stefan George, *Blätter für die Kunst*, for the crime of lèse-majesté in his translations of the Greek tragedians: to wit, for having transformed their poetry into prose. He was accused of deforming their specifically poetic values and being ignorant of art, of trivializing both tragedy and Plato. He spoke like a *Junker*, a landed nobleman, and that really displeased me!

And then he began citing and interpreting Plutarch and … well … his language was unforgettable! He captured the nuance of every word! How beautifully he interpreted what Plutarch said about Pericles! I was fascinated. It was a great impression that I will never forget.

After six months in Kiel, you returned to Heidelberg. But a year later, an invitation led you to leave your home university again for Hamburg. This invitation was no ordinary thing since it came from Ernst Cassirer, one of the great figures of German philosophy. How did this come about?

In Heidelberg I had met another student who was Cassirer's son, a remarkably gifted man, Heinz Cassirer,[29] who wrote on Aristotle's *De Anima*. He had spoken to his father of me. I knew the work of his father, whom I had met in Heidelberg when he was on his way to the Odenwald School to drop off his daughter. Ernst Cassirer invited me to Hamburg in 1926 to continue my studies there.[30] I lived and worked in his home and played chess with him. Life there was particularly sweet. All day long, he

1.7 / Ernst Cassirer. Photographer unknown, n.d. Private collection.

1.8 / Klibansky with Ernst Hoffmann (left) and Ernst Cassirer (right), Hamburg, 1927. Deutsches Literaturarchiv Marbach, Raymond Klibansky fonds.

1.9 / Lotte Labowsky, Somerville College, Oxford, 1926. Photographer unknown. Private collection.

worked in his office. He owned a magnificent library. Every evening, he received a select group of visitors. Mrs Cassirer was Viennese and a great hostess. It is hard to imagine the prevailing ambience at the Cassirers' home. That Hamburg circle, as I knew it, was happy, animated, cultivated. Musicians such as the pianist Arthur Schnabel were part of it. Mrs Cassirer's family had looked after him in Vienna when he was young and penniless. And there were painters … truly, there was no sense of impending catastrophe. I attended Cassirer's seminar on Kant and the way his ideas had influenced aesthetics. I spent a year in Hamburg before returning to Heidelberg.[31]

That same serenity, that simplicity in abundance, reigned in the family of my lifelong friend Lotte Labowsky,[32] who also lived in Hamburg and whom I had met when she was studying classical philology in Heidelberg. An unpretentious lifestyle, good cuisine, lovely furniture, silver platters covered with fruit. Germany was then going through a short period of prosperity before the 1930s, a period during which political tensions were less evident and social life seemed to be sheltered from external tensions. It had a gleam of the atmosphere that had reigned in Europe before 1914. It is often said that those who did not know Europe before 1914 do not know how sweet life can be. Obviously, this is only to repeat what Talleyrand said of France before 1789.

During my stays in Hamburg, I came to appreciate Mrs Cassirer for the remarkable woman she was. After Ernst's death, I persuaded her to write about her husband, and she wrote *Mein Leben mit Ernst Cassirer*, which is now, sadly, out of print. It was first distributed in mimeographed form, but the demand was such that it was published. It is a particularly interesting narrative because it describes Cassirer's encounter with Heidegger in 1927 – the historic Davos debate where, in some respects, the future of German philosophy was played out. Much has been written about this meeting, notably in French publications, but not with the sense of immediacy we find here.

Given that you were already working toward Saturn and Melancholy, *did Cassirer's ideas about art and religion as symbolism already interest you?*

1.10 / Portrait of Aby Warburg from the memorial book prepared by Lotte Labowsky for Warburg's funeral, 1929. Deutsches Literaturarchiv Marbach, Raymond Klibansky fonds.

They interested me, but I can't say their influence was decisive because I was already grappling with these questions. I came from Heidelberg, where I had, since 1923, been immersed in an extraordinary literary atmosphere. Prior to that, I had been influenced by a professor of literature at my school, Eva Cassirer, another of Cassirer's cousins and a friend of Rilke's; indeed, their correspondence has been published.[33] She taught German. She had not been to university but she knew her poetry, and it was with her that we became well grounded in German literature and poetry.

In Hamburg, Cassirer had introduced me to Aby Warburg, the founder of the library that now bears his name. He was a man of genius whose influence is still felt today in art history and in other areas of the history of ideas and symbols. This was a very important encounter for me.[34]

Warburg wanted me to help him with the library, and I did. I organized the philosophy section, the encyclopedia section, and also the section on classical studies. I met Fritz Saxl,[35] then Warburg's assistant, and Erwin Panofsky, who was a professor of art history.[36] They had written a book in 1923 on Albrecht Dürer's engraving *Melencolia I*, a terrific book, really interesting.[37] I took the risk and the liberty of critiquing it because, as it seemed to me, it did not sufficiently account for the philosophical and theological roots of the various conceptions of melancholy. To my great surprise, they acknowledged that my critiques had some basis and invited me to formulate them. And so the desire for a new book was born; I must of course tell you about it.

Aby Warburg, with financial aid from his family of bankers, had accumulated thousands of books while pursuing his various interests.

1.11 / Reading room, Kulturwissenschaftliche Bibliothek Warburg, Hamburg, 1927. Courtesy of the Warburg Institute, London.

He had opened his library to students and researchers, who discovered in it a paradise and a labyrinth. The elliptical shape of the main room had been inspired by his first conversation with Cassirer, about Kepler. Saxl, who became the director after Warburg's death in 1929, recounts that the first time Cassirer entered this library, in which books were sorted according to the principle of affinity – the unknown book on the shelf was often the one needed – he declared that he had two choices: run for his life, or become its prisoner for years! The creator of this paradisiacal labyrinth was a figure of rare, rich, encyclopedic knowledge and complexity. For him, magic and astrology were forces of the spirit that were intimately linked to other forces, and to the development of reason. He had devoted his life to exploring these connections. In his view, to comprehend the history of forms, one needed a great deal of knowledge, particularly in regard to rituals and superstitions. His method consisted in discerning the influence of antiquity: not merely the survival of texts, manuscripts, and statues, which are just the surface, but the influence that the ancients exerted on thought and action in the centuries that followed and up to our day. "The times are different, so their influence is different. Notably, the importance of symbols comes into play: they can be situated in an Olympian register just as well as they can embody superstitions and magical beliefs." Ideas such as these led Warburg to be the first to interpret the frescoes of the House of Este in the Palazzo Schifanoia in Ferrara, where he spotted the gods of antiquity in the form of demons. The conception of the work derives from the theories of the Arabic astrologers, Abu Ma'shar in particular, without which one cannot comprehend the artist's vision.

Warburg liked to spend his time in the library and he was in the habit of jotting down on little bits of paper the ideas and intuitions that guided his research. These fragments formed an immense, nearly incomprehensible file that gave the impression – at least superficially – of a fair degree of chaos.

Ernst Gombrich, in his biography of Aby Warburg, emphasizes this impression of chaos, of a labyrinth.[38] *He even stresses the phobic aspects of Warburg's character. What do you think?*

There is some justice to this position, no doubt, but it is incorrect to present this as a fundamental character trait. Aby Warburg had been through the First World War. For him, it was more than a tragedy. He found it simply intolerable that nations to which he had a deep feeling of belonging could be in conflict. "I am a Jew by blood, a Hamburger in spirit, and a Florentine at heart," he liked to repeat. The conflicts that arose between the German and Italian nations, after a phase of alliance, were traumatic to him, taking a further toll on his already fragile health. Yet this was the period of his most fruitful and original research.

Warburg was well acquainted with demons but he also knew that one ultimately overcomes them. He had reached the conclusion that the human soul constitutes a labyrinth. In Gombrich's interpretation, Warburg had not found a way out of this labyrinth, yet he was very much the one who, while acknowledging that the labyrinth constituted an original state of affairs, had searched for and knew the path to the exit. He was, in the words of a young Italian to whom I described him, "the great lord of the labyrinth." He was certainly not the only one to get lost in the labyrinth, but he was the only one who knew it well, and knew the way out toward the light.

1.12 / Gertrud Bing, Aby Warburg, and Franz Alber, Rome, 1929.
Courtesy of the Warburg Institute, London.

So it is inappropriate to describe this as a phobia; rather, it was knowledge of the fact that certain forces were present and that they could dominate men. This phenomenon has recurred throughout history. History also shows how it is up to people to acknowledge and exorcize these forces. The universe of thought and magic is the de facto basis for the history of astrology, which also intersects with the figures of Luther and Melanchthon. One sees the extent to which ancient symbolisms remain powerful when one considers, for example, their importance for Melanchthon: he sought to displace Luther's birthday by one year on the basis of an astrological interpretation, so that this birthday would coincide with the Great Conjunction, which would presage the occurrence of something that might very well amount to a shakeup of the dominant religion. For Melanchthon this prediction represented something worthy of belief, indeed a bona fide certainty, while for Luther astrology was a dangerous mistake. Luther, in contrast, believed in the signs of nature; for him these were authentic signs.

Not everyone shares Gombrich's point of view!

Edgar Wind's critique of Gombrich's biography deserves to be read.[39] For all those who, like Wind, knew Warburg well, Warburg was the opposite of chaos, of the labyrinth. True, he had experienced chaos, but when he spoke he managed to condense it, to exorcize it inasmuch as he transformed it into a form of expression, a language. He had a feel for the clear and original phrase, such as *Der liebe Gott steckt im Detail*, which might be translated without the colour of the original as "God lives in the details." When you listened to him, you were present at an act of creation. And you learned that a person who knew chaos better than most was also a person who understood this chaos and was capable of exorcizing it.

You were to maintain close ties to the Warburg Library, but Warburg himself died in 1929. As to Cassirer, did you see him again after leaving Germany?

I was in close contact with him and his wife after 1926. I returned to Hamburg very often. When they came back from Austria in 1933, I went to meet them in Switzerland – Mrs Cassirer mentions this in her book – to tell them it was impossible to stay in Germany. It was still believed at that time that Nazism would be a fleeting phenomenon. In 1933 I realized that, far from being fleeting, it had deep roots and that the situation would only get worse. I convinced him to leave Germany. We invited him to Oxford where I saw him every day. We spoke of problems in the philosophy of symbolic forms and the peculiarities of English philosophy.

Cassirer was very deeply rooted in German thought. He specialized in German literature, on which he had written lovely books, and was one of the foremost experts on Goethe. For a master of language like him to be forced to speak English ... He had read the English authors, of course; he had read Shaw – he had even written to him – but speaking and thinking in English did not come naturally to him. He taught at All Souls College. It was the era of the young Turks. Ayer was there, Austin, others. It was the beginning of analytic philosophy. When he spoke of Leibniz, discussed Leibniz in his relationship to Descartes, Leibniz in his time, his individuality as a thinker, they were totally uninterested.

They always wanted to ask the question: "Is that statement true?" They wanted to critique Leibniz, every statement by Leibniz, with reference to analytic philosophy.

That situation must have made him unhappy.

Unhappy is putting too fine a point on it, but he was not comfortable. That's why, when in 1934 he was invited to Gothenburg, Sweden, where the provincial governor had been his student, he decided to go. I prepared a Festschrift titled *Philosophy and History* in his honour and it was to have been published in August 1934 to commemorate his sixtieth birthday. I had wanted to ask philosophers from different European countries to use their contributions as a way of showing their solidarity with the German philosopher deprived of his teaching post by the racist legislation of Nazi Germany. I secured the collaboration of prestigious authors, among them Lucien Lévy-Bruhl, Léon Brunschvicg, Étienne Gilson, Henrik Pos, even Germans such as Theodore Litt and Ernst Hoffmann, and the Italian Giovanni Gentile who, although he had espoused Mussolini's ideas, insisted that Italy was, at that time, totally opposed to the Racial Laws.[40] The anti-fascist philosopher Benedetto Croce never forgave him for these fascist sympathies and withdrew from the project. But I want to warn you, in case you should ever undertake a similar project, that you are always beholden to the one who arrives last. This time, it was the Spaniard José Ortega y Gasset. He held up the whole project for over a year. His paper "History as a System" is noteworthy and has even been translated, but the publication of essays in honour of Cassirer was delayed until early 1936.

When did Cassirer leave Sweden for the United States?

He was in Gothenburg, and you know that during the war, after the invasion of Norway, Sweden was neutral, but the Swedish – and we must never forget this – had let the Germans use their trains to transport soldiers into Norway. So there were German soldiers on the trains. The fear was that this could become dangerous. Cassirer left Sweden on the last ship given permission to cross the Atlantic, which also carried a man whose name you will recognize, Roman Jakobson. It was a very risky voyage: at one point a German boat threatened to capture and search this Swedish boat. Nevertheless, Cassirer arrived safe and sound in the United States. I never saw him again, more's the pity. He died in April 1945 when the war was still on. It wasn't until 1946 that I was able to leave my post.

I believe you stayed in contact with his daughter.

And also with his wife. After my first visit to Canada, I went to New York to see her. I saw her often after that. I knew their daughter as a young girl at the family home in Hamburg. She did not go into philosophy but became a musician. The elder son wrote well-known commentaries on Kant that were published in England. The first job offer I received in England was to go to Glasgow as an assistant professor in the Department of Philosophy. I didn't want to because I was at Oxford and at the Warburg Institute, which was then in London. I recommended the younger Cassirer and he went. He wrote some of his works there before returning to Oxford, where something rather surprising happened: he converted to Anglicanism. He had close ties to Father Huddleston, a remarkable man who had been in South Africa and protested against the regime for religious reasons. After his conversion, Heinz Cassirer wrote on St Paul and Kant. Can you imagine? Ernst Cassirer's son demonstrating the superiority of St Paul! It was the revolt of the son against the father. He was well versed in Greek and produced a new English translation of the New Testament from the Greek. As you know, nearly all the translations are from the Latin. It stands apart for the quality of the translation, as Greek education was excellent in those days. He's dead now. He had a daughter whom I see in England from time to time.

2

LITERARY HEIDELBERG

You've alluded to the calibre of the intellectual atmosphere and the literary life pervading Heidelberg at the time you were studying there. You mentioned the salons. Did you attend others besides Marianne Weber's?

The first such event to which I was invited took place at the Curtius home. The professors' wives scheduled days when they were "at home" in Heidelberg. Most of these were actually evenings, although Mrs Weber was at home every other Sunday afternoon. Mrs Curtius, the wife of the archaeologist whose seminar I took, was a great lady. She had been married to a general but divorced him to marry Ludwig Curtius, which caused a scandal in Freiburg. She kept a salon in the great Weimar Palace that was their home in Heidelberg. It was there, in 1923, that a friend of André Gide's, Ernst Robert Curtius,[1] who was not a relative but a friend of Ludwig's (Curtius is a fairly common name in Germany), read passages from Marcel Proust to an audience of thirty. Only parts of *In Search of Lost Time* had been published by then. They wondered how to translate *À la recherche du temps perdu* and *Du côté de chez Swann*; the syntax of "Du côté de chez" is about as un-German as you can get!

They also organized memory games and the like. In a smaller room off the main room where the reception was held, sixty to eighty objects would be spread out on a table. Each guest had one minute to look at them and then had to list and describe the objects he or she had seen. Lujo Brentano, an economic historian in his late seventies, was the most frequent winner. He and his older brother, the philosopher Franz Brentano, were the nephews of Bettina von Arnim, who knew Goethe.

At these gatherings, there was always a moment when someone read a piece of literature, and sometimes musicians played.

So you knew Brentano?

He looked out for me when I was a student of seventeen. I was particularly interested in the debate that had pitted him against a French historian, Frantz Funck-Brentano, on the concepts of *Kultur* and *Zivilisation*. Romain Rolland and Thomas Mann had also taken opposing sides; Mann mentions it in his *Reflections of a Nonpolitical Man*, published in 1918.[2] In France at that time, the term *Kultur* was disreputable; it was a typically German word in its connotations. France was the land of *civilisation*. In Germany, by contrast, *Zivilisation* was limited to the outward habits of a society, to good manners, while *Kultur* referred to its creative spirit.

Did you meet Max Weber at his home?

No, but I met his brother, the economist Alfred Weber.[3] When I arrived in Heidelberg in 1923, I wanted to learn everything. I attended Alfred Weber's course and I remember his lecture on *Standorttheorie*, or location theory, the importance of a company's geographical location with respect to customers, communications, and raw materials. On 8 November 1923 we heard news of the putsch by Hitler and Ludendorff in Munich. He interrupted the class to tell us of the dangers looming over Germany. He was very nervous and kept mechanically reinserting a monocle that fell out over and over again.

Max Weber had been dead for three years but was still present in spirit in the home I visited as an intimate of his adopted children. His widow considered me a member of the family; my first job was to help her proofread the second edition of *Economy and Society*.[4]

2.1 / Marie David, *Marianne Weber*, 1896. Kurpfälzisches Museum Heidelberg.

She carried on her husband's celebrated salons, inviting professors, writers, and artists of the city such as Gustav Radbruch, the philosopher of law, former Social Democratic minister of justice, and penal code reformer; or Karl Mannheim, author of *Ideology and Utopia* and champion of the new sociology of knowledge, who presumed to serve as a spiritual guide to an uprooted European intelligentsia, to whom he preached nothing but contempt toward those who still held onto any moral certainties.[5] I have a clear memory of Pierre Viénot, a friend of André Gide's whom I met at Marianne Weber's on one of his trips to Heidelberg, saying that for Mannheim, "the only courageous attitude is a frank acceptance of inevitable nihilism." Viénot's book *Is Germany Finished?* (1931) is one of the subtlest and most brilliant analyses of German society at that time.[6]

2.2 / Home of Max and Marianne Weber, Heidelberg. Private collection.

It was my duty to serve as host and I attended discussions on themes dear to Weber. We were delving deep into our historical conjuncture in an attempt to gauge its consequences.

The monotheism that still characterized the nineteenth century no longer existed. There was no single religion, unique faith, or philosophy that commanded universal assent. We were in a "disenchanted" world, to use Weber's term; a world shorn of poetry, in which people felt lonely and abandoned. What were the consequences of this observation for society? Nationalism, new elitisms, socialist tendencies. These were the great problems that were central to all these discussions. Contrary to what some still believe, the ideas of Nietzsche and Schopenhauer had lost much of their power, and the question of God was not central, even if nihilism remained at the crux of our thinking.

In what ways did Germany's troubled situation make itself felt in daily life?

Inflation made life hard. Many students had to take odd jobs to make ends meet. I gave private lessons in Latin, Greek, French, and German. But bread that cost 20 million marks in the morning cost 40 in the evening. What was a person to do? I had a small fortune, 20 Swiss francs, set aside; to exchange them would have been a disaster – they'd have lost all their value. To survive, I found a solution: I spent two days buying up all the chocolate I could find in Heidelberg; in fact, I believe I even went to Mannheim to buy some there. I had a small mountain of chocolate in my room that I was able to sell during the day, as needed, so that I could buy bread.

But the circumstances, straitened as they were, did nothing to diminish interest in the literary life. Interesting women came to these salons; Else Von Richthofen, for example, who had married a Jewish scholar, Edgar Jaffé, the scientific editor of the *Archiv für Sozialwissenschaft und Sozialpolitik*.[7] Else Jaffé was an intelligent woman and a friend of Max Weber's – an intimate friend, it is said today. Her sister Frieda had left her husband to live with D.H. Lawrence – quite the soap opera, that story. During the First World War, their cousin, Baron Manfred von Richthofen, was the aviator who shot down the most enemy planes. There was also the admirable Marie Baum, a social reformer who introduced and organized *Familenfürsorge*, family assistance.[8] I'm fairly sure that Ricarda Huch came once, a great writer who wrote on the German Romantics. There were some really impressive women. One of them – who was to play an important role in my life on another occasion – was Wilhelm Fürtwangler's mother.

Going to the salons could not have been your only activity; what about student life, the student corporations, the duels?

In 1927–28 I lived in the *Gasthaus zur Hirschgasse*, which had a splendid view and a large garden. There was also an enormous room in which the student corporations met. In each corporation, the youngest, who was called *Fuchs*, fox, had to be initiated in order to join. The initiation consisted of a *Mensur*, a duel in which he had to strike his adversary with a sword. His utmost duty was to never retreat; retreat was a sign

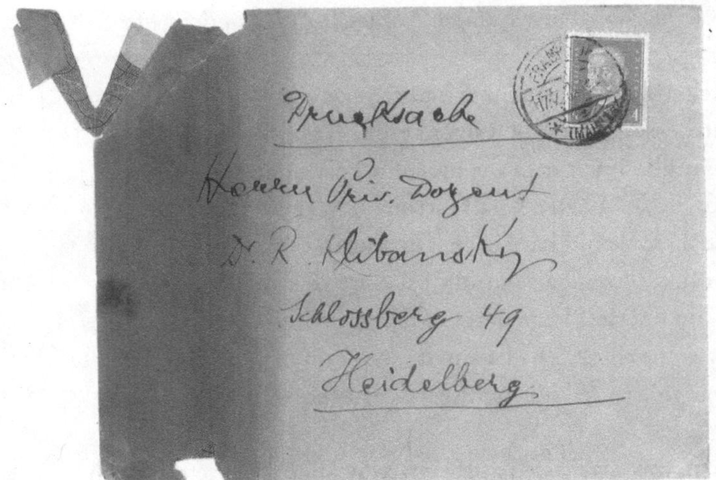

2.3 / Envelope addressed to Raymond Klibansky, *Privatdozent,* at his Heidelberg address. Postmarked Frankfurt, 27 July 1932. Private collection.

of weakness. So he inflicted, or received, *einen Schmiss,* a gash, a great mark of distinction in German society at that time.

One could watch what was happening in this big room from a balcony that served as a pilgrimage site for American tourists who wanted to see blood spilled. There were corporation banquets and initiation ceremonies, which took place every two weeks. On those days, I would run for cover. Those drunken rituals – the initiate had to drink – disgusted me.

Did these rituals pertain to all students?

Only those who insisted on preserving certain traditions, the sons of industrialists in particular. They formed a minority – quite a considerable minority, and a visible one, since these students wore uniforms. Those who were genuinely serious about their studies did not participate.

Who were your friends?

My dear friend Walter Solmitz was not in Heidelberg but in Hamburg with the Cassirers. He later retreated to the Bavarian hills near Czechoslovakia for two years to write his dissertation and produce other philosophical reflections. I was close with Heinz Cassirer, Golo Mann, who often came over for breakfast, and Lotte Labowsky. Labowsky was studying in Heidelberg and preparing her dissertation, which was published under the title *Die Ethik des Panaitios* and consisted of a detailed analysis of Cicero's *De Officiis* and Horace's *Ars Poetica*; it was an attempt to reconstruct the thought of the philosopher Panaetius, who was considered a Stoic, on the basis of those sources. She lived at Marianne Weber's after I did. Her father was a prominent Hamburg lawyer and she had begun by studying law. After realizing that this was not her field, she came to Heidelberg in 1925 to study classical philology and philosophy. In early 1934 she emigrated to England and took a job at the Warburg Library. She was then invited by Gilbert Murray to Oxford, where she taught at Somerville College, of which she would become a research fellow after the war. She greatly assisted me in my work on the *Corpus Platonicum*, and this collaboration would give rise to her great work on Bessarion's library.[9]

To assemble the sources of the Platonic tradition, one had to study the history of the Latin and Greek manuscripts. For the Greek manuscripts, the Byzantine scholar Bessarion, who became a cardinal, is one of the main sources. He is a fascinating figure. Even before the fall of Byzantium, he went to Italy in the wake of the emperor and the patriarch, who had been invited by Pope Eugene to the Council of Ferrara to bring about a union of the Christian churches. Nicholas Cusanus had gone to Byzantium bearing the pope's invitation, and he probably met Bessarion in that city or on the boat taking the Byzantine delegation to Italy. Bessarion took with him a certain number of Greek manuscripts. The Council concluded with a decree of union but the Byzantine clergy rejected it and revolted. Bessarion returned to Italy, this time with his whole library. He bequeathed it to Venice and it came to form the core of the Biblioteca Marciana. While he was alive and after his death, several successive catalogues of the library were prepared. Labowsky published them as part of her work, tracing and identifying the manuscripts, which had been dispersed to other libraries over the centuries.

Another of my friends, Heinrich Zimmer, was a man of genius.[10] He was an Indianist and wrote marvellous books that enjoyed great success in the United States. He developed a profound interpretation of Indian myth and thought. He did not limit himself to philological work, nor even to India alone. He also devoted attention to the great themes of human psychology, so the India he invoked and interpreted was very different from the India of other Indianists. He was deeply versed in world literature and poetry and was a spellbinding orator.

Zimmer married Christiane von Hofmannsthal, the poet's daughter, whom I met in Heidelberg. Hofmannsthal was Catholic but of Jewish descent. As such she was considered Jewish, so Zimmer could not stay in Heidelberg. In 1938 I invited him to Oxford. He came with Christiane and the widow Hofmannsthal, but it was clear that there would be no position for him at Oxford. He wasn't "academic" enough. In the United States, by contrast, he gained quick recognition. Unfortunately he died very young, in 1944.

You haven't mentioned your dear friend Friedrich Gundolf.

2.4 / Friedrich Gundolf. Photograph by Theodor Müller Hilsdorf, n.d. Private collection.

I did not meet him until 1928. When I arrived in Heidelberg I was very young and he was well known. His father had been a professor of mathematics at Darmstadt, and the son had written the first book to truly change the history of literature in Germany: *Shakespeare und der deutsche Geist* (Shakespeare and the German Spirit).[11] This was followed by *The Mantle of Caesar*, a book about how Caesar had been viewed, what had been made of him throughout history.[12] And that sense of history was everywhere in Heidelberg. When Gundolf entered the castle, he brought back to life the Romantics who had lived there – Clemens Brentano, Arnim ... But he also was aware of the danger of the Romantics, and when he spoke of Friedrich Schlegel, of that decisive time for the rise of subjectivity and irony in literature from 1797 to 1800, and of the Schlegel brothers' *Athenaeum*,[13] it was unforgettable. There was something of the prophet about him; he was a wizard, a grand priest of sorts.

How was he as a professor?

You know what a seminar involves, as we were just talking about it: the professor and his students sit around a large table; a student reads his work; the professor comments. Gundolf hated that whole routine. One day a man who was to become an influential professor in Germany and who sought admiration from Gundolf gave a big speech on Schlegel in the seminar, after which he sat back waiting for praise. Gundolf sat there silent for a long moment. Then, in the Darmstadt dialect, which he didn't always use, he said: "*Es war nit dumm, es war auch nit falsch, aber ganz nebensächlich*" ("That wasn't stupid, nor was it false, but it was completely inconsequential"). Gundolf really disliked people who put on airs.

He didn't do much to encourage students, but there were some whom he liked and who wanted to work with him. He had one notorious student whom he did not encourage, whom he didn't even know – after all, there were hundreds of people in his courses – and that was Joseph Goebbels. When the Nazis took power, I went to the library to read his dissertation. It begins with a quote from Gundolf.

Was it published?

No. It was a study of a run-of-the-mill Romantic poet, a couple of whose poems Schubert had set to music. Since Gundolf had academic responsibilities at that time and refused to advise graduate students, Goebbels had gone to an agnostic Jewish professor, Baron von Waldberg. Later, when Waldberg asked to be spared, Goebbels did nothing and the man died by suicide. Goebbels was nonetheless influenced by Gundolf's language.

What was Gundolf's situation during those troubled years?

His tenure as dean was marked by the unfortunate case of Emil Julius Gumbel.[14] A well-known, unabashedly pacifist, anti-nationalist Jewish statistician, Gumbel was the founder of the German League for Human Rights. One day, on the occasion of a commemoration of war dead, he said: "I want to talk about those who found their deaths … I won't say on a field of dishonour, but …" That phrase, "field of dishonour," was immediately picked up by Nazi propagandists. They demanded his dismissal from the university. This episode went on for years. The students demonstrated, demanding that Gumbel be kicked out. The university resisted. It consumed a great deal of Gundolf's time.

Was this when you were in regular contact with him?

Yes, between 1929 and 1931, almost every evening. He died on 12 July 1931. In 1930 he invited me to accompany him and his wife to Switzerland. That vacation was one of the great moments of my life. Mürren is a marvellous place with a splendid view of the high mountains. Gustav Cassel, a renowned Swedish economist, was also in Mürren. He told me of his utter contempt for most other economists. When I asked him if there existed a single one who rose to his ideal of a practitioner worthy of the name, he answered "Ivar Kreuger" (the "Match King"). Kreuger died by suicide shortly afterward when his empire crumbled. While Gundolf rested, I played chess with Cassel. He'd fly into a rage when he lost!

2.5 / Raymond Klibansky with Friedrich Gundolf and an unknown companion, Mürren, Switzerland, 1930. Deutsches Literaturarchiv Marbach, Raymond Klibansky fonds.

There were walks with Gundolf, and unforgettable conversations. It was at Mürren that he learned that he had been awarded the inaugural Lessing Prize, and I thought back to that day with great emotion more than fifty years later when I received the same prize myself.

After that stay in Switzerland, I went to Paris, to the Bibliothèque nationale, and to Chartres and Cambrai for my book on the School of Chartres. On my return, I went to Gundolf's every evening. He was very lonely. Stefan George had broken with him on his marriage in 1926. They had never spoken again. Yet I never heard Gundolf express the slightest criticism of George. His attitude could be summed up in these words: "Though you reject me, I shall not abandon you." He no longer saw George's acolytes, known as the "Circle" (*George-Kreis*), with the exception of Karl Wolfskehl,[15] who was his friend. When he came to Heidelberg, it was always a festive occasion.

Gundolf did not like making formal invitations and mostly stayed at home. But he did enjoy browsing in antique shops and bookstores. Every Saturday afternoon we went out looking for books. When Gundolf entered a bookseller's shop, it was magic. He found incredible things. He found the delights of Heidelberg. That human-scale city – you could do everything on foot – was full of treasures.

And he was someone you missed very much …

He was my dearest friend. Gundolf's death was a tragedy for me. He really marked the end of Heidelberg. I was twenty-seven and it felt like the end of an epoch. And it was.

Did Gundolf introduce you to George?

No. When I met him, the break between them had already happened.[16] I knew and admired George's works, of course; his superb poem collections, *The Star of the Covenant* and *The Year of the Soul*, for example. When you analyze the structure of one of George's poems, you see a total relationship between sound and meaning. The meaning ineluctably merges with the music of the phrase; the accent does not fall on one part of the line rather than another. The way that George and his disciples read verse was very

2.6 / Stefan George, 1928.
Photograph by Theodor Hilsdorf.
Private collection.

different from the way it is ordinarily read in German. A poem became a song; it took on a magical aspect. The Georgian poem is an *incantatio*: it has a magical, incantatory effect. The magic does not come from an analysis of meaning, but from sense and sound together, as in a Gregorian liturgy. There was something of the act of worship in Georgian poetry, and the disciples were in that ambience. It was the cult of the master and his poetry.

I knew some of the young people in his orbit well. George played a vital role for a certain young German elite, especially in Heidelberg. He was a dominant personality around whom cultured, admiring young people gathered. He was *the* master, the absolute master, who opposed lowest common denominators and everything he regarded as the false values of the modern world. His fervent adherents, the members of the *George-Kreis,* formed an elect gathered around him. Many others boasted of belonging to it and claimed to have intimate knowledge of it, causing Gundolf to say of it: "as of anything out of the ordinary: today, already, the rogues and the boors exploit it for their own aggrandizement. An unequivocal sign that someone does not belong to it is that he boasts of being a member and claims to be important by virtue of what he conceals or reveals. The circle is neither a secret society, nor a sect with bizarre rites and dogmas, nor a literary coterie, but a small group of individuals possessed of a certain attitude, a particular mindset, united by unforced devotion to a great man, who strive to serve the idea he embodies (without imposing it) with simplicity, objectivity, and conscientiousness, in their daily lives and their public actions. Everything whispered outside of the circle is just the gossip of fools, jokers, crooks, or slanderers."[17]

To get an idea of the *George-Kreis,* consider these characteristic verses:

Who ever circled the flame
Always shall follow the flame.
No matter how he may rove,
Reached by the rays he will not
Wander too far from the goal.
But when he loses their light,
Tricked by a gleam of his own,
Broken from bond of the core
He will be scattered in space.[18]

George is alluding to himself.

On a stopover in Holland en route to London when I was fleeing from Germany, I was invited to the home of the Dutch poet Albert Verwey in the town of Katwijk near Leiden. We spoke of George, whom he had known for a long time: "He has made a monument of himself," he told me.

The Georgians considered the *George-Kreis* to be a new empire, *Das Neue Reich*, which is the title of one of George's collections. Their ideal was not to create a new society but a covenant, a new empire, a new way of living in response to the values of the epoch. George was the guide to the elite of the "secret Germany." This latter phrase, owed to Wolfskehl, became the title of a section of *Das Neue Reich*. And Heidelberg was said to be the secret capital of the secret Germany.

What struck me most – and was perhaps most instrumental in my keeping my distance from them – was the total absence of humour and irony. Those people felt superior, they felt that they were the *elect*. That, plus their profound disdain for the Weimar Republic and democracy, goes some distance in explaining certain political developments. They believed they formed an aristocracy of the mind that rejected the very foundations of postwar Germany. One is reminded of George's verses in *The Seventh Ring*: "Return, O suave and clever fathers, though / With bane and dagger, for your ways outshine / The traitor's who backs equal rights."[19]

I could not but admire the force and beauty of George's poetry, but I could not countenance the attitude of those who wanted to be close to the *George-Kreis*. I despised their elitism. I made a point of telling them about George's intellectual origins.

At age twenty-one, in early 1889, coming from London, he went to Paris, where he immediately met a forgotten symbolist poet, Albert Saint-Paul, the author of *Les Encensoirs*;[20] Saint-Paul introduced him to Mallarmé, who invited him to his Tuesday gatherings in the rue de Rome. In parallel, he made the acquaintance of Verlaine. He discovered Baudelaire and that discovery was, by his own admission, a great event for him. He learned to value words for their sonic content.

He had discovered in Paris the symbolist journal *Les Écrits pour l'art.* He was to use this title for the journal he founded, *Blätter für die Kunst,* in which he published translations of Mallarmé, Verlaine, Saint-Paul, Rimbaud, and others. In 1907 he evoked in his poetry the memory of Auguste Villiers de l'Isle-Adam (whose funeral he attended), Verlaine, and Mallarmé, and he spoke of a return to "Frankish lands," where the Meuse and the Marne flowed.[21]

These contacts were decisive for his conception of poetry, which corresponded to the one expressed by Mallarmé in *Divagations,* where he says that the chief function of poetry is to achieve "the divine transposition, for the accomplishment of which man exists."[22] George would contrast this ideal with what he considered the German poetry of the time. In 1893 he wrote to Saint-Paul, "Germany is starting to disgust me."

But it would be ill-advised to draw hasty conclusions about the influence of France and his disaffection for Germany. It is best to let the poet speak for himself. In an unpublished letter to Stuart Merrill, probably dating from the late 1890s, which was kindly relayed to me by the director of the Bodmer Library in Cologny, just outside Geneva, George wrote: "Whereas I do acknowledge the influence of the French in my work, it must be of the vaguest, most general nature: the doctrine that in poetry, one must seek the highest beauty, purity, sublimity. Otherwise, in my *Hymnen,* simple outdoor tableaus, there is nothing foreign; on the contrary, they are pervaded by a sentimalism that can only be German. In *Pilgrimages,* you yourself remarked on the very German soul."[23]

In any case, the French influence was to diminish. It was the German poets, in particular Hölderlin's mature style, discovered by Norbert von Hellingrath, as well as the themes of Greek antiquity that were to become central in George's oeuvre. Among his acolytes especially, the Greek ideal and the notion of the great man took on increasing importance. These ideas influenced some of the best minds, authors of works that remain monuments of German scholarship in the fields of literature and history: works such as Friedrich Gundolf's on Caesar, Goethe, Shakespeare, and the German Spirit, or the Romantics, and Ernst Kantorowicz's on Frederick II.[24] For Gundolf, the "great man" was something decisive; in history, one had to look for the man, the great man, not material explanations. What mattered was what the man, the great man, did.

One always hears about the prevailing homosexuality in George's circle. Has this aspect been overestimated?

What struck me when I was seventeen, and already had a critical mind, was the slogan "the deification of the body is the embodiment of the deity." It is, to be sure, a lovely maxim, harking back to the Greek, but when I saw these people speaking at length of the living God, I was quite bemused. It brings to mind the story of Maximin, a thirteen-year-old boy whom George met in Munich and who died at the age of sixteen. After his death, George said that "God had taken human form."[25] I told myself the Georgians had taken things much too far, beyond the bounds of the acceptable. George had disciples who were fascinated by him. This can be clearly seen in certain impressive photos; he was surrounded by passionately devoted *Jünger*. I found this repugnant. I never wanted to be a *Jünger*. Disciple is *Schüler*. *Jünger* is more than that. An acolyte? An apostle?

Were there women around George?

Sure. Sabine Lepsius, for example, whom George had met as a fairly young man. During his youth in the town of Bingen, he had been close to Ida Coblenz,[26] with whom he had a warm but apparently platonic friendship. He dedicated several poems to her, as well as his translations of Verlaine. There was a break between them after several years, whose cause remains unknown. After a short-lived first marriage, Ida Coblenz married the poet Richard Dehmel, whom George detested. There were women, but no lovers. At the end of his life, Edith Landmann,[27] a woman I knew well in Basel, the author of an essay on the transcendence of knowledge who also published her conversations with George, was particularly occupied with philosophy in the *George-Kreis*. She was an intelligent and energetic woman whom George respected.

Some of George's disciples were ultranationalists. Did he have, or seek to have, political influence?

The tragedy of George had to do with the excesses of certain people in his entourage. One in particular, Friedrich Wolters, was the evil spirit.[28] A historian and a professor at Marburg, he wrote a book titled *Herrschaft und Dienst* (Royalty and Fealty), in which George is revealed to be the king in question. It was Wolters who insisted on the idea of a new *Staat* (state) of which George was the sovereign. He then published, with George's approval, a voluminous work titled *Stefan George und die Blätter für die Kunst*, in which the history of the German spirit is personified almost exclusively by George. The book made Gundolf quite unhappy. He said to me: "Das ist pfäffisches Geschwätz!" ("It's the chattering of a bigot!") And yet Gundolf was far from a wag.

This notion of the *Staat* did much to erase the French influence in the work of George and his disciples. Together with their unfailing elitism, it favoured certain political tendencies.

And National Socialism co-opted some of that elitism?

Certainly. But the conduct of the *George-Kreis* members is hard to pin down. There was a deep divide within the group. Among its members were a number of Jews, some of them – Wolfskehl, Gundolf, Ernst Kantorowicz, George's right-hand man Ernst Morwitz – widely renowned. But in later years, some of the disciples – the obvious examples being Kurt Hildebrandt and Albrecht von Blumenthal – had close ties to Nazism. But these were not very high-profile figures. There was also Woldemar Graf Üxküll-Gyllenband, to whom Kantorowicz had dedicated his book on Frederick II and who claimed to be his friend. When Hitler became chancellor, Üxküll-Gyllenband gave a speech revealing his Nazi sympathies.

But a case I found more dismaying was that of Max Kommerell, the brightest of the young literary historians.[29] Some eight years after the break with Gundolf, he had become the favourite among George's disciples. At first he expressed his sympathy for the enthusiasm of the young National Socialists, despite the crudeness of their speech. Later, after the party took power, the praise ceased, especially after he gravitated away from George. However, there is not the slightest allusion in his correspondence to the fate of those of his colleagues expelled from the universities or to those whose persecution he must have been aware of.

Another relevant figure is Claus von Stauffenberg, who was executed after the assassination attempt on Hitler.[30] In his youth, von Stauffenberg had shown his veneration for the master; it guided him throughout his life. It was from George that he derived his sense of having a mission. His brother's wife tells of how, after one of the major air attacks on Berlin, Stauffenberg, noticing from his balcony that a part of the city was on fire, recited a poem by George. He did oppose Hitler but, like the other rebellious officers, it was not because of the massacre of Jews, the execution of prisoners in Germany and the occupied East. It was only after the likelihood of military disaster provoked by Hitler's strategic errors became a certainty that the plot took shape. When I learned of its failure, it was not so much the existence of a plot that surprised me as the fact that these excellent officers did not know the most elementary principle of any attempt to take power by force, one that the youngest officers in my service had learned: that one must first take over the organs of communication and propaganda.

As to George himself, a profound ambiguity can be discerned in his attitude, a fundamental contradiction. On the one hand, the brightest of his adepts were Jewish, as was his childhood friend Ida Coblenz; on the other, and according to Edith Landmann,[31] George spoke quite guardedly about the Jews in September 1933, when he certainly knew about the regime's racial measures. There has been a recent tendency to minimize the critical remarks directed at Jews in his correspondence. For example, he wrote to Melchior Lechter, the illustrator of some of his poem collections, that in Munich there are "only people and youth, [which is] a thousand times better than this Berlin mishmash of low-ranking civil servants, Jews and whores."[32] The editors, albeit highly regarded George scholars, deleted all but "this Berlin mishmash." The George archives in Stuttgart kindly confirmed this fact, noted by Stauffenberg's biographer Peter Hoffmann.[33]

George seems not to have rejected all the ideals of Nazism; in a letter of 10 May 1933 after Hitler took power, when George was being asked to accept the presidency of the Academy of Poetry, he declared that he did not deny his role as an ancestor (*Ahnherrnschaft*) of the new national movement and did not rule out his spiritual participation. Yet he refused the honour offered him and preferred to go into exile at Minusio, near Locarno, where he died shortly afterward, surrounded not by the bright minds who had formed his circle but by two faithful youths.

Among the members of the George-Kreis, you have focused on Gundolf. Were there others whom you admired?

2.7 / Karl Wolfskehl. Photograph by Wilhelm Weimar, n.d. Stefan George Archiv Stuttgart.

I would mention one man of notable stature, both physical and intellectual: the poet Karl Wolfskehl, one of George's childhood friends, to whom he had introduced the young Gundolf. Wolfskehl was one of the foremost authorities on German literature and the history of the German language, without having majored in these areas at university, his comfortable personal income having made this unnecessary. He was very aware of his family's history. His ancestor Moses ben Kalonymos had saved the life of Emperor Otto II at the Battle of Crotone in 982 and had been invited to follow him to Germany, where he settled at Mainz. He was the first to take the Kabbalah north of the Alps.

From 1900 to 1914 Wolfskehl lived in a large house in Munich frequented by George, where he held antiquity-themed costume parties. George dressed up as Homer or Caesar, Gundolf as Dante, Wolfskehl as Bacchus, and so on. And the Georgians were very serious about staying in character.

In 1933 I met Wolfskehl again in Rome. I was there at the invitation of Auguste Pelzer, the scriptor of the Vatican Library, to work on certain manuscripts of Nicholas Cusanus from Subiaco. The intellectual collapse of Germany weighed heavily upon Wolfskehl. That same year he decided to go into exile in the remotest, most foreign country he could think of, poles apart from Europe: New Zealand.

No one other than he has brought the feeling of uprootedness so vividly to life:

On the Frankish Rhine I breathed in Latin air,
With Rhine wine I quenched, as our forebears did,
The Shabbat light.
...
Exile! I the vintner, wine's cellarer,
Of the wine called Spirit, thriving's dew,
I the appointed guardian of our shrine,
A wretch exiled and outlawed me,
Tore my heart and drove me into the night.[34]

In his exile, only one consolation remained to him, and that was to write poetry in German:

Wherever I am is German Spirit.[35]

He died in New Zealand shortly after the war without ever going back to Europe.

3

THE GERMAN MASTERS

ECKHART AND CUSANUS

You were twenty-one in 1927, the year you published your first scholarly work: a critical edition of the Liber de sapiente *by the French thinker Charles de Bovelles.*[1] *I notice two things in this work. First, you are already concerned with negative thinking, the whole question of* via negationis, *of how to approach the mysteries of nothingness. One senses that you have already set off on the path that will lead you to Eckhart. Second, this work was published at the same time, in the same volume, as Ernst Cassirer's* The Individual and the Cosmos in Renaissance Philosophy. *I would like to begin by asking if you could tell us what guided you toward these difficult authors, the theorists of negation, first Bovelles and later Proclus and Nicolaus Cusanus. Your first publications after this magnificent work on the* Liber de sapiente *were on Proclus and, that same year, on Cusanus. What led you to these authors?*

I wanted to understand German thought. To understand philosophy as a whole, one must of course analyze each particular philosophy to see how well what it says can withstand scrutiny. But one also has to realize that each philosophy is rooted in a historical moment. It is conditioned by history, the thinker's history. The questions asked are not absolute questions. They are informed by the situation in which the asker finds

3.1 / Unknown artist, portrait of Nicolas Cusanus, charcoal on Arches paper, 24 × 36 cm, from the tomb of Nicolas Cusanus (Rome, Basilica of St Peter in Chains). This portrait was given to Raymond Klibansky by the Cusanus Gesellschaft on 11 August 1964, in recognition of his work. Private collection.

himself. So, to understand both the questions and how to answer them, one must understand the genesis of these schools of thought. On this score, one can readily see how thoroughly German thought distinguishes itself from either French or English thought. What are these distinctions, what are they based on? To understand them, one has to take a step back, to see how this German school of thought was marked by Kant and the Kantian tradition on the one hand and by Hegel on the other.

To evaluate the links between Kantian thought and more remote tendencies – manifestly forgotten in Kant's day – we need only recall the work of the mystical thinker Valentin Weigel.[2] Consider, for example, the title of his 1618 book, which translates as "Knowledge or judgment comes from he who judges and knows, not from the object judged or known."

To understand Hegel, who is very important and has become increasingly so, we have to go back in time. How should one approach the dialectic? In this research, the importance of the German tradition becomes increasingly clear. It is a tradition marked on the one hand by Sebastian Franck and Jakob Boehme, but earlier by Cusanus and

Eckhart. And we cannot comprehend Cusanus and Eckhart themselves if we do not account, in ever-increasing depth, for the decisive influence of the Neoplatonic tradition. So it was this grand evolution running from Platonism to Hegel that formed the through line of my earliest research.

I'm hearing two things in what you've said. One is that you gravitated toward Eckhart and Cusanus as sources, for you, of the Hegelian tendency in German philosophy, inasmuch as it constitutes a fundamental expression of coincidentia oppositorum, *the idea of contradiction accomplished through the dialectic. But I'm also hearing, in terms of its relationship to Neoplatonism, what you already saw as the great importance of the whole question of the infinite and of divinity, the problem of the suprasensible, the longing for God.*

What is so distinctive in Germany is that tension between the importance accorded to reason and the value placed on that which surpasses reason, which can lead to irrationalism – and I say "can lead," for it does not always do so. But what is the source of this tendency, where does the need to go beyond reason come from? This we can only understand if we work our way back through the German tradition to Cusanus and Eckhart. This dialectic, found nowhere in English or Scottish thought, is obviously different as well from the grand Cartesian tradition. Even the Anti-Cartesians are entirely different from this German school. What typifies it, and why? Hamann, Kant's contemporary, always spoke of the coincidence of opposites. He saw this as a philosophical truth but he attributed it to Giordano Bruno. So those who knew Hamann took an interest in Bruno, and Schelling revisited this. But they forgot that Bruno was utterly beholden to Cusanus.

On another note, in the second half of the nineteenth century, the great Neo-Kantian Hermann Cohen, the leading light of the Marburg school, read Cusanus and affirmed that he was the source of modern thought: for the Neo-Kantians, the first modern thinker.[3] But he could only be read in old editions, the most recent dating from 1565. It had become urgent to produce a new edition. Ultimately, as I said, we can only understand this lineage if we go back to the Neoplatonic tradition and, in particular, to Proclus. Underlying all these thinkers, dialectics as a surpassing of reason takes our thinking in the direction of the infinite.

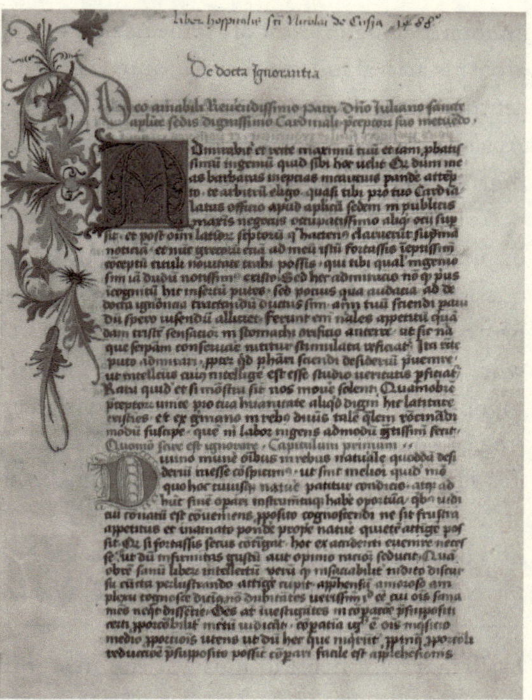

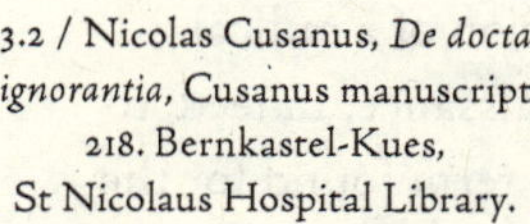

3.2 / Nicolas Cusanus, *De docta ignorantia*, Cusanus manuscript 218. Bernkastel-Kues, St Nicolaus Hospital Library.

To complete this work, you had to begin by questioning the traditional classification whereby a clear distinction is made between the Middle Ages and the Renaissance.

In Germany, Cusanus was always considered the first modern philosopher. Hoffmann,[4] for example, regarded him as the philosopher par excellence of the German Renaissance. As I studied him, I found that the division into Antiquity, Middle Ages, and Renaissance that is typically taught in school was fundamentally wrong. So I began to take an interest in the sources. Cusanus certainly knew some of the ancient literature in translation. When he speaks of Platonism, it is not the Platonism of Plato's time. I was able to show that references to Platonism in his earliest works are in fact to the masters of the School of Chartres, to twelfth-century Neoplatonism. But he was also conversant with interpretations of Plato from late antiquity: that of Macrobius and, what was even more important, that of Proclus in his *Commentary on Plato's "Parmenides."* He also possessed and copiously annotated a manuscript of Apuleius's philosophical works. It was only after his arrival in Italy that Cusanus discovered the early-fifteenth-century Italian translations of Plato's dialogues – the *Republic*, the *Apology*, the *Crito*, the *Phaedo*, and the *Phaedrus* – as well as the twelfth-century Sicilian translations of the *Meno* and the *Phaedo*.

You see how essential it is to modify the conception of a radical disjuncture between the Middle Ages and the Renaissance; indeed, to question the very conception of the Middle Ages, a term found for the first time in Bishop Giovanni Andrea Bussi's 1469 praise for Cusanus, who had long been his patron.[5] A close analysis shows that the rather vague term "Middle Ages," as used to designate the centuries between "the end of antiquity" and "the Renaissance" – another problematic term – has the effect of obscuring differences more than it reveals unity.

Did Proclus become important to you because he represents the link between the Neoplatonism of the founder, Plotinus, and the Renaissance?

I still maintain that Plotinus was the greater thinker, in contrast to Jean Trouillard,[6] who believed that Proclus was more accomplished. But from a historical point of view, Proclus is the one who is important to the medieval tradition for, apart from a few quotations, Plotinus was unknown.[7] He was only known indirectly, while Proclus's work was available in Latin translation in the thirteenth century, and it is essentially in Proclus that a concept that would become fundamental to German thought can be found. I'm speaking of the soul. In this grand scheme of thought, the soul is both God in the soul and *unum in anima*, the one in the soul. And it is the possibility of this "one in the soul" that binds man to God, enabling him to surpass the bounds of rationality. One can readily see how this idea of *unum in anima* would become central for Eckhart. Each man has that spark in him, that spark of the divine within man. This mystical foundation would later become secularized in those claims of dialectics that surpass rational reasoning. Too briefly put, this was what drew me to learn about the foundations of these German concepts.

Your oeuvre is immense. Its development comprises many different avenues of exploration and we have only examined a few aspects of it. The convergence of your work toward the interpretation of Platonism is the sign of a truly profound coherence, a great loyalty to Plato, to which we'll return. This loyalty is rooted in your work of the period from 1929 to 1936, work devoted to Cusanus and Eckhart. In a short book published later, in 1939, you showed the continuity of this Neoplatonic tradition throughout the Middle Ages. During this whole period, we see the importance for you of the concept of tradition, the importance of the heritage imposed on you as the central concept of your historical work. With profound fidelity to Cassirer, in whose thought you were well versed, this attention to tradition seems to me to evince great hopefulness and also a rejection of the monolithic character of Germany's culture of blindness, which was already darkening the horizon in the 1930s.

Could we dwell for another moment on your interest in negative thinking, to which the question of God is central? For example, starting from Rogier van der Weyden's now-lost painting of a face that appeared to be staring at you no matter where you stood,[8] *Cusanus evoked the infinitude of God, which is, for him, both necessary and impossible. I would like to ask you which aspects of Cusanus's thought were particularly compelling to you: his metaphysics, his theology, the* coincidentia oppositorum, *or questions of cosmology or epistemology?*

The answer to your question is simple. It is not any one aspect but the unity of all these aspects that distinguishes and characterizes Cusanus and is the reason why he is so important: in and of himself and also as a source of later developments, particularly in Germany. So to do him justice, we have to discern what is important in each of these domains. I will begin by speaking about his doctrine of liberty and the human personality.

Yes, that was important for you, because when you formed, in some sense, your own philosophical project, it was the idea of man that concerned you primarily; so, the idea of liberty in a world where necessity seems to dominate.

Absolutely. We can see that this notion of liberty and the human personality was, in the early fifteenth century, still dominated on the one hand by astrology, in which the stars, the heavenly bodies, the position of man in the whole cosmos dominated his fate. I found, for example, a long outline in Cusanus's hand in one of the manuscripts conserved in the library he bequeathed to the *Cusanusstift*, the hospital he founded in his native village.[9] It explains the great events, including the founding of religions, from the creation of the world to the Roman Empire, as a function of the constellations. This text shows the extent to which he knew the Latin translations of the Arabic astrologists.

But there was a much more profound doctrine, the grand doctrine of Augustine. Everything depends on divine grace. Cusanus's first writings are dominated by Augustinian doctrine, according to which the light of God's grace is the fundamental condition for any knowledge and the guiding principle of all human action. But Cusanus soon realized that the efficacy of this grace is closely related to the individual's personal acts. Thus, a striking difference manifests itself in his apparent return to Augustine. Grace is no longer a hidden divine power operating independently and without regard for reason and merit, but rather a force intimately linked to personal action. This idea is expressed with great lucidity and vigour in his treatise *De visione dei*, on the vision of God, a dialogue between man and God. "The power that I receive from you," Cusanus now declares, "in which I receive the seal of the Almighty, is my free will, by which I can increase or diminish my capacity to obtain grace."[10]

The fundamental point of view has undergone a significant change. Human will is no longer a mere consequence of grace. The emphasis is now strongly placed on the fact that it is at the same time a condition for receiving it. "It is my fault alone," he says, "if I do not find grace in your eyes." The manner in which divine grace itself is communicated to man is of the utmost importance. Man asks anxiously: "How does God reveal himself to his creation?" But God answers: "Achieve self-possession and you shall possess me" (*Sis tu tuus et ego ero tuus*). These words, in my view, contain the kernel of the doctrine of liberty. And when, after a long search, I obtained a copy of the first edition of Cusanus's works, I was not a little surprised to discover that a fifteenth-century reader had reached the same conclusion and had written these words as an epigraph on the flyleaf.[11]

But how does man obtain this self-possession that is prescribed as a condition and at the same time a consequence of grace? Here is the answer: The free will you have given me gives me the capacity for self-possession, if my will so desires; if I fail to possess myself, I cannot possess you. The key idea, found from then on throughout Cusanus's writings, is that for you to be in a state of grace depends on you and you alone. It is within your power to get there. In one of his last writings, *De ludo globi* (The Bowling-Game),[12] he revisits the theme of personal responsibility, widening its scope even further. Here, the primary causes not only of his conduct, but also of his entire destiny, are found within man himself. Man is accountable to himself, and himself alone, for his good and bad fortune. All the force and austerity of such a positive conception of destiny can only be fully appreciated if we recall the circumstances in which Cusanus made this affirmation. These are the words of an aging cardinal who had been deprived of his bishopric and lost all hope of regaining it. It is the attitude toward one's destiny that a later philosopher, Nietzsche, called *amor fati*, love of one's fate.

Closely related to the principle that man is master of his fate is the definitive rejection of astrological doctrines. The influence of the orbs extends only to purely physical events, natural phenomena such as time and the growth of crops. Man's personal, free, noble domain – Cusanus's phrase – eludes that influence. This work, *De ludo globi*, is a paean to the creative power of the human spirit, which demonstrates its intellectual liberty by creating the arts, an idea that was to play such an important role in the thinking of Leonardo da Vinci. For Cusanus, not only man's intellectual faculties, but also the possibility of his apostasy or suicide, are manifestations of human liberty.

In essence, Nicholas Cusanus became the apologist of reason even as he placed limits on it. What role does faith play in his thought?

On the relationship between reason and faith, it is important to stress the limits that Cusanus placed on reason and logic. God is beyond the coincidence of opposites, and one must aspire to God by making a personal effort that entails an act of faith. This act is not irrational; indeed, it is based on reason itself. What Cusanus calls intelligence, in the Neoplatonic sense, is not contrary to reason. But reason itself is what tells us that this leap of faith is necessary. Knowledge without faith is incomplete. Scientific research is precisely how reason proceeds to discover the traces of the divine in the world. God makes use of wisdom. God "ordered everything according to number, weight, and measure." It is the job of the human mind to discover this divine work by making systematic use of the numerical sciences. Cusanus was also a contributor to mathematics, making continual attempts throughout his life to square the circle, as can be seen in an autograph in the Vatican and in several writings on the subject. For him, mathematics was not an end in itself; it served as a symbol of the search for the infinite by the finite human mind. Like polygons that will never become congruent with the circle no matter how many sides are added to them, in an analogous fashion, human knowledge will increasingly approximate reality but never achieve coincidence, at least not in the strict sense of equality.

Perhaps, for you, the importance of this doctrine of responsibility and liberty had rather meaningful resonances with the context in which you approached it, and here I refer to the context of German culture in the interwar period. What was the path that led you to Eckhart? He is the source, is he not?

He is not the only source, but he is a great master who inspired Cusanus. It is said that his influence was handed down through the teachings of the Brethren of the Common Life,[13] from whom Cusanus apparently derived an ideal of secular piety, but this relationship is largely mythical. Yet he did study German mysticism – a vague and confusing phrase, ultimately a label that obscures more than it enlightens. At issue, in fact, is the fundamental relationship between the human soul and God. Cusanus had Eckhart's principal manuscript in his possession. He annotated a copy of it that can still be seen at the library of the *Cusanusstift*.

Let us come to the reasons why Eckhart's thinking became so important in interwar Germany. Can you say a few words about that, and particularly about the God-man question?

Eckhart's name was unknown to German philosophers. It was only in 1823 that Hegel, after hearing Franz von Baader wax enthusiastic about him, declared: "It has all been said already, everything that was important. The

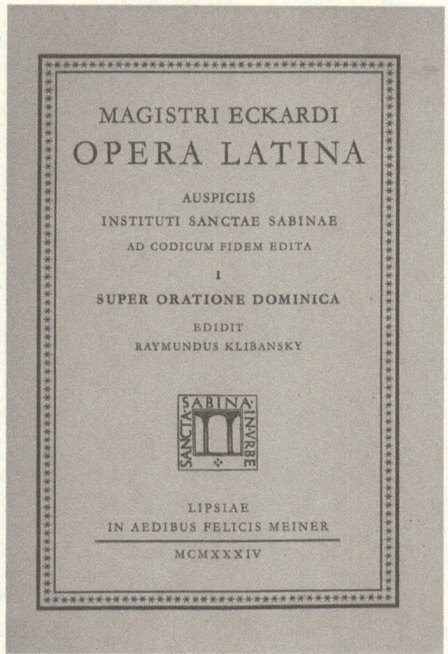
MAGISTRI ECKARDI
OPERA LATINA
AUSPICIIS
INSTITUTI SANCTAE SABINAE
AD CODICUM FIDEM EDITA
I
SUPER ORATIONE DOMINICA
EDIDIT
RAYMUNDUS KLIBANSKY

LIPSIAE
IN AEDIBUS FELICIS MEINER
MCMXXXIV

3.3 / Meister Eckhart, *Super Oratione Dominica, Opera Latina*, vol. I, Leipzig, Meiner, 1934, edited by Raymond Klibansky.

essence is to be found in Meister Eckhart."[14] But his thought was subjected to the most varied interpretations. The Nietzscheans invoked him, made a prophet of him, and this difference of interpretation turned dramatic when it became a political issue. Alfred Rosenberg, the ideologue of the National Socialist party, declared that Eckhart was the reincarnation of Odin;[15] that he was the creator of Aryan philosophy, the philosophy based on bloodlines as the most important element of identity and power; that he was Rome's enemy, the Nordic spirit, the Germanic man, and hence the source of true German philosophy; that those who did not wish to acknowledge Eckhart as such were people who did not want to see the truth.

Now, in early 1932 I had come up with a plan for an edition of Eckhart's little-known Latin works. Much emphasis was placed on the German sermons, which were popular. In the Latin writings, Eckhart spoke as a master of theology, a successor to St Thomas, whose chair in Paris he had occupied on two occasions, and here is where the core features of his thought come into view. He quoted the great Arabic and Jewish philosophers, especially Maimonides. That this man, the supposed founder of

3.4 / Raymond Klibansky, pencil drawing by his sister, Sonia, 2 September 1934. Private collection.

Aryanism, could have owed anything to Maimonides was of course heresy! So I recused myself from the mandate whereby the Heidelberg Academy had put me in charge of producing this edition, so as not to put the institution in a compromising position.

It is difficult to penetrate into Eckhart's thought on this question of divinity in humanity. Which work should one start with?

In his sermons, Eckhart wrote, for example:

> Know, then, that God is present at all times in good people and that there is a Something in the soul in which God dwells. There is also a Something by which the soul lives in God, but when the soul is intent

> on external things that Something dies, and therefore God dies, as far as the soul is concerned. Of course, God himself does not die. He continues very much alive to himself. When the soul is separated from the body, the body is dead and yet the soul lives on by itself. Thus God may be dead to the soul and yet alive to himself and one knows that there is an agent of the soul which reaches farther than broad heaven – so incredibly far that the distance is beyond telling. It goes even farther than that.[16]

Here is the theme of God in the soul, and this divine spark is what is immortal, this spark that allows us to say that man is in some sense God, a part of the divine. And some disciples, the Brethren of the Free Spirit,[17] separated this idea from its context; they denatured it, declaring: "I am God. I am not separate from God, and if you burn me" – as was done – "you cannot burn the real me. That me is God." There you have the God-man doctrine as a prefiguration of the Übermensch, the superman. These disciples wanted man to renounce what was human in him, and they believed that this renunciation led to union with the divine in him, with God.

4

LEAVING GERMANY

FROM HEIDELBERG TO OXFORD

You alluded to the vibrant literary life of Heidelberg in the halcyon days of your university career. Yet there must have been omens of the catastrophe to come.

In Germany those omens were visible right after the First World War. The Germans did not accept defeat. Crowds of people gathered to throw flowers at parades of soldiers. The propaganda started right away: that it was not a defeat; that the sickness came from within, from the socialists, the Jews, the internationalists … In Heidelberg, antisemitism was rarely blatant. In 1923–24, I was living in the home of a woman who rented rooms. Another student who lived there was a Nazi party member and he asked me in from time to time. This would have been unthinkable later.

Yet there were fateful signs: Philipp Lenard, the physicist who had received the Nobel Prize in 1905 for his research on cathode rays, had become an ultranationalist. In 1922 he refused to suspend classes after the assassination of Walther Rathenau, the foreign minister, not wanting to "interrupt his teaching for the death of a Jew."

When did you decide to leave Germany?

In January 1933, the Weimar Republic came to an end. Hitler was installed as chancellor of the Reich, essentially as prime minister. All the organs of propaganda were now in the hands of the party.

Sadly, it cannot be said that there was a major anti-Nazi movement among the professors in Heidelberg. But there was little active sympathy. The notorious election proclamation of 3 March 1933, signed by over three hundred university professors, obtained only three signatures in Heidelberg: those of emeritus professor Friedrich Endemann;[1] Philipp Lenard, of course, he too an emeritus professor; and professor *extraordinarius* Eugen Fehrle.[2]

The last relatively free general elections took place on 5 March. That morning, on the old bridge over the Neckar, I came across Dr August Faust,[3] one of the university's oldest *Privatdozenten* and the author of an excellent monograph on the concept of possibility. His democratic convictions were known to all. "I hope the democratic parties win a decisive victory," he said. Late in the evening, when it had become clear that the Nazi party had obtained an absolute majority with the German National People's Party, I met him again on the same bridge. "Who am I, as an individual, to oppose the will of an entire people?" he asked. He had converted to National Socialism. He soon became an active party member and obtained the chair he had long coveted.

It was clear to me that the youth believed in the advent of a new era. I thought of Jakob Burckhardt's *Reflections on History* (*Weltgeschichtliche Beträchtungen*),[4] in which he said that the cause of history's great upheavals is an aspiration toward something new that inspires the majority, especially the youth. This aspiration handily wins out over cool-headedness and forethought. And that was the case here. It shouldn't be imagined that party members alone cheered the new order; there were many young people who thought they were witnessing a new dawning. They were discouraged by the years that had just gone by, the Weimar Republic years, lacking as they had been in inspiring symbols. To start with, the republic had been unable to resolve the problem of unemployment and there was a tremendous gap between those who were earning a living and those who remained jobless. Second, students were very worried about the future. Half of the new graduates were unable to find jobs. Besides, it wasn't easy to pursue one's studies with barely a penny to one's name! The students held the government responsible for this situation; a considerable number of them had voted National Socialist. Neither the Socialist Party nor the bourgeois left parties offered an inspiring alternative.

The situation deteriorated rapidly. On the night of 9 March, a delegation of ten or twelve people belonging to the Nazi Party and the Steel Helmets (*Stahlhelm*), a nationalist group of First World War veterans opposed to Weimar, burst into the rector's office demanding that the Nazi flag bearing the swastika be hoisted. Incidents of this type multiplied at the university.

On 31 March, the Reich government passed a provisional law providing for the "unification" (*Gleichschaltung*) of the states, the *Länder*, with the Reich – their taming, to put a finer point on it. This was particularly useful in consolidating the new regime in the state of Baden. *Gleichschaltung* does not have a straightforward translation. Coordination, unification – these words only convey part of the idea. It was a general program designed to bring the states to heel, a program which, in several domains of civilian life, and particularly in university affairs, came to embody the central precept of Nazification.

On 1 April, all stores belonging or suspected of belonging to Jews or their descendants were marked with yellow stars and guarded by armed Brownshirts.[5]

Was there no resistance, no protest on the part of the intellectual elite?

When those events occurred, Professor Rickert invited me to his home and benevolently asked: "What do our Jewish friends think?" He misunderstood my reply, "They are ashamed," and responded with, "They need not be ashamed." I explained to him that they were ashamed that such measures had been taken without any protest, however modest, on the part of the spiritual leaders of the German elite.

He felt attacked: "What good would that do?"

So I said to him: "Professor, we learned in your courses and read in your books that the postulate according to which a thing should be done for its intrinsic value, not for its utility, is characteristic of German philosophy as distinct from French rationalism, English utilitarianism, and American pragmatism. In this critical situation, should the question of utility be the determining factor in taking action?"

This sad episode was characteristic of the gulf between the ideals taught in the courses and books and the teachers' personal conduct. Rickert, who had his whole life preached the Kantian message of an autonomous ethics, later wrote in *Die Probleme der Geschichtsphilosophie:* "If (a German's) conception of personal life does not accord with the demands of the hour and he finds his centre of gravity in cultural values other than the national state, he must adapt his opinion on the meaning of life today to the historical situation."[6]

Unfortunately, this attitude was shared by renowned scholars such as Eduard Spranger,[7] who wrote interesting books on the idea of humanity and on William von Humboldt. He had expressed his disapproval of what he regarded as outrageous statements by students, yet he later went on a mission to Japan to argue the case for a profound spiritual affinity between that country and Germany.

I've spoken elsewhere about the case of Heidegger.[8] This was perhaps one of the most serious because of his influence as a philosopher whose original ideas sought to overturn the foundations of modern thought. In 1929 I attended his lecture on the question, "What Is Metaphysics?" I was struck by the blend of real and apparent depth and by the casualness with which he ultimately did violence to Plato's *Phaedrus* in attempting to shore up his thesis on "philosophy and existence."

Shortly after Hitler took power, Heidegger became the rector of the University of Freiburg and announced his official membership in the party. One of his first measures was to decree that deans would no longer be elected but appointed by the rector. Going further, he stated in his rectoral address of May 1933 that academic freedom had to be banished from the universities. In this major speech to the professors and students of Heidelberg University, he essentially contended that the National Socialist university should not encumber itself with Christian and humanist ideas that might sap its primal force. At Freiburg, he adopted the party's racial laws, according to which all students of non-Aryan origin – including Christian students with only one parent and two grandparents of Aryan origin, even if the parents had fought for Germany – were to be considered Jews. He made an appeal to the students in which he said: "Let not propositions and 'ideas' be the rules of your being. The Führer alone is the present and future German reality and its law." Never before had reality been identified with the holder of power! Never had a philosopher prostituted himself so abjectly![9]

In France, where Heidegger still has fervent disciples, nothing has been learned. They explain away his conduct as a temporary aberration. Nothing of the kind. Karl Löwith, who discusses the episode at length in his 1940 memoir, told me that Heidegger had confided to him, when they met in Rome in 1936, that his membership in the party flowed from his philosophy itself, and from his conception of man's historicity.[10] Heidegger's position fooled no one: not Jaspers, as is clear from his correspondence and his deposition to the Denazification Commission, before which he was summoned as a witness in Heidegger's case; and not me either. Whether Jaspers was ever able to forgive him, I cannot say.[11]

Were you personally threatened?

At first it was my work that was affected. I told you that I had renounced the mandate given to me by the academy to edit the Latin writings of Meister Eckhart. At the Vatican, where I had gone in March 1933, I was put in contact with the Dominicans of Santa Sabina, who had offered to co-produce the edition. Travel to Rome that year was all but free of charge, as long as you could prove that you'd visited Mussolini's Exhibition of the Fascist Revolution! But the Nazi state had decided to give its support to the German edition for the greater glory of the regime, and I was asked to cease collaborating with the Dominicans, with the insinuation that I would obtain certain concessions. I refused what I viewed as a dishonest instance of horse trading and had very serious difficulties as a result. I was banned from entering my office and lost all my papers, the fruit of seven years of work. I continued, obviously, after emigration but our results were copied, the publisher was threatened, and the project had to stop after three instalments. The German edition is not bad; good scholars worked on it.

Were the papers stolen from your office? Did they use them?

Yes, my notes and papers on Nicholas Cusanus were used. I had had the chance to view one of the most important manuscript sources on Eckhart's Latin works: Codex 21, lent to me by the director of the *Cusanusstift*; I even had it in my office for a time. This manuscript had belonged to Cusanus and bore his precious annotations. I was to publish it. After the war I asked what had become of my papers and was told they'd been lost. In the 1970s I received a letter from the Heidelberg Academy reporting that they had been discovered and inviting me to come and get them. They had languished in an attic for decades.

I should say that I'm not certain whether the flap over the Meister Eckhart edition was the reason I was banned from my office. Things were coming to a head. The Reichskommissar for Baden immediately began applying the measures designed to achieve the goals of Nazism. On 5 April 1933 he issued a decree laying off all Jews from their civil service jobs. The university was hit hard by this measure. On 7 April, the day after the university was made aware of the decision, the Reich government passed its "Law for the Restoration of the Professional Civil Service" (*Gesetz zur Wiederherstellung des Berufsbeamtentums*), whereby civil servants of non-Aryan origin were forced to retire. This law also closed off the public service to communists. On 11 April, the university distributed a questionnaire asking all teachers, administrators, assistants, and employees the names, professions, and religions of their father, mother, and grandparents.

Everyone filled out this questionnaire, often unwillingly. I did not, but I did write a letter; it was recently found by a historian in the university archives and the archives of the government of Baden, and was published in Heidelberg. I declared that this questionnaire was incompatible with the requirements of science and that it was my duty as a *Privatdozent* to respect and publicize these requirements. I went on to say that racial origin simply could not be established as a function of religious observance over a mere two generations. I added that as far as I knew, all my paternal and maternal ancestors had practised the Jewish religion. The head of the *Gleichschaltung* agency responded to this bald challenge by demanding immediate measures against me.

In Heidelberg all the professors had been photographed; you could buy their pictures for 75 pfennig. I was at home when a young man came to the door saying he was from Mannheim, had been unemployed, and was now working as a photographer. He was trying to drum up work and wanted to photograph all the *Privatdozenten*. I told him this was futile because I had been suspended. Since I did need a passport photo and felt pity for him,

Ehefrau

Lichtbild

Unterschrift des Paßinhabers

Raymond Klibansky

und seiner Ehefrau

Es wird hiermit bescheinigt, daß der Inhaber die durch das obenstehende Lichtbild dargestellte Person ist und die darunter befindliche Unterschrift eigenhändig vollzogen hat.

Heidelberg, den 5. Nov. 1928

PERSONENBESCHREIBUNG

	Ehefrau
Beruf wissenschaftl. Assistent u. Privatdozent	
Geburtsort Paris	
Geburtstag 14 X 05	
Wohnort	
Gestalt mittel	
Gesicht oval	
Farbe der Augen	
Farbe des Haares	
Besond. Kennzeichen Keine	

KINDER

Name	Alter	Geschlecht

Ungültig

4.1 / Klibansky's passport, stamped Heidelberg, 5 November 1928, identifying him as *Privatdozent*. Private collection.

I let him take my picture. A week went by and I had received nothing. I called Mannheim and was told that they had never heard of him. It was all too clear that I was in danger. I received warnings from several sources that an attack was planned; I was advised to leave as soon as I could.

Was it possible to leave Germany?

It was still possible in 1933 if you were not personally in the authorities' sights. So as soon as I realized the gravity of the situation, right after the attack on Jewish stores, I decided to put my mother and my sister, Sonia, out of harm's way. My father, who was often away on business, was then in Italy and we decided to join him. I brought them to Heidelberg, where I knew a doctor who could issue the requisite medical certificate attesting that they needed to go abroad for their health. Without it, they could not have left the country. The next day, I took a car to drive them to Frankfurt. University professors, even lowly *Privatdozenten*, lived well in Germany. There was a garage near my home that kept a chauffeured car at my disposal round the clock. The chauffeur, a tall, very blond young man, was the spitting image of the German dear to the Nazis. We went by the bank – it was still possible to withdraw money at that time. I put them on the train to Switzerland, from where they would head to Italy, while I took the train to Hamburg. In 1935, with the situation worsening, the family went up to Belgium. My father died shortly afterward. Our family had a number of friends in Belgium, particularly the family of Jacques Pirenne,[12] son of the well-known historian Henri Pirenne. It was only after I myself had found refuge in England that I was able to bring over my sister and my mother.

Why didn't you accompany them to Italy?

I wanted to wait until 12 July, the anniversary of Gundolf's death. I also wanted to persuade the Warburg family of the need to move the library abroad. So I went to Hamburg to convince Fritz Saxl, the director of the library, to transfer the books abroad. The memorandum that I wrote at his request to the head of the Warburg family, the banker Max Warburg, had the desired effect. In a letter of recommendation to the Bodleian Library conserved among the papers of the Academic Assistance Council, Saxl explained that it was I who had come up with the idea for the Warburg Library to serve as a wellspring for studies of the history of civilization abroad, as it did in Germany.[13] Thanks to immediate action, the library was invited to London by English scholars. Edgar Wind played an important role at that point. Thanks to relations he carried on with an English family connected to his own, he had contacts in the field who put him in touch with the Academic Assistance Council. The negotiations to save the library bore fruit and, in late December 1933, the transfer was completed *in extremis*. It became the celebrated Warburg Institute, now part of the University of London.

Its influence was considerable. The institute introduced the English to a whole domain of art history with which they were unfamiliar – for them, art had been an object of connoisseurship. Wind, in his capacity as deputy director, held important international conferences and in 1937, with Rudolph Wittkower, founded the *Journal of the Warburg Institute*. Instead of being a purely aesthetic appreciation, or a history of styles, art now became a manifestation of the human spirit grounded in history.

From Hamburg, where I had stayed a week and a half, I went to Paris. I knew Marcel Cachin,[14] a founder of the French Communist Party, whose children had gone to the Odenwald School, so when I went to Paris I was invited to 4, rue Ordener. I attended the salon of Baladine Klossowska, a friend of Rilke's and mother of the writer Pierre Klossowski and the painter Balthus Klossowski. I was also invited by Charles Du Bos, who was often at home in his beautiful apartment on Île Saint-Louis. He had sung George's praises. He was a friend of another of George's admirers, André Gide, but had fallen out with him following the publication in 1929 of *Le Dialogue avec André Gide*, whose final chapter contains a rather harsh criticism of Gide's amoralism.[15] Du Bos had carried on a years-long correspondence with Ernst Robert Curtius, who had helped spread Gide's fame to Heidelberg and had translated some of his works into German.[16] Although not highly politicized, he was possessed of a rare sensibility that made him worried; it gave him a prescient awareness of the dangers looming in Europe's future. Germans opposed to Hitler were among his guests. At his home I met Harry Kessler,[17] who spoke of the situation in Germany with great lucidity. Thus, for example, he wrote in 1932 that that whole precinct of intellectual Germany that had sunk its roots deep into Goethe and Romanticism was thoroughly and unwittingly contaminated by Nazism.

I had a reunion with my father's friend Wilhelm Uhde, who had returned to Paris. I liked him very much. He was a German in the grand tradition who detested militarism.

In 1933 Alexandre Koyré,[18] whom I had met in Rome and who had produced a comparative analysis of my Nicolaus Cusanus, tried to persuade me to settle in Paris. Étienne Gilson,[19] who was influential and had been very kind to me, offered to secure a scholarship for me.

Didn't you later chance upon a letter from Gilson concerning you?

I was indeed surprised to find, among the Academic Assistance Council papers kept at the Bodleian Library in Oxford, a letter he had written in October 1933 recommending me to this institution. I was touched – so much so as to copy the letter – by his praise for my work, and even more by the profound understanding he evinced of the difficulties and dangers I had had to face. This man whom I had misjudged as somewhat cold was actually very welcoming.

Could you read it to me?

It is in English; in perfect English, for that matter. It begins like this: "I was asked for a letter of recommendation for Dr. Klibansky. There is nothing in the world I would do more willingly. I believe that Dr. Klibansky, even if he's still quite young, is one of the four or five greatest academics in the world of medieval philosophy." He had read my thesis on the School of Chartres, which circumstances prevented me from publishing, and he was kind enough to add: "I dare say that its publication will profoundly change the general opinion of that period." But what moved me was a more personal remark: "His attitude toward events and persons, which affords me the opportunity to write this letter, was, when I saw him in Paris this year, so deeply imbued with patience and dignity that it compelled my admiration. If I should ever find myself in similar circumstances, I hope I will be capable of following his example."

As I worked through the Academic Assistance Council papers to verify some dates for this book, I discovered, over sixty years after the events, how many people had gone to some trouble to help me.

Why didn't you stay in Paris?

That would have been the logical solution: I was born in Paris, I spoke the language, I had relatives there.

I remember a very nice evening at the home of Alexandre Koyré that was attended by Alexandre Kojève, Heidegger's translator Henry Corbin, Henri-Charles Puech, and others. They were worried about the situation in Germany, of course, but they had no idea of the real danger. I had also met Jacques Benoist-Méchin,[20] who invited me to his home on the avenue de Clichy. We had long conversations. He showed a keen interest in the German situation, about which he was very well informed. The standpoint from which he judged it gave me the impression that, far from seeing it as dangerous, he felt strongly attracted by the tendencies manifested in Nazism. I could not foresee then that he would become a minister in the Vichy government and an active collaborator. But his conversation opened my eyes to certain currents swirling within France. A curious character, Benoist-Méchin was possessed of an insatiable ambition that perhaps explains his collaboration, for which he was condemned to death in 1945. He was then pardoned and led a notable career as a historian. His *History of the German Army* was reprinted in 1993. One of his obituaries – he died in 1983 – recounted that he sometimes confided that his life was a failure because it was not he, "he and no other," who had put out de Gaulle's Appeal of 18 June!

So I took advantage of my stay to study French politics and the figures I knew. I could see clearly that France would not resist Hitler. The right detested the left much more than the Nazis. As to the left, it was all talk and no action! They stridently denounced Hitler but did nothing to arm themselves. I was left with the impression of a France divided by deep antagonisms that had been evident in the crises of the previous century and dated back to the revolution of 1789.

In any case, France looked none too safe.

You went back to Germany, where the situation soon became dangerous for you. How did you manage to escape?

Shortly after the anniversary of Gundolf's death, on 12 July, I left Heidelberg. I made it in time to a place where I would not be looked for, the village on the Moselle where Cusanus was born and where his manuscripts were located.

Leaving Germany called for methodical planning. It would take courage and a willingness to do something unpredictable. Too many people were applying for the medical certificates that would permit them to go abroad for their health. That wasn't working any more. So I applied for a diplomatic passport to go and see the books I needed for important research. As luck would have it, the ministry was not yet entirely in the party's hands and I got it. At the Dutch border, I ploughed through with high-handed disdain. The Nazis noticed the "diplomatic baggage" inscription and asked me if everything was okay. I made it through without a hitch.

Did you cross Holland and sail for London?

Not right away. I had to finish a paper and I worked at the library in Leiden. I had a bit of Swiss money. As you know, Dutch breakfasts are a feast. I packed up bread and cakes and lived on those for the rest of the day. The university library in Leiden is marvellous. Once my work was done, I took the night boat to London. I landed in late August 1933 with my suitcases and just enough money to pay for a taxi to the hotel.

5

LONDON AND THE FIGHT AGAINST NAZISM

Why did you choose to live in England?

I had realized that Nazism was not a passing phenomenon and that it was a threat to civilization, to the whole world, but that one thing kept it in check: the force of arms. No other argument was persuasive. It was only in England that I saw the possibility of resistance. So I went to a country where I did not speak the language and strove to learn it so that I could sway influential intellectuals. At first, no one wanted to listen to me. All Souls College, Oxford, was one place where I found a sizable pocket of appeasement. It gave me an acute sense of bitterness to find these highly intelligent people whose big idea was "Anything but war!"

I had not forgotten, for example, a debating contest at the Oxford Union that had taken place in March 1933. The theme of the debate, which I followed in the German press, was along the following lines: "Never again will this House fight for King and Country." Churchill's son took the contrary position, but his adversary was a much better orator and won. Non-insiders, not knowing that the debate had been decided on the basis of eloquence rather than substance, misunderstood. It made headlines. In Germany and Italy also. We know that Hitler and Mussolini saw it as a sign that the English would do nothing, that they wouldn't budge. So, you see, these little episodes do after all have historic influence: that one debate encouraged the dictators.

You said that you preferred England to France because the anti-Nazi movement in France wasn't strong enough. Wasn't it hard to tell which of the two countries would turn out to be the last line of defence?

England, too, had a schism between right and left, but the antagonism about it was less deep. The elements advocating for appeasement did not represent England as a whole, only a segment of official England. England resisted admirably. The spirit prevailing during the war can be illustrated by a personal anecdote. During the blackest period of 1940, when Germany was invading France with dismaying speed, Sir William Beveridge,[1] Master of University College, Oxford, convened a meeting of experts on Germany, which I attended. The purpose of the meeting was quite simply to discuss what was to be done with Germany after the Allied victory!

Furthermore, it must be acknowledged that what England did for the intellectual refugees was outstanding. Many people, professors foremost among them, gave generously for the refugees. There is no parallel in the modern history of intellectual movements. Thousands of refugees arrived in England: Germans, followed by Austrians and Italians. They were received and given assistance thanks to the work of the Academic Assistance Council, founded in 1933 under the impetus of Beveridge. Some of them continued on to the United States; but it was through Britain that they came, and many of them obtained university positions in Britain. Musicians were less fortunate because there was a union, and wherever there is a union, there are constraints; interests are at play. But the British academics conducted themselves most admirably.

I remember attending a major event at the Royal Albert Hall on 3 October 1933, a fundraiser for refugees featuring prestigious speakers under the presidency of Lord Rutherford. Einstein spoke on "Science and Civilization."[2] Conservative party leader Sir Austen Chamberlain, the Nobel Peace Prize laureate and former foreign minister (not to be confused with his infamous brother, Neville), spoke some words of thanks. The room was packed.

5.1 / Albert Einstein, Royal Albert Hall, London, 3 October 1933. Keystone/Zuma.

We also need to understand that the First World War had been very hard for Britain. English casualties had been enormous, especially among the officer class. It can be said that a large part of the British elite had been wiped out during that war, for the officers were on the front lines and were cut down. This led to the conviction that any war is a disaster because elite bloodlines are severed. Britain never fully recovered from that loss of its best and brightest. This sentiment was, quite clearly, very keenly felt by those who wanted nothing to do with war or anything leading to it. On another note, there was a political calculation: German Nazism was bad, but communism was no better. It was hoped that Germany's ambitions would turn toward the communist world and that Britain would keep out of it. It was a Machiavellian gamble and the resulting disappointment was all the greater. The pact with Stalin was a decisive factor.

People in Britain were very kind to me. In April 1934 I was made an honorary lecturer at King's College, University of London. I was also an active member of the Warburg Institute. I then went to Oxford, where the very fine Oriel College offered me hospitality.

In parallel with my work, I led a very interesting social life. I enjoyed the friendship of Jenny de Margerie (née Fabre-Luce), a Rilke enthusiast, and her husband, Roland, who was secretary of the French Embassy in London.[3] They came from Berlin, where they had been attachés in the French embassy from 1922 to 1933 and where they had maintained close ties with German literary circles. Charles Corbin,[4] the ambassador to

London, being a bachelor, the role of hostess fell to Jenny and she played it admirably. She regularly welcomed French writers and others to her salon, where I met Jacques de Lacretelle[5] and Nikolai Berdyaev,[6] among others.

One day she told me she would like to come to Oxford with her friend, the poet Edmée de la Rochefoucauld,[7] who wanted to meet a select group of students interested in literature. I got together a small group at Balliol College. "If you could meet one French writer, who would it be?" she asked them, expecting to hear names like Gide, Claudel, or Valéry. Not at all! The students unanimously chose Henry de Montherlant.[8] It should be said that at the time, his tetralogy *Les Jeunes Filles* (published in English as *The Girls*) was so popular that every young aspiring seducer took himself for Costals from *Pity for Women*!

When the war started, Jenny wanted to entrust to me her collection of items related to Rilke, the poet dear to her. Alas, I could not accept. My service was calling me to London.

Academic and social activities were not all that kept you occupied. You were later to be recruited by the British secret service.

My work on Plato and other academic work came second. I had acquired British citizenship in 1938, five years after my arrival. At the start of the war, I was invited to do some top-secret political intelligence work as part of what was called the Political Warfare Executive.[9] The job consisted of keeping accurate, strictly objective track of the enemy's intentions, which is to say, the intentions of the enemy leaders, and their morale. I worked near Bletchley, which was, as you know, the major cryptography centre. Have you heard of Enigma, the encryption machine used by the Germans for their most secret messages?[10] But that is another story. While the people hard at work at Bletchley lived under rather Spartan conditions, my service was housed in one of England's most beautiful castles, Woburn Abbey, the family seat of the dukes of Bedford. I had a superb Canaletto in my office.

Philosophy is of great help in ruling out overly subjective and hence biased judgments, to the extent that this is possible. I saw how the generals, officers, and politicians let themselves be caught up in their emotions and how inadequate was the role played by judgment, logical reasoning. Prejudices too often won the day. What I saw during that war gave me a very poor opinion of military men; during the Italian campaign, for example, which did no honour to the judgment of the military high command, and on many other occasions as well. What was needed was to develop methods that eliminated subjective judgments to the greatest extent possible, in regard to the events in Germany and, unfortunately, also Italy.

When you were in Britain, you were safe of course, but you knew that many of those left behind in Germany were threatened, suffering and, in some cases, murdered. Were these matters the subject of much discussion in London? Were the persecution of non-Aryans and the later systematic extermination of Jews topics of discussion?

There was no talk of extermination because the plan for the Final Solution only emerged at the Wannsee Conference of 1942. But there was no ignoring the threats and the dangers. To mention one case that hit close to home: in May 1939 I received a visit in London from my cousin Erich Klibansky,[11] whose father ran the boarding school I had attended on my arrival in Frankfurt as a child. Erich was himself the author of works on the sources of historical knowledge[12] and the headmaster, in Köln, of the first Jewish *Gymnasium* of Rhineland. He had been offered a position at Cambridge and I urged him to accept, convinced that the situation in Germany would inevitably worsen. He refused to leave until all the students at the *Gymnasium* were safe. The goal of this trip to Britain, like several others, was to find placements for the students. He decided that he would leave Germany when the last student had reached safe harbour. He had got about 135 students out of the country. His furniture was already on the boat when war broke out and he was barred from leaving Germany. His books were taken and then, in 1942, he was deported with his whole family to the vicinity of Minsk, where they were all executed. To this day the Belarusian authorities have refused to allow a commemorative plaque to be erected.

There were young people in Germany during the war, a group of students calling themselves the White Rose, who were among the first to denounce the regime.[13] These were authentic resistance members, not soldiers with weapons who mobilized later when they knew Germany was lost. They were youths who harboured a principled opposition to the

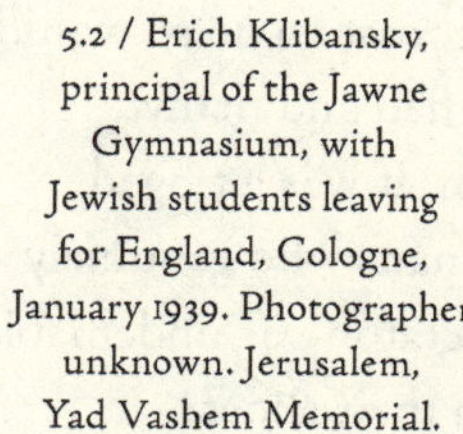

5.2 / Erich Klibansky, principal of the Jawne Gymnasium, with Jewish students leaving for England, Cologne, January 1939. Photographer unknown. Jerusalem, Yad Vashem Memorial.

regime. In 1991 I was very moved to attend a commemoration of the White Rose movement in Hamburg alongside those who were still living and the relatives of those who had been killed.

We know that there was never any effective resistance against the regime. There were, however, people whose disapproval of Hitler was such that they went into voluntary exile, even though they did not belong to any threatened group: my dear friend Bernard Groethuysen,[14] a student of Dilthey's; the Anglicist Walter Hübner,[15] a student of Edmund Husserl's; and the classical philologist Kurt von Fritz.[16] Others suffered: Karl Jaspers, for example, who was stripped of his teaching post and ready, with his Jewish wife, to take the liberating poison if the threat of deportation should materialize. Still others, like Ernst Robert Curtius, the philosopher Theodor Litt, and the classical philologist Karl Reinhardt, chose what was called "internal emigration," avoiding all involvement with the regime, anything that could be taken for a sign of approbation. There were heroes: the members of the White Rose, as we have seen, and Pastor Dietrich Bonhoeffer,[17] who returned from England to oppose the regime and was executed.

We know too that there were upstart officers who tried to get in contact with Britain. We were wrong not to take them seriously, to have rebuffed them. Many German émigrés were also treated as enemies; the situation was not easy. It's not a question we can resolve now, because to do so would be to rewrite history. Be that as it may, they were rebuffed and many Germans are quite bitter about it. We distrusted them. It was a tragedy. We condemn "the Germans," and yet there were Germans who genuinely wanted to get rid of Hitler. Their opposition to the dictator was undeniable, but what could they do? What would we have done in their shoes?

On the Allied side, there was no understanding before the war of the danger and the cruelty of Hitler's regime. We knew the situation was bad and that the refugees had to be helped and welcomed; however, this was not always straightforward.

One day at Oxford, I received a letter from a fellow Odenwald School student named Fuchs telling me that he and his family were persecuted and asking me if I could help by offering hospitality in Britain. Without hesitation, I said yes. I did not like Fuchs because he had been a communist of a sort I did not approve of, someone who thought that everything should be collectivized. He was opposed to the idea, so dear to my school, of respect for the individual, whereby the individual must be allowed to develop his potential. A second letter came asking me not to say that his brother Klaus (who was already in England) and his sister were communists.[18] It would have been unconscionable to mislead the English authorities on these matters. When I learned some time after the war that Klaus Fuchs had taken part in the construction of the atomic bomb at Los Alamos and that he had passed nuclear secrets to the Russians from 1942 to 1949, I could hardly believe it. Did my warnings make any difference? I cannot say.

I suggest we take a look at the consequences of the war for scientists: those who took refuge in Britain or the United States at the outset, with the rise of Nazism, and those who stayed in Germany and were ultimately manipulated by the regime into doing certain things.

A serious and complete answer would be the subject of several books, so I'll limit my answer to my own experience. In 1933, just after my arrival in England, I met a Hungarian scholar arriving from Germany who spoke German very well. I met him at the offices of the Royal Society in London, which were then located at Burlington House, in Piccadilly, which also housed the secretariat of the Society for the Protection of Science and Learning (the successor organization to the Academic Assistance Council). This man, named Leo Szilard,[19] invited me to his hotel on Russell Square. He told me that he had had to flee. This was surprising at the time. I had had to hide and flee because my edition of Meister Eckhart and my response to the official questionnaire concerning my origins had provoked the hatred of the National Socialists in Berlin. But it seemed strange that a scientist involved in physics research should have had to flee. I asked him why. He told me that he had worked at the Kaiser Wilhelm Institute, the centre for theoretical research in physics at Berlin-Dahlem; that he had worked with Einstein for a time and that his research concerned the prospects for atomic energy. In fact, it had been on the eve of our encounter, while waiting for the light to change on Southampton Row in front of the Imperial Hotel, that the idea of a chain reaction had come to him, even before knowing that it was possible to split the atom.

The prospects for atomic energy were such that the consequences were unimaginable. Any government that got hold of the results of such research would have power unequalled by anyone else in the world. That was the subject of his research. We know today that his approach, the method he then had in mind, was wrong. But he came up with the idea. At first I thought he was exaggerating. He had a way of speaking that seemed to … I won't say embellish, but amplify things. Yet, as I questioned him further, he gave me the impression of knowing what he was talking about. Eloquent he was not, but very serious he was, and the impression was so strong that I took notes in my notebook, something I do not generally do. I met him again just ten days later, in early September 1933, and several times after that. He often came to Oxford where he was close to Professor Francis Simon,[20] who was later to be knighted and had produced the lowest temperature yet reached, at the Clarendon Laboratory in Oxford. Szilard spoke to me of his own work. He was unhappy because he was unable to devote himself fully to his research. He had to content himself with working at St Bartholomew's Hospital in the City of London and using the instruments found there.

I recall meeting Professor Simon at the start of the war in 1939, while on my way to London for an interview. We travelled together and he told me about the use of atomic energy. For me, discussing this aloud was unthinkable; the war was starting and everyone was conscious of the possibility of espionage. There were posters everywhere urging silence and here was someone talking about the atomic bomb! I said: "Shouldn't we be keeping quiet about this?" He looked at me and answered: "The German physicists know the possibilities very well. We're not keeping any secrets from the Germans."

Later, in February 1943, the Battle of Stalingrad was the first great catastrophe for Germany, a catastrophe that could not be kept hidden from the German people. We know Hitler's aptitude for stagecraft – the parades, all that Wagnerian theatre – but this time he had not only to preserve but to raise the public morale. How could he do that without a stirring military victory, for which the prospects now seemed remote? That was when talk of a secret weapon began to appear in German propaganda. And it was clear that this propaganda was coming down from the upper echelons. The secret weapon was intended to compensate for this sensation of defeat and give people hope. Now, a dictator cannot lie to such an extent as to put out utter fabrications without some concrete basis. If he does, he stops being believed and disaster ensues. So there had to be a kernel of truth to this. What was the secret weapon? That was the crucial question.

Technically, there were two possibilities: either the V1 or V2 rockets, or the atomic bomb.

We didn't yet know what it would be. So from that moment on, efforts were mobilized on a worldwide scale to find out what the secret weapon consisted of. This preparedness work had many ramifications. There was worldwide censorship. All German correspondence leaving Europe was intercepted and analyzed to see if it contained any clues. For one thing was clear: a secret weapon cannot be built out of nothing. It demands concerted effort on the part of a sizable number of people. Where could these people be found? In what fields had a special silence been imposed by the authorities? These were the two important factors. We were looking everywhere for the slightest indication or evidence. Alongside the foreign missions and the diplomats, there was another very important source of information: the numerous foreign workers, many from France, including some who had been forced to work in Germany and others who had gone there voluntarily. Well-paid jobs were to be had in Germany and people went there to work. Some of these workers realized what was happening and had contacts with nationals of their countries. There were considerable concentrations of these foreign workers in some regions.

So there was a whole group of intelligence sources that I won't enumerate, some more secret than others. One important one was the aerial photographs taken every day using a method based on what was called in Britain "operational research," whereby the maximum area was covered with the minimum number of aerial movements. A vast sector of German territory was photographed every day. These photos were interpreted at a centre not far from London, where the job of the staff was to say whether they observed anything out of the ordinary. One day, a member of the Women's Auxiliary Air Force (WAAF) named Constance Babington Smith[21] noticed an object on the ground, a catapult of sorts, that she was unable to identify but clearly had to do with aerial manoeuvres. This was the first indication of rockets.

Next, the Polish resistance found some unexplained shrapnel, an oblong object, some kind of a shell, that we hadn't seen before. It was in fact a rocket that had been launched into the Baltic Sea and overshot the target, falling in Poland. They had copied it and taken measurements that could scarcely be believed. The drawing was successfully brought to Britain. And there were other clues as well. It was known that there were many foreign workers along the Baltic Sea near Peenemünde. Peenemünde was attacked in what became known as the Peenemünde Raid,[22] causing enormous destruction and delaying the rocket program by six crucial months, time enough to make preparations for the invasion. Sadly, a great many foreign labourers were killed.

The second possibility concerns the signs pointing to the production of a nuclear weapon. The importance accorded to heavy water by the Germans was known.

The rocket was obviously of great importance, but we also knew, as you say, that special interest was being paid to heavy water. Even before the onset of war, an item in an official German newspaper had attracted our attention: an official public order banning uranium exports from

Czechoslovakia. Second, we had reports from Norway on the great importance attached to these heavy water facilities by the Germans. As you know, uranium comes from the Congo; the Germans couldn't go there, so Norway was the main source of heavy water. We could see that every effort was being made to exploit it, and we had to find out why. What good was it, if it was only for theoretical research? The Germans were going to use it. So it was clear that the danger of the nuclear bomb was real. It was well understood in scientific circles that the Germans had pioneered this research and that the experiments of Hahn and Strassman in Berlin had led to the first instance of fission in late 1938. The word "fission" had yet to come into common parlance. In early 1939 Hahn had written to his co-worker Lise Meitner,[23] who had had to seek asylum in Stockholm in 1938 because she was Jewish, that fission was now a reality. She immediately notified her nephew in Copenhagen, Otto Frisch,[24] a man of great intelligence who worked with Niels Bohr.

Frisch wrote to his friend Mark Oliphant[25] in Birmingham asking if he could come to England. By that point the prospects for the use of nuclear energy had become real. Szilard was now in the United States. He had said that he would move there "a year before war was declared" and had indeed done so at the start of 1938. He went to see Einstein, whom he had known in Berlin as a very young man. Einstein understood the alarming possibilities of this discovery and they wrote a famous letter to Roosevelt saying, in substance: "The Germans are working on it, of that there is no doubt. If we don't get there first, they will gain a decisive advantage." This was the origin of the Manhattan Project. Szilard devoted every effort to producing the chain reaction. It was he who persuaded Enrico Fermi to request the money that would be needed to do the necessary experiments. They managed to obtain it in Chicago; they worked tirelessly, and succeeded in producing the chain reaction on 2 December 1942.

Do you know Richard Rhodes's book about the atomic bomb?[26] It is an excellent book that won the Pulitzer Prize, a great book based on primary sources, in which we see the difficulties experienced by Szilard in the United States. This man truly gave his life to building the atomic bomb; yet, after managing to alert the Americans, he still found himself in a rather difficult situation because General Leslie Groves, who had military responsibility for the project, was deeply suspicious of him. He believed

Szilard to be a spy and kept him under surveillance. There are reports from the US police saying that he had been observed meeting with two other scientists and speaking a foreign language. These were Edward Teller and Eugene Wigner and they were speaking Hungarian! It must be admitted that Szilard had a tendency toward indiscretion.

After the success of the bomb, he did everything, really everything, to gain access to President Truman and convince him not to drop the bomb on populated countries, on people, but to warn the Japanese and show them what would happen. Truman refused. Szilard was so disgusted that, as you know, he abandoned all work on nuclear power and began studying something completely new to him: biology. He became a great authority on dolphins. He wrote about them. He became one of the most active participants in the Pugwash Conferences[27] and devoted all his energy to the problem of human survival. He founded the Council for Abolishing War (today the Council for a Livable World), whose role was to raise funds to help congressional candidates who committed to working for world security. He shared the 1959 Atoms for Peace Award with Wigner. I had invited him to Montreal in my capacity as founder and president, for some fifteen years, of the Canadian Society for the History and Philosophy of Science. He was unable to accept, being already ill, and died in 1964. So for everything relating to the atomic bomb, he is one man who should not be forgotten.

And you also contacted Einstein himself, did you not? Did you have any interviews with him?

Yes, in 1933. You know that Einstein was detested by official Germany. He was persecuted in the papers and individually targeted by propaganda. So Elisabeth of Bavaria, the Queen of Belgium, a great lady with a lively interest in music, invited Einstein to Belgium. When it was realized that the German secret services had him in their sights, the Belgians didn't think they had the power to protect him, and Elisabeth advised him to go to Britain.

I met him because I was then living in London at the home of A.S. Yahuda,[28] a great friend of his whom I had known since Heidelberg. Yahuda was a member of the Sassoon family, an old family of Baghdad. He himself was from Jerusalem. An excellent Hebraist, he had become the first Jewish

Lieber Herr Klibansky!

Ich habe Ihr so rasch ausgefertigtes Memorandum sorgfältig gelesen und bis auf einige Einzelheiten recht gut und zweckmässig befunden.

Es wäre nun gut, wenn Sie einige unserer besten Leute aufsuchten und sie über die wahre Lage der Universität instruierten. Sagen Sie dann nur, dass Sie es auf meinen ausdrücklichen Wunsch thun.

In der Hoffnung auf künftiges gemeinsames Wirken bin ich mit herzlichen Grüssen

Ihr

A. Einstein

Dies ist am 7. X auf der Fahrt zum Dampfer geschrieben. Verzeihen Sie das hässliche Papier.

THE INSTITUTE FOR ADVANCED STUDY
School of Mathematics
FINE HALL
PRINCETON, NEW JERSEY

England

Dr. Raymond Klibansky
Western Central District Office
poste restante
London W.C.1,

5.3 / Letter from Albert Einstein to Raymond Klibansky, Princeton, New Jersey, 20 November 1933. Private collection.

professor to be appointed by the king of Spain since the exile of the Jews in 1492. He had left Spain to do research in Saint Petersburg. His book *The Language of the Pentateuch* made waves in 1932–33, particularly in the British press. In it he developed a revolutionary thesis: by means of an analysis of Hebrew metaphors in the five books, he reached the conclusion that the metaphors from the ancient Hebrew, at a time when it was becoming a literary language, were all based on Egyptian. The author of the Pentateuch must therefore have been proficient in that language and could only have been Moses. Einstein greatly appreciated this highly controversial work.

I kept abreast of what was happening in Germany at the time, among other things by reading the *Frankfurter Zeitung*, the German newspaper of record. It was a liberal paper, one of the great European papers, and was of course taken over by the Nazis, but it remained an important paper. The day of my meeting with Einstein, the front page carried a vehement diatribe against him by the physicist Philipp Lenard, riddled with coarse, violent libels and insults.[29] When I saw Einstein that evening, I asked him: "Did you know that there is a very personal attack against you in this newspaper?" I showed him the article. Einstein replied, with a serious air: "Lenard has accomplished great things." That and no more. So I asked him what he was referring to, and he explained to me what Lenard's merit consisted of.

Around 1933, several émigrés, including Szilard and myself, had discussed the potential positive side of this flight of intellectuals from the Nazi regime, as long as the best of these minds could be gathered at a model university. Some thought it should be in Switzerland, while I had the Hebrew University of Jerusalem in mind. Szilard had taken many steps to move the idea forward. As for me, I had had a long conversation with Einstein, who shared the idea of a university of exiles and was interested in the prospect of creating an institute of physics in Jerusalem. He wrote on 30 May 1933 to his friend Max Born,[30] then a professor in Göttingen, that it would be splendid for such a project to lead to the creation of an internationally renowned institute but that the prospect was unlikely because "utter charlatanism" held sway in the relevant circles at Hebrew University. He was highly critical of the university, whose chancellor, Judah Leon Magnes,[31] had turned it into an American college of sorts. At the time it relied on an international committee of directors, among them the Italian physicist Tullio Levi-Civita[32] and the French mathematician Jacques Hadamard,[33] a cousin by marriage of Captain Alfred Dreyfus.

Einstein had written mandating me to go and see these directors and explain the project to them, so I went to Paris and Rome. They proved largely in favour of the idea and I produced a report containing some proposals.[34] All that remained was for the money to be found and, most important, for Hebrew University to agree to reform its curriculum. But there was sharp dissension within the institution. In a memo written on 7 October while en route to America, Einstein thanked me.[35] And on 18 November 1933, he wrote me to thank me for my "not especially pleasant, but marvellously clear" report. Let me quote the end of his letter: "If the majority of those concerned are not driven by the will to serve the cause without reserve, it will be impossible to drain this swamp. It seems, then, that we are up against the sad truth that we Jews produce eminent individuals but are incapable of forming a normal collectivity. Cordially yours, A. Einstein."

In any case, the deciding factor was Einstein's willingness to move to Jerusalem. He approved of my recommendations, as he had occasion to tell me before his departure for the United States, but preferred not to commit. Instead, he accepted the prestigious position offered him by the Institute for Advanced Study at Princeton, where he could devote himself fully to his research.

To return to the development of the bomb, there were, as you've rightly pointed out, undeniable signs of the Germans' general intention to succeed in building a nuclear bomb one day or another. But were there clear signs of progress on this project? Wasn't the use of heavy water in fact a sign that they had made only limited progress? Was there an idea at the time, or at any point during the war, of how far the Germans had gone?

5.4 / Raymond Klibansky in British army uniform, 1945. Private collection.

We faced an enigma. Naturally, I am looking at the situation solely from my point of view and I make no claims to omniscience. But I did have the impression that the Germans were busy. What exactly they were doing, we learned later. Shortly after the German surrender, I found myself at Field Marshal Bernard Montgomery's headquarters at Bad Oeynhausen in Westphalia.[36] I learned that important papers discovered at the German headquarters had been brought there and that Major Simmons,[37] a librarian at Birmingham, had even classified them.

In just a few days, this man had done something brilliant. The whole collection was organized. The first thing I saw was a big map. Huge. It depicted Operation Sea Lion (*Seelöwe*), the plan to invade Britain, with coloured pins showing the first day of the invasion, the second day, and so forth. A small printed manual intended for the military police gave a list of people who were to be apprehended immediately, with all the places where they might be found. The number of names it contained was astonishing. When I opened it, one of the first names I saw was my own. This list was published in the *Manchester Guardian* in September 1945.

The second thing I found among these papers was a voluminous report on the prospects for the use of nuclear energy, signed by Werner Heisenberg. Too bad I can't tell you where it is today; probably in the archives in Alexandria, near Washington, DC.[38] I read this large report but, not being a physicist, I cannot speak of the details. Simmons, who is now at Oxford, gave me all the information for other research. However, I do clearly recollect that the document said that atomic energy was a certainty but that the practical difficulties were very significant, and that large sums of money and, especially, plenty of time would be necessary. The report concluded that the prospect of producing this bomb in the near future had to be ruled out and that it was not practical for the purposes of this war. I'm certain that that was the overall thrust of the report.

On that note, I wanted to ask you what you thought about the attitude of Heisenberg who, on the one hand, in his autobiographical works such as Physics and Beyond, *explains that he was so opposed to the production of the nuclear bomb by the German government that he unceasingly tried to persuade that same government that the project was almost certainly unviable, and tried to forestall it. Whereas, on the other hand, in a recording made at Farm Hall near Cambridge in 1945,[39] when German scientists were being held in a country house, we have this sentence from Heisenberg: "It can be said that the first time significant funds were made available in Germany was in the spring of 1942 after that meeting with Rust, when we convinced him that we had definite proof that it could be done." So we have a sentence seeming to attest to the fact that Heisenberg was, on the contrary, trying to convince the Nazi government that it could be done. Wasn't he simply trying to cover his tracks?*

There can be no doubt that Heisenberg is deliberately misrepresenting his own attitude. We know that the German scientists worked intensely, no longer in Berlin because the situation there was difficult, but at Hechingen, to the south, not very far from Stuttgart, and that they were looking for money.

There were two things. They wanted to obtain the necessary resources and they wanted to convince the leader, Hitler. But Hitler wanted nothing to do with the atomic bomb. We know this from the best authority, his own minister of armaments, a source of the highest quality, Albert Speer, whose memoirs are required reading.[40] Why? At first glance, one might assume that a secret, decisive weapon would have captured Hitler's imagination, he who loved this sort of surprise. But it didn't – not at all – because everything connected with the atom was looked at askance, since it was considered Jewish; everything relating to relativity and nuclear energy was Jewish physics. In this connection, Lenard played an important role. Hitler respected him. He was the most famous of the scientists, the Nobelist, the one who had gone to see him and told him that relativity was at odds with German morality, that it was a factor in its disintegration. Meanwhile, Werner von Braun won Hitler's enthusiasm with the idea of the rocket.

On this score, moreover, one of Heisenberg's remarks from the Farm Hall recordings is noteworthy. Heisenberg asks how the American physicists managed to gain such a lead over the German physicists. He totally forgets to mention that among the "American physicists" were a number of German Jewish physicists who had, unsurprisingly, emigrated with their know-how. This omission by Heisenberg in 1945 is quite extraordinary after everything we've learned.

It is very important to emphasize that great minds like Heisenberg had an aptitude for forgetting unpleasant facts. Heisenberg visited Francis Simon after the war and told him: "You know, had we given the Nazis fifty more years, they would have become entirely reasonable." This is a man who misunderstands, as we can see from his comments, and then all of a sudden turns into a moralist. It was the *others* who had sinned. It was *they* who bore the responsibility. But the Germans did want to build their bomb! It's easy to pretend the contrary now! Quite simply, Heisenberg and his ilk were trying to transform "couldn't" into "wouldn't."

From a psychological standpoint, it must be said that these people knew the terror that reigned. They didn't know of all the horrors, of course, because they didn't want to know, but the horrors existed and they all knew it. Obviously, they did not approve. So later, they told themselves: "Well, we never had any use for that regime anyway!" But there had been none of that during the war. They worked unstintingly at their facilities in Hechingen to make progress on the use of nuclear force. To claim the contrary is false.

There are other accounts corroborating what you say. Max Dresden's biography of the Dutch scientist H.A. Kramers[41] contains a very interesting anecdote: Kramers, who was in Holland during the Occupation, heard that Heisenberg was arriving in the capacity of a Nazi dignitary and that he wanted to meet up with his former colleague, who had collaborated on so much of the work leading up to matrix mechanics. Kramers told Heisenberg frankly that as the representative of an enemy occupying Holland, he had absolutely no desire to see him again. Heisenberg replied: "Look, no big deal. We'll get together anyway, and talk of physics." Kramers acquiesced. When he opened the door, the first thing Heisenberg said was: "But why do you oppose Germany's plan for the domination of Europe? Germany is the country that will reunite Europe." And so on. Kramers shut the door in his face.

Niels Bohr,[42] who was not a great diplomat, also had the impression that when Heisenberg paid him a visit he wanted to sound him out: that he wanted statements, he wanted information. Bohr was very, very careful. Heisenberg's attitude was typically that of a great German scientist; he was not, however, a violent Nazi. He was no partisan of the excesses of National Socialism, but he was nonetheless its servant. And those who served the regime are culpable, because without them, the regime could not have done what it did.

In any case, the secret weapon for Hitler was not the atomic bomb but the V1, V2, and even the V3. We don't know enough about the V3, which is said to have been something truly horrific. They were working on it. I know what the V1 was. I escaped it twice by the skin of my teeth. As long as you could hear it, it was harmless. It was only when the noise stopped that danger was imminent. So you had some time to get away from the windows before the glass shattered. Unless the device landed right on top of the house, you were safe, you could do something. With the V2, there was nothing to do. The destructive power of the V3 was such, I'm told, that it would have been a true disaster.

So that was the secret weapon we were all concerned about. We practised a truly intelligent form of intelligence. We gathered and interpreted all the signs as broadly as possible, following wherever they led.

Since you've begun to indicate some of the methods, by default as it were, that could be used to apprehend the enemy's secrets, let us return to the philosophical aspect of the method.

What we call "intelligence" is merely a synthesis of historical and logical methods. It is similar to the work of the historian. The historian wants to know the past, but the past is largely beyond direct recall. So how can it be known? Through the interpretation of documents in the broadest sense of the word: stones, fossils, if we are talking about ancient times, or written documents. One must strive to eliminate all subjectivity from this interpretation. It is not a matter of understanding a thing in one sense rather than another; rather, you have to abide by a rule of interpretation. Well, the situation is the same in wartime as far as philosophy is concerned. You interpret the present. It is a present that you cannot evoke as such. It is a present that you want to know but to which you do not have direct access. How can it be known? Fundamentally thanks to the interpretation of documents in the broadest sense of the term. What are these documents?

They are, above all, the enemy's statements, his propaganda, whatever it is that he says. The interpretation of propaganda is vital because all totalitarianism, all dictatorships, are highly vulnerable. Their propaganda follows certain dictates. We can deduce with some accuracy what they are trying to make their followers believe. We knew that every Friday throughout the war, the German government issued directives for the coming week's propaganda. So we could deduce, up to a certain point, the meaning of the directives and what they showed us about the enemy's intentions. I don't want to get into the fine details, but that is the general idea, the approach.

You can deduce the enemy's intentions by analyzing what is said about certain subjects in the press and on the radio (there was no television then). This propaganda must of course be studied intelligently by doing something I do not particularly like to do, which is to quantify quality. Take the invasion of Norway. We followed what was said about Norway from week to week. We plotted graphs. At first, some of the discussion about Norway was even rather laudatory – at any rate, there was no hostility. Then the tone changed. The praise gave way to a certain coldness, then to remarks about the fact that Norway was sheltering enemy vessels. These remarks did not remain isolated. Why this sudden change? The nation was being readied for an attack. And so by quantitatively gauging the emotional tone of what is said, by making comparisons from one week to the next, one can deduce intentions. That is the application of a historico-logical method. I could offer many examples and I can tell you that the method gave good results.

I find this example particularly interesting in that one generally tends to assume that democratic societies are more vulnerable to external analysis.

Quite the contrary! In democracies, what you have is disorder; every newspaper says something different. If the enemy wants to make deductions, he has to decide that one paper is more important than another. That will obviously have some value, but it does not lend itself to accurate deductions.

So isn't there at least one philosophical lesson to be learned, which is that regimes whose ideology leads to a radical curtailment of human freedom prove infinitely more predictable than others? And this might serve as a segue to your own research on freedom. Isn't there a relationship between your studies on freedom and the method that you employed?

In regard to the possibility of prediction, certainly. However, you always have to consider that the person holding power can change his mind. We cannot be sure that he will be reliable. With Hitler, we knew he had an *idée fixe*, which was to never give ground. We knew it, but we could also see that there was a gap between him and his generals. So it was possible to make deductions. Hence, of course, the importance of spies, people placed high up in the enemy camp who could send intelligence. To summarize, I would say that it is simply the application of certain logical procedures to historical knowledge; it is the historical method, in which there is nothing miraculous, nothing surprising. It is a matter of applying the techniques by which we can know the past in a manner that excludes, insofar as possible – never totally – the subjective element, the interpreter's interest, the interpreter's conditioning, the interpreter's experience; these are always in play and always constitute subjective factors. But we must minimize them, as must historians, who remain creatures of their time, prey to their own prejudices. We must eliminate these prejudices, to the greatest extent possible, as we attempt to discern the facts of the moment.

Ultimately, it means strict adherence to rigorous analysis, whether one is studying the past or the present. Put another way, it means, in analyzing whatever "depth" a regime or an ideology may possess, strict adherence to the surface, to what it shows openly – to its propaganda, that is. Can we say, then, that the entire reality of a totalitarian regime is to be found in its propaganda? Doesn't it give the whole game away, provided that we are able to interpret it using the methods you've discussed, by focusing on its propaganda?

Yes, of course, but there is also the possibility that things will go awry and that they will then try to persuade their followers that things are going pretty well after all. That attempt is in itself meaningful. They would not be at such pains unless the leaders feared that the people believed that things were going awry. Turn the statement around: Things must be going awry if they are working so hard to show that all is well! There is no propaganda without a kernel of truth. What is that truth? We can ascertain it with a high degree of probability. Much more important than the study of propaganda is the analysis of how power is actually being wielded. We must study the actual status of the decision-makers, the plans of those who hold power, how these are being received by the generals and the army who carry them out, the manner and the material means of execution.

But we have only spoken of the enemy regime's propaganda. We must not forget the importance of Allied propaganda, especially British propaganda, during the war. The BBC was broadcasting in Germany. Planes were dropping leaflets. The administration of this direct propaganda had been entrusted to Richard Crossman,[43] a member of New College who had had to leave Oxford as a result of his turbulent marital life. He had made a successful entry into politics and would surely have begun a career as a Labour cabinet minister right away if the Ministry of Economic Warfare had not recruited him to spearhead the propaganda effort against Hitler. He was particularly gifted for this task. He was fluent in German, having spent time in Germany before the war as a reporter for the BBC. During the war, his programs reached many listeners in Germany. One day, after he had mistakenly announced the bombardment of one of Berlin's train stations, some Germans wrote via Switzerland to upbraid the BBC for disseminating false news!

There was also indirect or black propaganda, whose purpose was to sabotage the German war effort by spreading false rumours. It was directed by the journalist Sefton Delmer,[44] a brilliant man who had done part of his education in Germany. He had known Ernst Röhm, the chief of staff of the SA, and had been the first to interview Hitler in Munich. He invented "Der Chef," a fictitious German officer, patriot, and nationalist opposed to Hitler who broadcast over the radio – supposedly from Germany – to the members of his secret organization. In 1942, after the construction of the powerful Aspidistra transmitter at Crowborough, he inaugurated his most famous program, titled *Soldatensender Calais,* whose content, consisting of popular music and anecdotes about the rather scandalous conduct of certain officers, became popular among German soldiers.

You were the expert on German questions. How did it come about that you were assigned to Italy?

Right, I had developed these methods with Germany, not Italy, in mind. I had spent a bit of time in Italy and had always been well received. As you know, prior to 1938 the stance of the Italian fascists was very different from that of the Nazis. We spoke earlier of Giovanni Gentile, the most important Italian philosopher after Benedetto Croce.[45] Gentile invited me over one day and told me how much he hated the Nazis. He asked if he could contribute to a work I was editing, a *Festschrift* for Cassirer, and sent me his essay "The Transcending of Time in History."[46] When Croce, who had also agreed to participate, found out that Gentile was submitting a paper, he withdrew. For Gentile, it was a gesture of solidarity; he wanted to show his opposition to the racial policies. This happened in 1934–35.

The end of October 1942 saw the Second Battle of El Alamein, on the Mediterranean coast near Alexandria. This was the first British victory, the first great victory after so many defeats. The battle had not yet even been won when it was decided that the next target would be Italy, the invasion and occupation of Italy. For this operation, nothing had been prepared from an intelligence standpoint. To occupy a country, you have to understand it from an administrative standpoint – its roads, its agriculture – from every perspective. We also had to study the key figures in the regime. None of this was known! It strained belief. An Italian intelligence file had to be built from scratch. Since it was known that I had done something on Germany, they said, "Let's give him Italy," and I was asked to take on this responsibility. I strenuously objected, arguing that this would be precisely the kind of dilettantism I had always condemned. Sure, I spoke Italian. I was familiar with some Italian libraries, I knew a bit of Italian poetry, and I had visited Italy and the Vatican. I also knew some Italian philosophers. So I was introduced to the person who'd been responsible up to that point. His Italian was halting; he was friends with the king's cousins; he owned a villa near their residence; they took tea together … I was forced to admit that my qualifications were better than his!

But knowledge of Germany gave me no special insight into Italy. I had to work literally night and day. I was very familiar with Nazism, but not with the organization of the Fascist Party. We had to produce a whole set of guides to the regions of Italy, one for each of the eighteen *compartimenti* and one for Italy as a whole, in three volumes. The first thing we needed was staff. I had made my acceptance conditional on choosing the staff myself. For me, the writing of these manuals was a supplementary task. My main work consisted in finding out what was happening in Italy. And I did succeed, little by little over a period of two years, in becoming an expert on the country's political and military figures. We ultimately became well informed about the figures who mattered, the intrigues that divided them, and the power struggles among them.

Here again, it was simply an application of the method. We needed to have archives. I had excellent archivists – my friend Richard William Hunt, for example,[47] a great scholar who became Keeper of Western Manuscripts at the Bodleian Library.

Of course, it wasn't just a matter of compiling the archives. They also had to be interpreted. To cite a trivial example, the Americans urgently wanted to know how many Croats there were in Germany – men of military age, not children but people aged eighteen to sixty. This had become important for some reason. I still remember the urgent telephone call. My assistants smiled; that was an easy one. Our archives concerning foreign workers in Germany contained a file on Croats in which a newspaper clipping indicated the monthly salary of a worker. Since the Germans boasted in their Croatian-language radio broadcasts about the amount paid out each month to Croatian workers, it was quite simple to deduce the number of Croats working in Germany.

I'll cite another small example. The Americans wanted to know details about the harvest in Tuscany. This too was quite simple. One of my assistants said: "The peasants do such and such on such and such a date, and have done so since the time of Virgil. The peasants do not change."

A great deal of very detailed intelligence was needed, mainly data about people, and this was a new application of the method. The information had to be carefully classified and subtitled. It had to be divided up, replicated under several carefully classified headings. In short, what was needed were well-kept archives.

So did you keep abreast of all the events of the Italian campaign?

The preparations were secret, obviously. It was forbidden to mention anything, except in code. The Sicilian campaign was codenamed "Operation Husky." This campaign went off quite smoothly. The same was not true for the Italian campaign. When I learned that they were getting ready to cross the Strait of Messina and go north, I couldn't believe it. From Hannibal to Garibaldi via Byzantium and the Goths, history has shown that to conquer Italy, you have to attack from the north or the centre. To begin with, there is only one road running between the sea and the rocks, and several rivers to cross, posing dangers each time. The plans had been made at Eisenhower's headquarters in Algiers and approved in Washington. They showed a total ignorance of history. But I was a political intelligence officer and my opinions on military matters carried no weight. At every river crossing and at the Battle of Monte Cassino, the mistake was dearly paid for. So many Allied soldiers were killed. I am thinking in particular of the Polish army – the Poles, who were not even invited to the Victory Parade held on 8 June 1946!

I recall listening to a speech given by Gentile at the Theatre of Marcellus in Rome during the Calabrian campaign. He exhorted the Italians to go to the trenches; he tried to persuade them that they had wanted the war and that it was their duty to defend the country. I was dumbstruck by this speech given by a man whom I knew, and whom I knew to be intelligent.

You published Mussolini's diary for the years 1942 and 1943. How did it come into your possession?

The first copy of this diary[48] that reached Britain was brought to me by an officer who had escaped from a POW camp. It had been published in the form of a little green book as a supplement to the *Corriere della Sera* on 9 August 1944. I augmented it with the account of Admiral Franco Maugeri,[49] who had accompanied Mussolini to his place of captivity after he was deposed in July 1943. Maugeri, who had been chief of the naval secret service, was a brilliant man with a subtle intelligence; he took part in the resistance against the Germans during the occupation of Rome. I met him after the German defeat in 1945 and we spoke at length of Mussolini and the war.

I had studied the rise of Mussolini from schoolteacher, socialist agitator, and admirer of Nietzsche – whose ideas he interpreted in his own personal way – to party leader showing a notable talent for detecting and exploiting others' weaknesses, to the brilliant orator who bewitched crowds and impressed not only journalists but also some eminent ambassadors and foreign heads of state. It seemed vital to me to publish a text that revealed him as he truly was, and thus to avert the birth of a myth. The memoirs that I edited covered the events running from the First Battle of El Alamein to the fall of the dictator, while tracing the history of Europe from the birth of fascism. We find ourselves in the presence of an unscrupulous opportunist, an actor playing the role of Napoleon one last time, a cynic full of contempt for his compatriots, and finally a gambler who senses that his luck has run out. By his own admission, it stopped smiling on him on 28 July 1942, the day General Claude Auchinleck's troops halted Rommel's march toward Alexandria. The arrogance is gone; what's left is the visible desire for propaganda, vengeance, and apologetics.

For me, Mussolini's importance, the influence he had on the course of the war, resides in his personality conflict with Hitler. Whereas his seniority as a dictator should, at least in his eyes, have enabled him to serve as an adviser to Hitler, his pride was deeply wounded by the fact that Hitler didn't even bother to inform him of his military enterprises. So, in October 1940 he decided to declare war on Greece, a fact Hitler only learned about in the newspapers. Instead of the rapid, victorious march to

Athens Mussolini had envisioned, his campaign stagnated dangerously. The Germans had to intervene. In April 1941 they crossed Yugoslavia and occupied Greece in six weeks – brilliantly, from a military standpoint. But Operation Barbarossa, the invasion of the Soviet Union, had to be delayed by six weeks from its scheduled beginning in May to the morning of 22 June. This delay was fatal to the German army, which reached Moscow in December, suffering from the effects of a particularly cruel winter.

Right after the war, when I had an opportunity to interrogate German officers, two of them confirmed that they had come within sight of the Kremlin cathedral domes. All means of transportation were frozen. They had to beat a retreat.

The Allies were already on German soil in 1944 when Hitler wrote to Mussolini a bitter missive complaining that his untimely initiative in Greece had prevented Germany from conquering Gibraltar, causing events to take a different, ill-starred turn.

What interested me first and foremost was to observe that neither factors of a sociological nature, nor military strategy, nor natural resources, nor the courage of the combatants and the morale of the population suffice to explain crucial decisions. The impact of individuals – in this case the antagonism between Mussolini and Hitler – must be taken into account. As proved by the minutes of the secret council of war convened by Mussolini, which I also published, the decision to invade Greece was made by one man.

You haven't mentioned the French government in exile. Did you not have any contact with the French in London during the war?

I did have contact with it. I was in touch with Maurice Dejean,[50] who was in charge of foreign affairs in de Gaulle's cabinet. Without betraying secrets, I tried to give him some advice that might help reduce friction.

Contact with the general and his entourage was not straightforward, as it happened, and de Gaulle's personality made it no easier. I remember one of my rare days off, which I spent at Oriel College, Oxford. The provost, Sir William David Ross, editor and translator of Aristotle, who was then also the vice-chancellor of the University of Oxford, told me: "Too bad you weren't there last week. The college invited General de Gaulle to lunch. He is lacking the conversational sixpence."

More seriously, de Gaulle's failure at Dakar on 23–25 September 1940 had complicated Franco-British relations. Certain French officers, as courageous as they were, didn't realize that a Vichy spy might be concealed behind the smile of a ravishing young woman. When de Gaulle's fleet, supported by an English battlefleet, reached Dakar in the hope of taking the city and thus establishing a bridgehead in Africa, the cannons of Governor General Pierre Boisson, loyal to Vichy, were ready.

In November 1942 the landing at Casablanca as well as at Oran and Algiers took place without de Gaulle being notified. I recall the total secrecy surrounding the plans for this operation, codenamed "Torch." De Gaulle's wounded pride – exacerbated by the choice, at President Roosevelt's behest, of General Giraud to administer these African territories – probably had something to do with his policy vis-à-vis the "Anglo-Saxons" in the years that followed. Yet another example of the impact of one individual on world events.

6

THE CHILDREN OF SATURN

Did you resume your academic work after Germany's surrender?

I had never entirely interrupted it. Before the war, I had devised a plan to publish the texts of Plato and the Neoplatonists, the *Corpus Platonicum Medii Aevi*.[1] The first volume appeared in 1940. I had also founded *Mediaeval and Renaissance Studies* with my friend Richard Hunt; the first two volumes were published during the war. The German version of *Saturn and Melancholy* was completed before the declaration of hostilities. The last proofs had been sent back to Germany in July 1939, as had those of my book *The Continuity of the Platonic Tradition*. Before the end of 1939, I received a copy of the Plato book from the German printer. He had managed to send it to Holland before the invasion of that country and it was sent on to me from there. By contrast, it had not been possible to print *Saturn and Melancholy*. After 1945, when I returned to Hamburg as an officer, I met the printer. He shed tears as he told me he had had to destroy the type metal, which had been requisitioned for military use. We had to start all over again.[2]

When you left Germany in 1933, Saturn and Melancholy *was already well underway. Did you finish it in England with Panofsky and Saxl?*

It wasn't that simple. Panofsky had lost his position as a professor in Hamburg in 1933 and emigrated to the United States. The obligation to start a new life – the fate of so many German intellectuals – monopolized all his energy and he stopped working on the book. So Saxl and I continued. It was Fritz Saxl who, during the years that Warburg spent being treated at Kreuzlingen, the clinic run by the psychiatrist Ludwig Binswanger,[3] had kept the library running and stewarded it into becoming a public institution. He was the great specialist on the astrological manuscripts, first producing a catalogue of the ones in the Vatican collection, then those in British libraries. These are masterpieces.[4]

In 1937, as I was just saying, we had been able to send the manuscript of *Saturn and Melancholy* to the German printer. We received the last proofs during the summer of 1939. War broke out in September, and after it ended, everything had been destroyed and no one wanted to read German anymore. So we had to work on the drafts still in our possession. Saturn is said to delay every endeavour; the ancients would surely have found one more proof of this dictum in the fate of this book.

6.1 / Fritz Saxl, photographer unknown, n.d. Warburg Institute, London.

6.2 / Erwin Panofsky, Hamburg, 1932. Photograph by Emil Bieber. Deutsches Literaturarchiv Marbach, Raymond Klibansky fonds.

6.3 / Raymond Klibansky, London, ca. 1945. Photograph by Elise Saxl. Private collection.

6.4 / Albrecht Dürer, *Melencolia I*, copper engraving, 23.8 × 18.9 cm, 1514.

Saxl died in 1948. Translating from the German was an extremely difficult enterprise, especially the parts written by Panofsky. It took nearly twenty years. The English translation was published in London and New York in 1964.

For you and for Panofsky, who took an interest in Dürer's engraving Melencolia I, *what was the meaning of this deep-seated interest in melancholy? What was the meaning of this philosophical melancholy tied to the history of genius, and also to the doctrine of temperaments?*

This was unquestionably a fundamental theme in art history, and it was a central theme for Dürer. Few works of art have been given so many interpretations as his engraving; there have been alchemical, astrological, religious, numerological, and other interpretations, in keeping with the concerns of the interpreters. Panofsky was the great expert on Dürer,[5] whereas Dürer was not central to my work. I was more interested in the history of melancholy from the time of Greek medicine and philosophy to our day. Melancholy differs from all other concepts. In general, when we examine a concept, we see the truth of Horace's maxim that words are like leaves on a tree: they sprout, grow, and die.[6] With melancholy, the situation is entirely different. The word is ancient; it has been with us since the fifth century BCE. The word endures, but its meaning changes all the time. So the often-asked question, "What is melancholy?" is ill-formed, for it presupposes some intangible core of melancholy. There is none.

You established the main differences between these conceptions of melancholy in the doctrine of the humours, in physiology, in Greek medical philosophy, and then in the doctrine of temperaments. Tell us something about this evolution.

This theme illustrates the fundamental problem of the relationship between the physical and the mental: how humans and their actions, their behaviour, are linked to their physicality, their temperament, how these things are determined by one's constitution. "Temperament" translates the Greek word *krasis,* meaning a mixture of humours. Among the four humours, the one that causes the most problems is black bile, *melan choly*. So depending on the role it plays, the weight it carries, it has a greater or lesser influence on character.

Certain physicians of antiquity considered black bile (μελαινα χολη, *melaina kholé*) to be an unhealthy byproduct of the decomposition of either bile or blood. It offered a characteristic image of morbidity. At the other extreme from this totally negative aspect, the text of *Problema* XXX.I, attributed to Aristotle but actually due to Theophrastus, paints a complex picture of the various possibilities of melancholy, beginning with the question of why all eminent men in philosophy, politics, poetry, or the arts are manifestly melancholic.[7]

Plato had formulated the notion of the divine madness (θεία μανία, *theia mania*) of the poet. Aristotle's pupil, for his part, could not concede that this madness had a supernatural origin. Plato's divine madness evoked the vision of a hereafter bathed in a supercelestial light, a realm that could only be regained in moments of ecstasy. Theophrastus's notion of genius, by contrast, lacked this transcendence; it acquired legitimate status by being reduced to a sequence of causes and effects. To him, melancholy became a form of experience in which divine light is a mere correlate of shadow, and the path leading to the light is strewn with demonic perils.

Only the distinction between divine madness and madness as a human malady, as established in Plato's *Phaedrus*, could allow one to differentiate between natural melancholy and the pathological melancholy sketched out in Theophrastus's *Problemata*. While for Theophrastus, melancholy predisposes one to pursuits of the mind, for the great physician Rufus of Ephesus, a primary source for Arabic medicine who lived several centuries later, pursuits of the mind predispose one to melancholy.

A conception disputed by the Church?

Vigorously, inasmuch as, with the Christian era, the negative conception of melancholy prevailed. It was considered a vice akin to the culpable *acedia*, the mother of *tristitia*. It was all the easier to make this equation in that the outer symptoms of the sins of fear and despair form an image very similar to melancholy.

More radical still is the portrait presented by one of the most remarkable women of the twelfth century, Hildegard von Bingen.[8] She conceived of melancholy as a celestial element inflicted by divine providence on humanity in general and on certain individuals in particular, to punish them for past sins and to prevent future ones by forcing them to undergo a painful experience. She ascribes its origin to the Fall. She relates how the melancholy humour was formed in Adam's body as a consequence of the Fall, hence essentially deriving from the serpent's breath and the devil's suggestion. If human beings had stayed in Eden, they would have been protected from all harmful humours; but they became sad, timid, and fickle; neither their constitution nor their behaviour was good. Among her clinically precise diagnoses of the four temperaments, that of the melancholic is notable for the particularly sinister atmosphere he emanates. The composition of these portraits revolves around a single point: sexual behaviour and how it is contingent upon temperament. The abbess was the first (and for a long time the only) author to treat masculine and feminine types as distinct. Writing with rare precision, she describes the melancholic individual as a sadist driven by a demonic desire, a being who goes crazy if he cannot satisfy his craving and who, hating women while at the same time loving them, would willingly kill them in his wild wolf's embrace. He is someone whose children, conceived without tenderness, are just as unhappy, perverted, lawless, and misanthropic as their father. But at times – and here is a surprising positive aspect – they are careful, skilled craftsmen who put their heart into their work.

There are many other descriptions of the melancholic besides this extreme view, which contrast with it by highlighting the melancholy person's pensiveness and suffering. Boccaccio describes Dante as *malinconico e pensoso;*[9] Dante himself admitted that he saw things in a negative light. As for Petrarch, he brought new nuances to melancholy, seeing its influence as permanent: to wit, the paradoxical effect that it creates by provoking both despair and delight.

And let us not forget a new form of melancholy introduced in the West even before Petrarch by physicians, particularly those of the Montpellier School and in a special treatise by the Catalan scholar Arnaldus de Villa Nova:[10] lovesickness. It makes its appearance under the strange name *amor hereos* or *amor heroicus,* an expression that originated in the Latin translation of Avicenna (Ibn Sina), which, in its Arabic original, had preserved the Greek root *eros,* describing "erotic" love as a *sollicitudo melancholica.* This *amor heroicus* was to be adopted into the vocabulary of poets such as Chaucer.

How does Saturn figure into evolving conceptions of melancholy?

A new element was developing in parallel with the irruption of astrological thought in Europe, arriving via translations of the Arabic authors. Melancholy was linked to Saturn, the malevolent planet of misfortune, which, in the Neoplatonic tradition, is at the same time the orb of sublime contemplation. Thus, in canto XXI of Dante's *Paradiso,* souls who pass their lives in contemplation appear to the poet in the sphere of Saturn, and from this sphere rises the scintillating ladder leading to a vision of divinity.

Several centuries later, Marsilio Ficino[11] produced an outstanding synthesis. The melancholy that he feared derived from Saturn, but it was in fact a unique gift for the same reason that Saturn, besides being the most elevated of the planets, is also the most noble and, at the same time, the most dangerous. The children of Saturn possess the qualities necessary for intellectual work, but intellectual work in turn exerts an influence on humans by placing them under the dominion of Saturn. Consequently, intellectuals are condemned to melancholy. Saturn guides human beings toward the contemplation of the supreme realities, producing exceptional philosophers who are strongly attracted to all that is transcendent. Ficino is nonetheless obliged to emphasize that thinkers who devote themselves to the most intense contemplation suffer from melancholy to an unusual degree. He was too closely beholden to the established doctrines of medicine and astrology – and his personal knowledge of the painful effects of bitter melancholy and Saturnian malevolence was too intimate – for him not to highlight their negative aspects. All of Ficino's efforts are therefore directed toward the practical goal of protecting the melancholic *viri literati* from the dangers inherent in their temperament: instability, weak-mindedness, depression, and dementia.

What a contrast between the astral preoccupations of Ficino and the approach adopted by Giovanni Manardo![12] This physician of Ferrara had, during his youth, helped Pico della Mirandola with his critique of astrology. Manardo, later called "one of the glories of Italian medicine," wrote in one of his *Epistolae medicinales* to a friend "tormented by the black bile": "Do not procure medicines from the shores of India, do not bring Asclepius back from hell that he may free you! You have within yourself the necessary antidotes (*Intra te ipsum habes antidota*); no one better than you can be your physician ... You hold healing in your hand," by lifting the spirit toward those timeless realities standing outside this world. He did see fit to add a list of "human remedies which God Himself created on earth, and which must not be neglected."

For Pico della Mirandola, what constituted human existence was the possibility of becoming either a god or a beast, of manoeuvring on a narrow crest between two chasms – a situation that, for Ficino and his many sectarians, typified the Saturnian, melancholic type. The members of this elect group were given the impression that they had been lofted high above the comfortable level of banality.[13]

Thus, the spiritual status of Florentine humanism, the consciousness of a freedom experienced in the tragic mode, gave birth to the notion of a genius who could claim to be unbound, in life and work, from the criteria of normal morality and the rules of art.

Was melancholy thought to be a sign of superiority?

This mode of thought had a European influence, but nowhere as vigorous as in the Elizabethan writers. Many figures seeking recognition did indeed consider this temperament to be a sign of intellectual superiority.

The most nuanced and finished portrait is presented by Robert Burton,[14] a clergy member and fellow of Christ Church, Oxford, in his *Anatomy of Melancholy*. The world is a theatre; every man stands on stage, playing his role, and no one can withdraw of his own accord. All our lives are a play that we perform for ourselves. So, how can one escape the madness of melancholy? By being active through literary production? But what is the character of this production? "We weave the same web still, twist the same rope again and again; or if it be a new invention, 'tis but some bauble or toy which idle fellows write, for as idle fellows to read, and who so cannot invent?" There is nothing new under the sun: a deep conviction of the melancholic whom Burton knew himself to be.

The close connection between madness and melancholy is evident in the successive stanzas of the poem summarizing his work, whose first refrain is:

All my joys to this are folly,
Naught so sweet as melancholy.

Only to become:

All my griefs to this are jolly,
Naught so damn'd as melancholy.

Melancholy is thus the source of both the deepest sorrow and the joy bound to that sorrow. The mask of Democritus, the laughing philosopher, whose persona Burton adopted in writing this book, takes on the traits of his opposite, Heraclitus, the weeping, melancholy philosopher. The theme of the two faces will reappear in one form or another in the centuries to follow.

In his study of the symptoms of melancholy, Burton put forward the hypothesis that melancholy is a social malady. In the conclusion to his work, he proposed that it be treated by changing the entire structure of society.

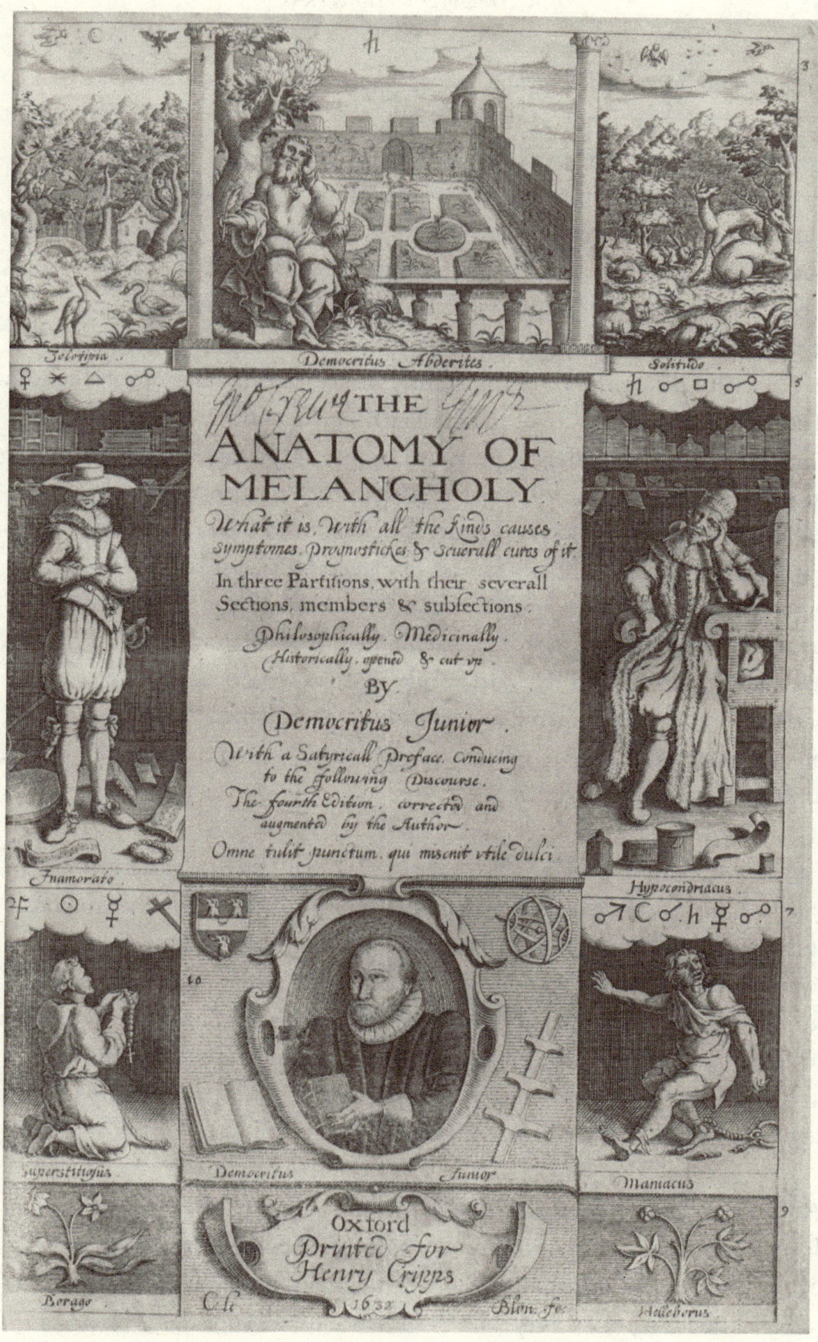

6.5 / Robert Burton, *The Anatomy of Melancholy*, frontispiece to the 1632 edition.

So some authors regarded melancholy as a hazard?

Of course, and one that was emphasized by Luther. Faith in God must be joyous. He who is tormented by sadness must feel the greatest fear, for Satan is the *spiritus tristitiae* and melancholy is the bath prepared by the devil. Dürer's *Melencolia I*, inspired by Ficino, links melancholy to Saturn, while by contrast, the four canvases by Lucas Cranach, the painter closest to Luther, link this phenomenon to Satan.

So with Luther and the Protestants, we see another face of melancholy. The most striking feature of the history of melancholy is its protean character. It can be suffering pure and simple, intolerable suffering leading to suicide, as in Goethe's *The Sorrows of Young Werther*, a work that had an unprecedented impact and which Napoleon claimed to have read six times. Others may see it as a source of delectable pleasures. In the early eighteenth century, the English essayist Joseph Addison[15] averred that he derived great pleasure from beauty when it is softened by an air of melancholy. His friend Richard Steele[16] speaks of the calm and elegant satisfaction, vulgarly treated as melancholy, that is the particular pleasure of erudite, virtuous men. "Melancholy pleasure" became a common phrase among the century's literati.

In this study of melancholy, which you pursued even after the book was published in 1964 by reorganizing and expanding it, and in other writings as well, we find your interest for what, in human beings, depends on them and what, on the contrary, as we saw in regard to Nicolaus Cusanus, represents a form of necessity. So does your interest in melancholy fundamentally overlap with your philosophical concern around freedom, the freedom to be oneself and to not let ourselves be ruled by the part of us that constitutes our physical temperament; that is, the aspect of necessity?

Absolutely, and you find this line of thinking coming up again in Kant. It becomes clear in his *Anthropology* how attached he is to the doctrine of the four temperaments. It plays a fundamental role. For him, the melancholic is a personality who has a sense of the sublime, who has a sense of freedom. It is always threatened, of course, but Kant accords it a very noble position. The melancholy condition is the one that appears to harmonize best with "true and principled virtue." To the melancholy person, "all shackles, from the golden ones worn at court to the heavy irons of the galley-slave, are abominable."[17] In the nineteenth century, however, the notion became entirely different, except of course among physicians. In nineteenth-century poetry and in Kierkegaard, for instance, the physical no longer plays any role. It is a feeling of distance from God. It is *Schwermut,* or *Tungsind,* as Kierkegaard puts it. We find here a basic aspect of human existence, the divide between humans and God, which has nothing to do with their physical constitution. Melancholy takes its place as a tragic pillar of nineteenth-century existence, which is expressed in poetry, and it is this aspect in particular that drew me to it. You are right to emphasize this; the clash between freedom and necessity remains a constant.

Did psychoanalysis play a role in the culture that was yours?

It certainly had an influence. Freud's ideas were familiar in academic circles but they were not accepted. When writing on historical matters, Freud always produced interesting constructs, of course, and he also happens to have been a master of the German language. But compared to the force of the poets' expression of melancholy as found in Baudelaire ("Get rid of this Saturnian book / Of orgies and despondency"), or Verlaine, Freud seems very superficial, far from what is truly threatening for the French poets, from what they perceive as forming the tragic element of melancholy.

In the nineteenth century, ignorance of the reasons things are as they are became a frequent and worrying theme. We find it in Leopardi,[18] in the Austrian poet Nestroy, and later in Verlaine. And Kierkegaard was to write: "If a depressed person is asked what the reason is, what it is that weighs [*tynge*] on him, he will answer: I do not know; I cannot explain it. Therein lies the limitlessness of depression."[19]

This theme had been forcefully expressed in fourteenth-century French poetry. It pointed to the discovery of subjectivity, as may be seen in the verse of Eustache Deschamps, a high-ranking officer in the court of Charles V. In the ballad he wrote about his own melancholy, each stanza ends with *Muser souvent et si ne say pourquoy* ("Often I ponder, and do not know why"). This same motif is found in Charles d'Orléans and other poets of the time.

Not knowing why is the basis of sorrow. Why is this fact of such importance for Western thinkers? In the centuries following Plato and Aristotle, a fundamental conviction reigned that every action had a reason. For the Platonism of late antiquity, *voluntas dei est origo certissima rerum* (God's will is the most certain origin of things). Each thing has its logos, and this logos can be known; whereas, for modern melancholiacs, reason eludes us, and the loss of meaning is intimately linked to the loss of reason. The Italian philosophy student Carlo Michelstaedter expressed this feeling of loss in a fragment written some time before he died by suicide in 1910: "Melancholy is a slow and steady rain, for it tells man of the infinite monotony, the immutability, the purposelessness of all things."[20]

Does this sentiment still prevail in the literature of our own fin de siècle?

Despair at not knowing why presupposes that one believes in a fundamental order; the anguish provoked by the loss of meaning is founded on the conviction that life and history have, or should have, some kind of meaning. Today, these questions no longer seem relevant. Certainly, human beings will always suffer from the divide between what they want and what they can have, and depression in the medical sense is still with us. But melancholy as a fundamental human attitude toward the world is not limited to select literary circles. Certain sociological philosophers, the founders of the Frankfurt School, for instance, tried to place the responsibility for human melancholy on society. This attempt on the part of comfortably established authors to amuse themselves by chronicling the progressive ruin of contemporary society makes one smile.

With the terrible experiences of this century, the climate that gave rise to the melancholics of old has fundamentally changed. What meaning can melancholy still have after Auschwitz and Hiroshima, after the systematic application of the most advanced techniques of mass destruction of human beings?

A new set of problems has been created.

7

FROM OXFORD TO MONTREAL

After your extensive contributions to the war effort, what were your feelings on returning to university life?

I did not leave my service right away; it was not until early 1946 that I returned to Oxford. In 1945 I was sent on a mission to Germany. The mandate was to take the pulse of various segments of the population, university professors in particular, in regard to the collapse of the regime. I was attached to General Montgomery's headquarters at Bad Oeynhausen, as I already mentioned. It was there that I encountered Nicolas Nabokov,[1] whom I'd met in Paris at the home of Wilhelm Uhde when I was a student. A highly gifted musician, he had composed a ballet for Diaghilev. The American general commanding the occupation forces had entrusted him with cultural affairs in the American zone. In this capacity, in the ruins of Berlin, he had held the first great symphony concert with a motley group of musicians. He was also in charge of reviewing the conduct of orchestra conductors under the Third Reich. It was the time of denazification.

This was how he came to focus on the case of Wilhelm Furtwängler,[2] who was presumed to be a Nazi. It is true that Furtwängler had accepted from Goebbels the title of *Preussischer Staatsrat*, Prussian councillor of state. He had conducted the Berlin Philharmonic in Stockholm, and Nazi propaganda had used this event as proof that great German musicians supported the regime. In short, the Americans regarded him as highly suspect. However, there were several accounts suggesting that he had helped a certain number of Jewish musicians. What had struck Nabokov was his discovery, among the official documents, of a 1933 letter from Furtwängler interceding on my behalf and requesting that my dismissal from the university be rescinded. A note in the margin from a senior officer in the Ministry of Culture left me no chance, but spoke volumes about Furtwängler's conduct: "Can you name a single Jew on whose behalf Furtwängler has not intervened? But, on a more serious note, I could do nothing for this Dr Klibansky even if I wanted to, for he is an unsalaried staff member of Heidelberg University whose case is therefore outside of my purview." Prieberg's and Shirakawa's biographies of Furtwängler cite this letter, which is now in the state archives at Koblenz. However, the details given by the reviewer of these biographies in the *New York Review of Books*, according to which Furtwängler helped me write my curriculum vitae, are utter fantasy!

I wondered – and both biographers asked me this question – why Furtwängler, who hardly knew me, had taken such an interest in my fate. I had met his mother a few times at Marianne Weber's. She'd been very nice to me. It is possible that she spoke of me to her son and expressed her indignation at my dismissal.

In any case, it's clear that Furtwängler was far from an antisemite. The only thing that interested him was music. He felt it was his duty, under the circumstances, to preserve the quality of music by staying in Germany and continuing to conduct the country's most prominent orchestra.

What sort of people did you survey in Germany?

A very wide variety. I first went to the Bethel Institution for epileptic children near Bielefeld to meet the director, Friedrich von Bodelschwingh.[3] He had managed to save his patients despite the Nazi policy according to which the incurable had to be exterminated, and I wanted to pay my respects. He told me that the head of the SS Medical Corps had sat down in his office and said: "Didn't you know that Plato said that abnormal children should be eliminated?"

"How did you manage to save your patients?" I asked, and this brave, dignified pastor said simply: "The Lord erected a fortress around us."

In Hamburg, I met with Professor Emil Wolff,[4] a well-known Anglicist and friend of Cassirer's with whom he later had a falling-out; he told me with bitterness that the émigrés were lucky in comparison to those who had had to stay in Germany.

I then attended, as an observer, the trial of the commander and staff at Bergen-Belsen, a notorious concentration camp not far from Lüneburg, south of Hamburg. During the sessions, I was sitting a few steps away from the defendants, across from the torturer Irma Grese,[5] a woman with eyes of unforgettable cruelty.

We had stressed to the local authorities that citizens of Lüneburg should attend and hear the testimony. They were there with their sandwiches and I can still hear the noise of crumpled paper when they opened their lunch during the accounts of the atrocities.

During recess, we went to the town square and I struck up conversations with the residents:

"Bergen-Belsen isn't far from here. How much did you know about what was happening there?"

"Nothing."

"You don't remember that a train was bombarded by English planes on a certain day in March and the prisoners escaped because the guards had left the train?"

They were surprised at what I knew, and even more when I told them that it was the residents of Lüneburg who had caught the prisoners.

"But those were criminals! They were wearing stripes!"

I was also struck by the large number of refugees, displaced persons as they were then called, coming from the eastern camps – Polish Jews and others who had survived. There were very young girls who spoke a little German. One of them told me she had an uncle in Brooklyn but was unable to get in touch with him. I asked for his address. I still have the uncle's reply. I cannot erase the image of those haggard faces.

You returned to a country in ruins?

I was appalled by the ruins, yes, and also by the contrast between the wreckage and what was left standing, such as the magnificent Hotel Atlantic in Hamburg, all in white, which housed the Allied officers and whose cellars overflowed with fine wines that the Nazis had stored there. In Frankfurt, the train station had miraculously survived the bombardment that had almost entirely destroyed the city's beautiful old quarter. It was all lit up when I arrived there one evening. There were hundreds of people, groups of soldiers and groups of women, casting overlapping shadows … From afar, I had the impression of a ballet.

I left my car and my orderly at the hotel and I went off on foot through the familiar blacked-out streets toward my parents' home. After a few minutes, I heard a woman's cries; I hastened and found myself face-to-face with a black soldier brandishing a revolver. Just in time, my electric torchlight showed him my uniform. The woman had run away. I reached home without further adventures, finding only ruins along the way.

However, the splendid headquarters of IG Farben, the chemical company that had put people to work in Auschwitz, stood intact in the middle of Grüneberg Park. It had become the headquarters of the American army.

Luckily, Kues was spared.

Luckily! I had feared that I would find the *Cusanusstift* destroyed. As you know, Cusanus had founded a hospital to accommodate thirty-three people, corresponding to Christ's age when he died. The tradition has survived to our day. The bulk of the library, including Cusanus's manuscripts, is located in that hospital. However, it is situated right near one of the few bridges over the Moselle, between Koblenz and Trier, also right near the old Roman road that went from the *Limes Germanicus* (fortifications) into southern Gaul and toward Italy; during the war, it connected the industrial zone of Frankfurt to the theatre of military operations in western and southern France. Given the strategic importance of this bridge, it would likely have been targeted for bombardment, which would have caused the total destruction of the hospital and its riches.

Every time I met British or American air force officers, and at all the meetings with members of our American counterpart organizations, I tried to get them to understand that the destruction of this historic monument would go down in history as a crime against culture. I always asked the Americans what they would think if the Statue of Liberty were destroyed. The first time I returned to Kues, shortly after the German surrender, I had the surprise of being considered a saviour by the mayor and the old women of the village. A US air force commander had told them that an Englishman familiar with Kues had interceded.

My surprise increased when I read, a little over ten years ago in an otherwise serious book, *Deutschland deine Denker*, that it was I who had approached Air Marshal Arthur "Bomber" Harris and asked him not to bomb Kues.[6] Since he knew nothing of the great German thinker, he was thoroughly unimpressed and I went away believing I had failed. But officers who attended the interview struck the name of Kues off the list of targets behind Harris's back. All that is utter fantasy! I never approached Arthur Harris. The same story had appeared a little earlier in *Stern*, and also in a Köln paper. That is how myths are created. Another that I read in a local paper is popular in Kues among older people of simple hearts and faith: that an angel had taken human form to protect the hospital.

Did you see your Heidelberg friends again on this trip?

I went to Heidelberg after Frankfurt with a large sack full of provisions: coffee, sardines. I was on a mission but I wanted to visit Marianne Weber. She cried when she saw me. She had suffered great hardships toward the end of the war. My duties kept me too busy to see other friends or former professors.

On my first visit to Heidelberg, I went of course to the university library and saw a considerable number of boxes sitting on the central staircase. The American officer in charge – Heidelberg was the headquarters of the Seventh United States Army – told me: "We don't know what to do with this stuff. It came back from Italy with the German army. Nothing we need."

I open a box and what do I find? The diary of Vittorio Ambrosio,[7] chief of staff of the Italian Armed Forces, and other documents of great interest for the history of Italy during the war. "You're interested in these? You want them?" When I objected that I couldn't carry it all, he offered to put a plane at my disposal. We still had to find a place in England to store it. I no longer had my large office suite; after the surrender of Italy, my office had been moved across from St James's Park, not far from the Foreign Office. I knew I would be returning to London in two weeks; the officer kindly agreed to wait.

On arriving in London, I went to the Foreign Office and asked to see the head librarian. Unfortunately, my good friend Sir Stephen Gaselee,[8] a distinguished Latinist famous for his *Oxford Book of Medieval Latin Verse*, among other works, had died. The woman serving as his interim replacement did not want to take responsibility, but she said to me: "We have here Professor Woodward, who writes on war. You would need to talk to him. He will be delighted with this still-unknown material." Unfortunately, he was absent. This was the renowned historian Llewellyn Woodward,[9] later Sir Llewellyn. A few days later I learned that, far from being delighted, he was furious at a discovery that interfered with his publication schedule. He refused to accept the material and I was forced to communicate this refusal to the Americans. These treasures are now, I am told, in the the National Archives in Alexandria, Virginia.

A few months after your return to England, your tour of duty ended and you returned to Oxford, but you were to leave for Montreal, where you settled permanently, in 1946. Why this departure?

The war had been a difficult period for me. It had demanded all my energy, since I had a job associated with great responsibilities that showed me the horrors taking place. When it was over, the quiet, sophisticated atmosphere of Oxford was agreeable enough, but it had become vaguely foreign to me after the pressures of war. When I received an invitation to Canada, a country of which I had only a foggy notion, I accepted.

What was Montreal to you when you agreed to come in 1946?

First of all, I didn't want to make a firm commitment. There was Oxford, but I had also been offered the post of director of research at the Warburg Institute. I accepted on condition of being allowed to return to England for a few months. After two years, I had to make up my mind and I chose Canada. Why did I settle on McGill? The Oxford libraries were better, especially for my own work. However, this entirely new atmosphere was more beguiling to me. The students pleased me, with their fresh faces and their desire to learn. So I packed up my library and made a permanent move to Montreal.

I found the city particularly interesting because of the English and French elements that coexisted side by side with almost no communication between them. I also met remarkable Russians and Poles who had fled the Bolshevik regime. I felt at home in Montreal. I got to know the francophone students and teachers at the Université de Montréal, where I became a visiting professor in 1947 and would remain one for twenty-one years. I worked at the Institut d'études médiévales on the Conférences Albert-le-Grand;[10] it was, as you know, a very fine, I would even say unique institution. There were Dominican masters there of great worth, great breadth. It was inhabited by a spirit both vigorous and discerning.

I deplored the absence of sustained dialogue between the two communities. So I invited young professors of philosophy to take part in my courses at McGill, and francophone students to attend my seminars in French there. We had discussions of considerable interest. We read books of interest to the francophones that the anglophones had never heard of, for those authors were absent from their university curricula. I invited French scholars, Michel Foucault and others, and we had exciting discussions in which the students took an active part.

Montreal seemed to me an extraordinary city. As I wrote then, it was the only city where for a dollar – the price of a taxi ride from McGill University to the Université de Montréal in those days – you could go not just from one university to another, but from one world to another. These were in fact two worlds that, unfortunately, hardly spoke to one another, two very rich worlds, possessed of great traditions but lacking essential relations. I felt that these young people had unique possibilities if they became aware of both traditions, their own and each other's. But I also saw the difficulties, primarily on an institutional level: there was no way to transpose part of the education into the other setting. Moreover, there was a certain weakness on the francophone side, a lack of grounding in the great French tradition. The language teaching seemed deficient to me; their knowledge of great French poetry, great French literature, was limited. They tried to grapple with the present instead of studying the effects of this tradition, which would, in my opinion, have enabled the francophone students to play a high-profile role on the American continent. If they had been better versed in the spiritual and literary riches of their own tradition, they could have adapted the other tradition to their needs.

To improve the teaching of the language, one had to start at the source, and so I agreed, in the early 1960s, to give philosophy courses at a primary- and secondary-school teacher training institution (*école normale*). I made the students do a lot of writing!

It was not the only time that your teaching diverged from traditional university teaching.

Indeed. An active and intelligent Jesuit priest at Loyola College, Father R. Eric O'Connor, a man of remarkable enthusiasm and energy, had the idea of founding an institute, the Thomas More Institute,[11] to enable adults who had to earn a living or had not been able to go to university because of the war to get a university education; they took an intensive reading program and attended evening classes. By doing so they could get their bachelor's degree from the Université de Montréal in seven or eight years. The Thomas More Institute gave many adults the chance to find jobs for which an undergraduate degree was a prerequisite. I taught hundreds of students at the institute. People still come up to greet me on the streets of Montreal and tell me that they have fond memories of those courses.

You had thousands of students. Did some of them leave special memories?

Certainly. I'll mention just one. Shortly after arriving in Canada, I had an outstanding student, a Costa Rican named Daniel Oduber Quirós,[12] who was doing his master's thesis on Plato's dialectic. He had been imprisoned by the dictatorship in his country and then escaped. His studious, mature character made him a pleasure to work with. He often came to my office to discuss the coup d'état that he and a group of friends were planning in order to restore democracy to his country.

7.1 / Raymond Klibansky, Montreal, McGill University, 1979. Photographer unknown. Private collection.

When, in late 1948, he was abruptly called back to Costa Rica to put this plan into effect, he was about to take an exam. He had fortunately already finished writing his thesis but had not yet proofread the typescript. I remember writing to request that he be exempted from the exam and be allowed to submit the thesis in that form: "His sudden departure is due to force majeure; he has responded to the call of duty, and feels obligated to return to the country of his birth." I knew how devoted he was to his studies, but he wanted to contribute to restoring social justice while preserving individual freedom. Shortly afterward I received a telegram: "Victory!"

I kept the proclamation of the Junta Fundadora de la Segunda República, of which he was secretary general; he sent it to me on returning from the front, along with the draft constitution of 1949, an exceptional document for the time. It provided not only for full equality of rights and duties for men and women, but also the right to health and social security. It even abolished the army as a permanent institution, a noteworthy achievement in the context of Latin America. Oduber wrote to me that he had borne in mind the principles taught in his philosophy courses while writing these documents and that he had tried to apply them, to the extent that he had understood them.

He had a brilliant political career, becoming president of the republic in 1974. At the end of his presidency in 1978 – the constitution prohibited sitttting presidents from running for a second term – one of my colleagues launched the idea that McGill University could award him an honorary doctorate. Unfortunately, the Vesco affair[13] in which his predecessor had been mixed up – although he had not – scared off certain parties, and this plan came to nothing.

After his presidency, Oduber remained active on the national and international scene, devoting some of his abundant energy to environmental protection. Costa Rica is the only country in the world where 20 per cent of the territory has some form of protection as a nature reserve. Oduber was, sad to say, greatly aggrieved by US interference in his country's political and economic affairs. He died in 1991.

I had other students who went on to excellent careers in many fields, even in philosophy! Some became dear friends. I always found Canadian students endearing for their enthusiasm, vitality, and spirit of enterprise. At McGill, they had founded a philosophy students' society. As director of the department, I was always able to procure some money so that they could invite philosophers they wanted to get to know. I always insisted that they meet them alone over lunch, with no professors present. In the aftermath of 1968, they invited a man who was quite famous at the time, Herbert Marcuse.[14] I had met him earlier, in 1968, when the regents of the University of California were refusing to renew his contract because he was on the left. He was a visiting professor at San Diego. The president of the department asked me to intervene on his behalf and I wrote to the regents that I had just come back from the World Congress of Philosophy in Vienna where I had drafted a declaration affirming that freedom of thought is essential for any academic practice. And there they were in California, trying to adopt the methods of communism!

The president of the philosophy students' society was a smart young man. He knew that philosophers – some philosophers, at any rate – are not above vanity, so when he invited Marcuse, he asked two of the prettiest female students to linger near the entrance to the restaurant holding copies of his book, on which his photo appeared. Which they did. When he arrived, one of them said: "Look, there's Professor Marcuse. We have your book and there you are!" He was charmed. He called these McGill students the smartest he had ever met. It succeeded beautifully because he was vain, a very bourgeois man in his private life, albeit very anti-bourgeois in his outward politics.

At the Université de Montréal, the students' enthusiasm was also expressed in a different way. Around the 1960s, I saw in them a reflection of how Quebec society was changing. They were becoming politicized. They would discuss their aspirations to independence with me. Quebec was awakening. To give you an idea of the prevailing atmosphere at the time of the regime of Duplessis, who died in 1959, remember that he asked the Vatican to recall the Archbishop of Montreal[15] and the request was granted, simply because the archbishop had called for prayers on behalf of the striking asbestos workers. In the early 1960s, francophone students were in the front ranks of the political and cultural movement that would produce spokespersons such as the writer and filmmaker Hubert Aquin,[16] whose renown reached France.

Was the philosophy education at the Université de Montréal different, at that time, from the education provided at McGill University?

There was obviously, among the francophones, the influence of a certain clerical tradition, but there was also a degree of openness on the part of the Dominican professors. One of them, Father Noël Mailloux,[17] introduced the study of psychoanalysis to Quebec. He wanted to show how psychoanalysis spoke of nature and fit very well into a broader whole. Alongside professors who embodied a Thomist tradition, the eminent Scotist Camille Bérubé,[18] a Capuchin priest, initiated the students to another tradition. In addition, the university regularly received visits from eminent French professors such as Henri-Irénée Marrou[19] and Paul Vignaux.[20]

In regard to McGill University, the history of the philosophy department and its teaching is too long to recount here. When I arrived in 1946, the department was small. I watched it grow, and was able to guide our hiring policy in such a way as to foster this growth. I was personally able to attract Mario Bunge,[21] the great philosopher of science, and Harry Bracken,[22] who wrote on Berkeley and on language, among other subjects. After the events of 1968 in Poland, I was able to welcome Leszek Kołakowski,[23] who had been forced to leave the country in great haste. Unfortunately, the university couldn't afford to keep him and he accepted an invitation to Berkeley. He is now at Oxford.

7.2 / Raymond Klibansky and Leszek Kołakowski, Montreal, McGill University, 1968. Private collection.

Your concern with dialogue was not limited to the classroom. You also founded the Canadian Society for the History and Philosophy of Science, bringing together groups that you wanted to see communicating among one another. At the time of its founding, it was the only bilingual philosophical institution of its kind in Montreal. Since then, as we know, it has extended to the whole of Canada. In its early years, this society prospered at McGill – thanks to an excellent sherry, I'm told, among other things.

First of all, the society was founded in 1959 and I was its president for a long time. I resigned in 1972 to become honorary president. The basic idea was that history and philosophy should not be isolated from each other. I found that in North America, as elsewhere, historians of science risked becoming antiquarians. History was the important thing to them, with no consideration for the value of scientific truth. Philosophers, meanwhile, were debating in a vacuum without realizing that their point of view is historically conditioned. They were blind to the fact that the concepts they were employing were concepts formed in particular situations, often debatable, not at all absolute. The historical aspect was intended to make them aware that they too are the product of a certain historical constellation.

I am and always have been concerned with the relations between science and history; or, to put it another way, the historical character of all science, history's claims to scientificity, and their common goal of seeking truth. I had been working on these problems since my youth. I was already discussing them at the time of my meetings with Einstein before the war. And the reason I founded the Canadian Society for the History and Philosophy of Science was to subject them to detailed examination.

That there can be any knowledge of history at all leads one to consider the question of how objective that knowledge can be, which leads to an in-depth examination of the very concept – in fact a rather vague one – of objectivity. I had previously addressed the question in "The Philosophical Character of History," an essay published in *Philosophy and History*, the volume I co-edited in honour of Ernst Cassirer in 1936.[24] In the 1975 volume of the *Revue internationale de philosophie* dedicated to me, the problem is studied from different angles.[25] To what extent is historical judgment determined by the prejudices and interests of historians? To what extent are we conditioned by our own situation and that of the society to which we belong? The fact that judgment is conditioned by numerous factors makes it all the more critical to gain a full understanding of objectivity.

Objectivity, then, must not be construed as a matter of fact but as an intent to exclude subjective elements reflecting our own desires and fears. It is an idea in the Kantian sense of a regulative principle governing our judgments, but also in the Platonic sense of a norm, a model to which we voluntarily submit.

The society was and remains a fruitful idea. The historians listened to the philosophers and the philosophers listened to the historians. At the same time, it was a meeting place for anglophone and francophone scholars as well as for non-specialists. One of the innovations of the society, to which you are no doubt alluding, was to begin sessions with a sherry cocktail hour, during which people met and mingled. Fruitful discussions ensued. The sherry put people at their ease and made them more indulgent toward the speakers they were about to listen to. But we started out with almost no money. Membership dues were minimal, much too small to

7.3 / Osler Library of the History of Medicine, McGill University. Photograph by Klaus Fiedler, McGill Library.

afford good wine. Luckily, the secretary of the society was a chemist and he had the ingenious idea of buying some South African sherry and then mixing it with a bit of better-quality sherry. Some of our Montreal connoisseurs wanted to know the name of the particularly fine brand we were serving! From that point of view as well, the society was a success.

We were fortunate enough to be able to meet in one of the most beautiful rooms in Montreal, the Osler Library of the History of Medicine, where our discussions took place amid precious books and manuscripts displayed in showcases. The setting had nothing of the banal and dreary traditional conference room; rather, it helped make the lectures an elegant event that ambassadors would often travel from Ottawa to attend.

In Montreal, you continued your work on Platonism and your untiring efforts to make the great texts on tolerance better known. Let's talk about both of these things. In 1954 you published a volume of David Hume's letters, which occupies a special place in your oeuvre. What exactly does he represent for you?

To begin with, he was my way of learning English. To learn a language, you have to read good literature, and in that way gain access to the humanity represented in and by this language. This work can be done by devoting time to someone's biography and I chose Hume as a philosopher of great importance. When I arrived in England, my English was very poor. I grew up with Latin and Greek, French and Italian. Apart from German, I could read English but not speak it and I had to learn the philosophical vocabulary as quickly as possible. So I started reading Hume. He was also very important to German philosophy because it was he who, as Kant put it, "interrupted my dogmatic slumber." Hume is a master stylist and I began by devoting time to his correspondence. I was struck by the fact that the editor of the Oxford University Press edition of Hume's correspondence, albeit a great scholar, had ignored a particularly interesting letter found at Oxford itself, in the Bodleian Library. That impelled me to seek out others; I embarked on a systematic study leading to the discovery that many of Hume's letters remained unpublished. I compiled and published them in collaboration with Ernest Mossner,[26] the great Hume specialist who was a professor at the University of Texas. Meanwhile, still more letters turned up. I even succeeded in getting the library at my own university, McGill, to acquire certain letters.[27] Hume's correspondence shows, as do his philosophy and his philosophical writings per se, a critical mind alert to all dogmatism. I was drawn to this mind that is so nobly on display in his writings, even though I do not at all subscribe to his philosophy.

One could, after all, find that there are, in Hume, too many premises or propositions contrary to your own Neoplatonic propositions.

Yes, but he interested me as a man, for the relations he carried on with France and especially for his biography. I managed to persuade my university to acquire the manuscript containing his correspondence with the woman who mattered the most in his life, the Countess de Boufflers, with whom he corresponded from 1761 to 1776. She was an extraordinary woman with an intellect as great as her beauty, whose advantageous station as mistress to the king's cousin, the Prince de Conti, made her one of the highest-profile hostesses in Parisian society. She was admired by Rousseau. Sainte-Beuve attributed the following remark to her: "I want to restore to virtue by my words what I take from it by my actions." In the era when Hume was often in Paris, she was known as "the idol of the temple," the Prince de Conti's house. Later, "when the passions of the mind succeeded in her to the passions of a tenderer age," she was also known as "the wise Minerva."[28]

Horace Walpole's description of her was less charitable: "She is two women, the upper and the lower. I need not tell you that the lower is gallant, and still has pretensions. The upper is very sensible, too, and has a measured eloquence that is just and pleasing, but all is spoiled by an unrelaxed attention to applause."[29]

Hume harboured loyal affection for her throughout his life. A few months after leaving France, he wrote expressing his hope of returning and embarking on a journey with her that would take them to Italy and Greece. "Might we not settle in some Greek island, and breathe the air of Homer, or Sappho, or Anacreon?" Was this his actual intention, or was it just one of those dreams one cherishes from the safety of distance?

Did they see each other again?

Never, and their correspondence dwindled. This has been blamed on the effects of time and separation, but recent work has found that another correspondent, King Gustav of Sweden, had attracted the countess's interest.

Hume, when he learned on his deathbed of the Prince de Conti's death, wrote one of the loveliest letters in the history of philosophy.[30] It caused Sainte-Beuve to opine that "the woman who inspired a dying sage with such supreme sentiments of concern and friendship was not an ordinary soul."

The story of the manuscript containing the thirty-seven letters from Hume to the countess and her thirty-nine letters to him, along with the eleven letters written by Jean-Jacques Rousseau to this remarkable woman, is worth telling. I told it in a paper that I wrote on some of the numerous treasures to be found in the Rare Books and Special Collections Department of McGill University's McLennan Library, which contains stunning treasures for a North American university.[31]

Among the letters of Hume that I published are those that he wrote as *chargé d'affaires* in Paris, dealing with the consequences of the Treaty of Paris. These are in the archives of the Department of Foreign Affairs. But in contrast to the letters, Hume's diary from the time when he was to take part in an expedition to invade Canada has not yet been published. Hume was the advocate and adjutant of General James St Clair. This projected expedition to invade Canada is interesting. Great confusion reigned in Britain at that moment. The expedition was halted and replaced by an invasion of continental France. The Lorient raid was successfully repelled and is not a very glorious episode in British history.

Hume has some importance for Canada because, as *chargé d'affaires* in the ambassador's absence, he was in charge of peace negotiations with the French ministers. One important point for Canada had to do with the Newfoundland fisheries. The British complained that the French were flouting the peace treaty. Hume intervened but did not succeed in resolving everything; he can hardly be criticized, however, since the problem is still with us today!

He also had to look after a matter of great importance for the French population remaining in Canada: determining the exchange rate for the redemption of outstanding colonial paper money. In all these negotiations, Hume found himself testing his mettle against the Duc de Praslin, the French foreign minister, a veteran politician with long practice in the shrewd art of diplomacy.

Is Hume of special interest at McGill?

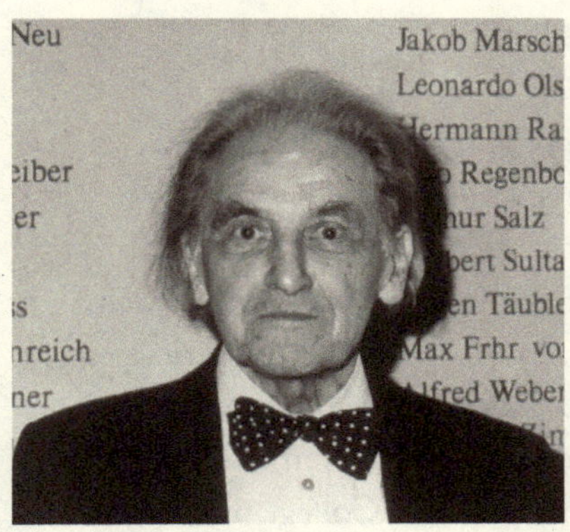

7.4 / Raymond Klibansky in 1991, standing in front of the plaque installed by the Senate of the University of Heidelberg commemorating professors expelled on account of the racial laws. Photograph by Michael Schwarz, Archives of the University of Heidelberg.

Yes, in fact the university owns a good collection of Hume-related documents. It began with a discovery. Shortly after my arrival in Montreal, I noticed nine elegantly bound eighteenth-century volumes, each bearing Hume's *ex libris*, in a closet at the Faculty Club. It was the Dauphin's Cicero, published by Olivetus in Paris in 1740–41.[32] This was the starting point for a collection which, in many respects, is only surpassed by those of Edinburgh and London. Professor David Norton of McGill's

7.5 / Oriel College, Oxford.

Department of Philosophy,[33] the author of several works on Hume including the *Cambridge Companion to Hume*, helped to enrich the collection. He himself has just published a book on Hume's library.

Your time has been divided between several continents and institutions, and yet you consider yourself Canadian, am I right?

I am deeply European by training and tradition. I go back to Germany, mostly to Heidelberg, where the university made me an honorary senator.[34] And I've recently been back to Oxford quite often; in 1976, when I became an emeritus professor at McGill, Wolfson College named me a fellow. And somewhat later, my beloved Oriel College made me an honorary fellow. Wolfson is an attractive, modern-looking college for graduate students, set in marvellous surroundings along a river, and I spent enjoyable times there, several months a year. But when I come back to Montreal, that's when I come home. Perhaps a synthesis of the old world with the new has been effected within me.

8

THE NEOPLATONIC TRADITION

We now come to a central domain of your work, the Neoplatonic tradition. In 1939, you published The Continuity of the Platonic Tradition. *Prior to that, you had produced an outline for the* Corpus Platonicum Medii Aevi, *the first volume of which appeared in 1940. The others followed after the war and you devoted yourself to this task in Montreal. What is the source of this constant quest for Neoplatonic thought and its transmission?*

Plato played a major role during my German university career. I was mainly interested in his influence, in the Neoplatonic tradition. How did Plato influence philosophy? How was he received? When I was at school, scholars believed in an abrupt disjuncture between the Middle Ages and what is called the Renaissance. There were two opposing tendencies. One group thought that everything Plato-related that was written in the Middle Ages was Platonism, without stopping to wonder what exact relationship these writings bore to the ideas of Plato himself; the other group thought those medieval scholars who cited Plato were utterly blind to his true message. To me, both these tendencies were mistaken. I wanted to demonstrate what seemed clear to me: that what we call the Renaissance was, in many respects, a continuation of trends that developed over the preceding centuries. To discover what belonged to this putative renaissance, one also had to emphasize what it shared with

8.1 / Raymond Klibansky, *Ein Proklos-Fund und seine Bedeutung.* Heidelberg, 1929. Doctoral thesis.

what came before; only by doing so could one perceive what was new. So we had to look to the sources, look at how Plato had survived and how, even though the actual Greek Plato had lain forgotten for centuries in the West, he remained a powerful force. The only way to discover this was by studying the Latin translations. These had never been compiled, never been published in a critical edition. So the first task was to publish the translations of Plato's works themselves as well as those of his commentators, the commentators of antiquity who had been translated into Latin. Second, it was important not to neglect the transmission of Platonism through Arabic authors.[1]

As a student, I had already begun to discover, in Latin translation, an important piece of classical philosophy that had been lost in the Greek: a work by Proclus, the head of the Neoplatonic school in fifth-century Byzantium, a great commentator on Plato and an important philosopher of mathematics in his own right.[2]

Where did you discover it?

In the library of the *Cusanusstift*. One imagines, incorrectly, that such finds are a pure stroke of luck. While studying the Neoplatonic tradition, I dwelt on Proclus's commentary on Plato's enigmatic *Parmenides*.[3] In late

8.2 (*left*) / Postcard showing the library of St Nicolaus Hospital, Bernkastel-Kues. Undated, without postmark, sent from Raymond Klibansky to Frau v. Muschwitz, Berlin: "It is sometimes as if the spirit of Cusanus hovers over the building he founded. I work in the Cusanus library every day. It's very beautiful here. Many buried treasures are crammed into these manuscripts! Warm greetings, yours truly, R. Klibansky." Private collection.

8.3 (*below*) / View of Bernkastel-Kues, undated postcard. Private collection.

1927, I went to Kues to see the manuscript of this commentary that had belonged to Cusanus. It contained a different ending from the one found in the Greek manuscripts published until that time – a lengthier ending. That is, this Latin translation differed from the Greek text published by Victor Cousin, who had paid no attention to the Latin translation. I went to Oxford to see the Digby 236 manuscript and observed that it also contained this ending, which I announced in the publications of the Heidelberg Academy in early 1929. It is a central piece of ancient dialectic. One can see the importance of this tradition for the history of dialectic, one that must be known in order to understand the background to modern philosophers such as Hegel.

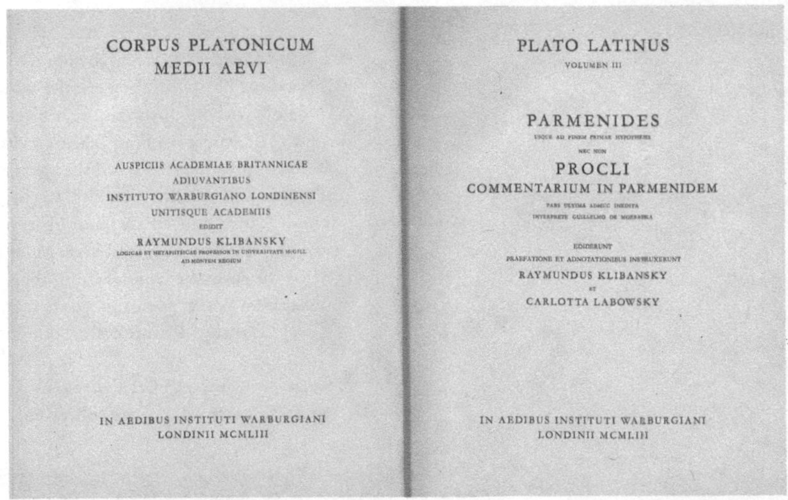

CORPUS PLATONICUM
MEDII AEVI

AUSPICIIS ACADEMIAE BRITANNICAE
ADIUVANTIBUS
INSTITUTO WARBURGIANO LONDINENSI
UNITISQUE ACADEMIIS
EDIDIT
RAYMUNDUS KLIBANSKY
LOGICAE ET METAPHYSICAE PROFESSOR IN UNIVERSITATE MCGILL
AD MONTEM REGIUM

IN AEDIBUS INSTITUTI WARBURGIANI
LONDINII MCMLIII

PLATO LATINUS
VOLUMEN III

PARMENIDES
USQUE AD FINEM PRIMAE HYPOTHESIS
NEC NON
PROCLI
COMMENTARIUM IN PARMENIDEM
PARS ULTIMA ADHUC INEDITA
INTERPRETE GUILLELMO DE MOERBEKA

EDIDERUNT
PRAEFATIONE ET ADNOTATIONIBUS INSTRUXERUNT
RAYMUNDUS KLIBANSKY
ET
CARLOTTA LABOWSKY

IN AEDIBUS INSTITUTI WARBURGIANI
LONDINII MCMLIII

8.4 / Proclus, *Commentary on Plato's "Parmenides,"* ed. Raymond Klibansky and Carlotta Labowsky. Warburg Institute, *Corpus platonicum Medii Aevi*, London, 1953.

The fact that Cusanus included in one of his philosophical sermons verbatim reproductions of summaries he had written in the margins of his manuscript of the *Commentary on Plato's "Parmenides,"* and that his work is full of reminiscences of his reading of Proclus, affords a striking illustration of the role played by this author. A not inconsiderable number of these ideas were handed down from him to Giordano Bruno,[4] who most often fails to mention their provenance and in turn passes them on to modern philosophy.

Cusanus's marginal notes show, for example, the importance of transforming a rational approach into one that acknowledges the limits of reason and the coincidence of opposites in the One, the supreme principle.

Why did you choose to begin the work of publishing the Corpus Platonicum *with the* Meno*? Was there a special reason, or was that simply the text for which you had the best manuscripts at the time?*

The two works of Plato that had been fully translated in the twelfth century were the *Meno* and the *Phaedo*, so we started with them. We know, for example, that the *Phaedo*, and to a lesser extent the *Meno*, were read by Roger Bacon and by scholars and literati of Paris, who had a manuscript of the first dialogue in the Sorbonne library as of 1271.

The most important text was the *Timaeus* but it had not been completely translated – only partially, with commentary. This dialogue, or rather its first part, had been studied and quoted throughout the Middle Ages, and there were few libraries of a certain calibre that did not possess a copy of Chalcidius's version, dating from the fourth century CE, and in some cases also a copy of the fragment translated by Cicero. With its attempted synthesis of the teleological religious justification of the world with the rational exposition of the origin of the world, *Timaeus* constituted a guide to the first gropings toward a non-mythic cosmology. Where Plato says, "nothing comes into being that is not preceded by a cause," Chalcidius renders this as "nothing comes into being that is not preceded by a legitimate cause and reason." In his Plato, God's will is the most certain origin of things, which obviously constitutes the approach of Christianity. Around this dialogue and the accompanying exposition by Chalcidius found in numerous manuscripts, there developed a copious literature of commentary whose existence was almost completely ignored, despite its great value for the history of the beginnings of scientific thought.[5]

It was of the Timaeus, *I believe, that you wrote in regard to the modern philosophers – modern at the time of Chartres, that is – who averred that they stood on the shoulders of giants?*

I had written a book on the School of Chartres that was to have been published but, when Hitler came to power, I held it back since I did not want to publish in Germany. Subsequently, this text remained unpublished.[6] I had embarked on an intensive study of Chartres, whose central figure was the master, Bernard de Chartres, who had extensively studied the classical authors. This study is reflected in Chartres cathedral, where the classical authors associated with the seven liberal arts are carved into the structure of the building. The school was characterized by the central importance it accorded to the interpretation and reading of certain classical authors. When asked why it did so, Bernard answered, "We are dwarves standing on the shoulders of giants."[7] Our own size is tiny compared to that of the ancients, but if we sit on their shoulders, we are capable of seeing beyond their horizons. We must undertake an intensive study of the classical authors in order to see more clearly than they could themselves. Without them we would be nothing, but they alone do not suffice. We must build from where they left off. Consequently, there was this sense of continuing in the tradition of classical philosophy; not servilely imitating it, but rather building on its foundation. That was the central idea of Chartres. The image has often been repeated without realizing that it comes from Bernard de Chartres. You will find Newton, for example, employing the same image as a central theme in his work.[8]

The Latin *Timaeus* and its commentary were largely responsible for the fact that the striving toward a more rational explanation of the universe found expression in attempts to harmonize the Neoplatonic and the Mosaic accounts, and in essays interpreting the story of *Genesis* in terms of Greek scientific categories and concepts that had begun to be integrated into Western thought. These tendencies culminated in the twelfth-century School of Chartres, which exerted a profound influence over the teachers of the Faculty of Arts in Paris for a century. The *Timaeus* was read in this faculty with explanations drawn from the commentary by William of Conches until it was replaced in the official curriculum, sometime before 1255, by the Aristotelian corpus.

The influence of the Chartres masters, latent for two centuries, is found in the doctrines of Cusanus, who perhaps more than any other thinker contributed to the formation of what we know as modern cosmology. This connection between the philosopher of the Renaissance, the *grande platonista* as his contemporaries called him, and the twelfth-century Neoplatonists is a striking example of the continuity of the Neoplatonic tradition. Through Cusanus, some of their theories came down to Copernicus, as we can prove using the marginal notes appearing in his copy of the *Liber de intellectu* by Bovelles.[9] This book was found in the cathedral of Frombork (Frauenberg), where Copernicus was a canon. The Swedes captured it as a war prize in the early eighteenth century and it is now in the Uppsala University Library.

I believe you discovered another Neoplatonic text as well.

In the course of my research, I was lucky enough to discover, in the Vatican Library, an unknown text from classical antiquity, an anonymous summary of the works and doctrines of Plato. It had been copied into a manuscript containing, among other things, the philosophical writings of Apuleius, at the end of his *De Mundo*, with no title and no indication that it was a different work. The beginning is clearly lacking. The numerous scholars who have had this manuscript in hand had not noticed that it was a different text. It is quite probably the Latin translation of a Greek text from the epoch of Apuleius. He wrote in the second century of our era and is universally known for his novel *The Golden Ass*, but he is also one of the most important authors for the transmission of Neoplatonism. A German scholar and I wrote a book on the transmission of this author's thought, containing a description of over a hundred manuscripts.[10] Some of them, such as those that belonged to Petrarch, Cusanus, and Marsilio Ficino, proved particularly interesting and contain annotations by their owners. This was a stage in the history of Platonism.

I am preparing the publication of the manuscript that I found, a particularly difficult text whose story I was able to trace, and a rather interesting story it is. This manuscript was unmistakably mentioned for the first time in the *Biblionomia*, written shortly before 1250; it is the catalogue of the library of a curious figure, Richard de Fournival, who was chancellor of the cathedral chapter of Notre-Dame d'Amiens. This poetic catalogue compares the library to a beautiful garden in which the most precious ornaments are the books by the best authors. Fournival, a distinguished man of letters and an inspired author of pornographic prose, bequeathed his library to Gérard d'Abbeville, who in turn left it to what became the Sorbonne library. The book then disappeared, only to turn up in the library of Christina, Queen of Sweden, which she brought to Stockholm from Rome after her abdication. At the queen's death, the books fell to Cardinal Decio Azzolini, of whom she said: "The Cardinal is a divine and incomparable man. He is dearer to me than life." The Cardinal's nephew sold it all to Pope Alexander VIII (Pietro Ottoboni), and the manuscript came into the Vatican.[11]

In all this research, the question arises as to the extent to which traditions are the reflection of their creative sources. This is the problem that I strove to examine in a study published recently in Paris, "Regagner Athènes à partir d'Alexandrie?"[12]

I was your student – and it was of course a great privilege – when you taught at the Institut d'études médiévales, which was then directed by Father Benoît Lacroix, a marvellous man of warmth and rigorous intellect. You revived an old bond with the Dominicans, of whom we spoke in connection with your work on Meister Eckhart, and I have vivid memories of your lectures on Plato. In fact, what you taught was the importance of the Neoplatonic tradition. You did well in keeping yourself out of the picture so that we could focus on the greatness of the text. I'm thinking in particular of the text from the Timaeus *on human nature and the importance of reason, which you commented on during the first class I attended.*

Yes, it is a text of the first order – a famous text – in which the ties binding man to divinity are affirmed by Plato in such a strong and imagistic way. Shall we recite it?

> And we should consider that God gave the sovereign part of the human soul to be the divinity of each one, being that part which, as we say, dwells at the top of the body, and inasmuch as we are a plant not of an earthly but of a heavenly growth, raises us from earth to our kindred who are in heaven. And in this we say truly; for the divine power suspended the head and root of us from that place where the generation of the soul first began, and thus made the whole body upright. When a man is always occupied with the cravings of desire and ambition, and is eagerly striving to satisfy them, all his thoughts must be mortal, and, as far as it is possible altogether to become such, he must be mortal every whit, because he has cherished his mortal part. But he who has been earnest in the love of knowledge and of true wisdom, and has exercised his intellect more than any other part of him, must have thoughts immortal and divine, if he attain truth, and in so far as human nature is capable of sharing in immortality, he must altogether be immortal; and

> since he is ever cherishing the divine power, and has the divinity within him in perfect order, he will be perfectly happy.[13]

As you know, this text proved central to the whole medieval Neoplatonic tradition, and that is where the moderns got it from. Its importance cannot be overstated.

In rereading this text from the Timaeus, *one may wonder as to the value of Platonism today. When we hear this paean to humanity, as we found it in the thought of Meister Eckhart, which in fact has deep roots in Plato's text, one wonders if it is still possible, after Auschwitz, to see ourselves in this celestial plant. Does Platonism still have a force that makes it a form of truth in your eyes?*

For Plato, Auschwitz would certainly have proved one thing: that the negative side won out. That makes it all the more important, all the more necessary, to remember that human beings cannot be reduced to what the National Socialist regime made of the tradition. It is the nadir of human evolution, the place where that spark was entirely obscured, but there was – Plato would say there always has been – some small minority in which that spark did not go out, who were conscious, who suffered. The majority, for Plato, is never an argument against his philosophy. On the contrary, he would say that this shows the necessity of recalling this divine origin, that which binds man to what allows him to transcend his quotidian needs, his ordinary passions and the will to dominate, the will to self-aggrandize at others' expense. Only this faith, Plato would say, allows for the survival of humanity as a force for good.

9

THE ENGLISH MASTERS AND THE QUESTION OF TOLERANCE

From Hume, you went on to Locke. You published his A Letter Concerning Toleration *in your Philosophy and World Community series and that edition was translated into numerous languages. I wondered as I read this letter, and seeing the importance it had for you, whether this work on toleration (or more colloquially, tolerance) was a reaction to the Cold War or to other ideological forms that you wanted to combat at that time. Why did tolerance become absolutely essential to your thinking after the war?*

It took on great importance for the following reason. During the war, I wondered how it could be that individuals who seemed in no way morally inferior to others should have behaved as they did. I interrogated German and Italian prisoners of war. As individuals they were not criminals, yet they had shown themselves capable of committing criminal acts. Numerous Germans, in particular, did so in the name of the state. How can we explain that people who were honest and good husbands and fathers, individually speaking, could commit atrocities in the name of the state? You have to go back to their education. And on that score I noted that even those who had been to university were not at all conversant with the tradition in which the state is not regarded as a supreme master but only as a means. For a German, the state commanded respect.

This notion was rooted in German nineteenth-century philosophy; the German educational system almost completely ignored the existence of a different tradition that teaches tolerance of other people's ideas. The notion of the state pervaded all of German culture and teaching, at school and university alike. If you look for the reasons why this was so, you discover that schoolchildren and university students were totally unfamiliar with the authors who became the advocates of freedom of thought and the right of each person to form his own opinion. So it's important to know what young people are learning at school or university, as well as in the home.

The whole tradition of tolerance was unknown in Germany. If you have some familiarity with the literature, with nineteenth-century German philosophy, and also with a certain particular culture of policing, you find that the notion of authority, *Obrigkeit*, reigns supreme. To this authority, one must submit. There is a very sharp distinction between the individual and his morality on the one hand, and the individual as a social and political being on the other. Absolute submission to the will of the state goes back to Luther – the mature Luther, that is, not the young man.[1] Luther stated, in sum, that religion, that faith in God, resides in one's inner being; that the authorities have no right to interfere with the immediacy of the individual's relationship to God. But in regard to the individual as a social and political being, one must render unto Caesar the things that are Caesar's. Luther based these ideas on scripture and opposed all the revolutionaries of his day. So human beings were split into two parts, one capable of having faith and the other acting in the social and political sphere.

And that is bound to have an influence on the conception of the state?

This dualism characterizes the whole of German culture. The state becomes a force that is entirely different from the naïve conception of the state in France or Britain, where it is conceived of as a mere means toward an organized, civilized life. In Germany, the state is not a means: it is an end and it demands reverence. This supremacy of the state is very

NICOLAI DE CUSA
OPERA OMNIA
IUSSU ET AUCTORITATE
ACADEMIAE LITTERARUM HEIDELBERGENSIS
AD CODICUM FIDEM EDITA
VII
DE PACE FIDEI
EDIDERUNT
COMMENTARIISQUE ILLUSTRAVERUNT
RAYMUNDUS KLIBANSKY
ET
HILDEBRANDUS BASCOUR, O.S.B.
HAMBURGI
IN AEDIBUS FELICIS MEINER
MCMLXX

9.1 / Nicholas Cusanus, *De Pace Fidei*, ed. Raymond Klibansky and Hildebrand Bascour, Hamburg, Felix Meiner, 1970.

important to an understanding of everything that happened in Germany. This conception can be found expressed in philosophical language in Hegel, where the state is the embodiment of the spirit, the reality of the spirit. In no other country has such a philosophy developed. This does not mean that Hegel was personally very intolerant or cruel. True, he behaved quite badly toward the mother of his illegitimate son, an accident from which one cannot derive significant conclusions for his philosophy. But in the *Introduction to the Philosophy of History*, the state is seen as all-powerful, embodying the spirit at a certain moment in its development.[2] This conception of the state as the entity commanding active submission was handed down to the universities, the teachers, and also to families who had not read the philosophers.

I took Locke on tolerance as an example. I attended one of the best universities, if not the best – Heidelberg, the cradle of the great historical school dating back to Hegel's lectures of 1816 – a university where there were great masters such as Kuno Fischer[3] and others. I noticed that Locke was not read at all in Heidelberg as the twentieth century began. To be sure, the seventeenth-century edition could be found in the library, but one had to go there and there was no translation available. Locke's work was not part of the curriculum. Philosophy students were of course familiar with his *Essay on Human Understanding*. They knew that this work was important to the history of the philosophy of language and especially the theory of knowledge (it emphasizes the primacy of sense impressions, a thesis that would be opposed by Leibniz). Locke was seen as a predecessor, not an important author in and of himself. In Germany, Italy, and other countries as well, this tradition of tolerance was unknown, whereas it was available in France thanks to the great writings of Voltaire[4] and various nineteenth-century works.

So you published Locke in several languages?

I felt it necessary to make the texts embodying the idea of tolerance available in various countries of the world. So in 1957 I founded the Philosophy and World Community series under the auspices of the International Institute of Philosophy in Paris. The purpose of this series is to show how philosophy can serve the idea of a world community. The texts propagating this idea must be readily accessible; thus, they must be published in low-priced editions that teachers and students can easily purchase. So, we published texts like Spinoza's writings on liberty and others,[5] some of them in dual-language editions with the Latin presented alongside translations into Hungarian, Japanese, and other languages. For the purposes of this series, the most important texts were indeed Locke's *Letter Concerning Toleration* and the edicts of Asoka, the great Indian emperor of the third century BCE, who reconquered a part of North India that had been lost to Alexander.[6] The first thing he did was to declare that one must not kill for religion; nor must any religion be imposed by force. When the terrible cruelty of war impressed itself upon him, he resolved to promulgate a series of edicts throughout his empire ordering an end to wars of religion. These edicts were engraved on stones. Thirty years ago, a monument was found at Kandahar with these edicts written in Prakrit, a vernacular form of Sanskrit; Aramaic, which was the *lingua franca* of the Near East; and Greek. For the first time, respect for the faith of others was proclaimed.[7] This text is little known in India, although Asoka's likeness can be found on Indian banknotes. It was one of the texts that needed to be disseminated.

As to John Locke's *Epistola de tolerantia*, it was translated into numerous languages, including English, German, French, Polish, Japanese, Hungarian, Italian, and Spanish, for the Philosophy and World Community collection. The most surprising thing is that the Arabic translation, published shortly before the Hebrew translation, was printed in Beirut during the terrible events of that day. Obviously, books themselves change nothing; there have to be people capable of interpreting them, people who believe in these texts and who can use them in their school and university teaching. The texts by themselves accomplish nothing, but they are indispensable to teachers and are the necessary condition for the teaching of any tradition.

Couldn't one dispute the very term "tolerance"? After all, doesn't "tolerate" mean to endure something that one really doesn't like? In Latin particularly, doesn't the term refer to an idea close to "gritting one's teeth"? Doesn't the word contain a dual assessment, both positive and negative, of another person's opinions?

Tolerance in Latin is not just physical endurance, as is often said, although it is that too. When Cicero speaks of *tolerantia rerum humanarum,* he is talking mainly about endurance, stoicism in the face of life's vicissitudes. But his letters, written in the vernacular, contain some quite interesting phrases. At one point he writes, *cum … me cogerem illa ferre toleranter,* . "how I tried … to bear it all with patience, with fortitude" (*toleranter*). This is not physical endurance but patience in the face of something negative. It is always used in this sense. Thus, in the *Tusculan Disputations,* he says that the Greeks endure diseases *toleranter,* with patience. In English, one would say "to put up with."[8]

So is it solely and only putting up with something one cannot fully endorse?

It is the ability to endure something disagreeable, painful. It is quite clear that the connotation is negative. The article on the verb *tolérer* in Diderot's encyclopedia illustrates this point: "They *tolerate* things who, knowing of them, and having the power in hand, fail to prevent them; they *suffer* them who, having the power to prevent them, fail to oppose them; they *permit* them who authorize them by formal consent. *Tolerate* is said only of bad things, or things believed to be so; *permit* is said of both good and bad."[9]

Mirabeau, for his part, objected to the note of condescension contained in tolerance: "The most unlimited freedom of religion is, in my view, so sacred a right, that the word tolerance, which affects to express it, appears to me in some sense tyrannical in itself, since the existence of an authority, which has the power to tolerate it, keeps guard over liberty of thought at the very same time that it tolerates it, and so has the power to suppress it."[10]

The declaration of one of Mirabeau's contemporaries, Thomas Paine, the celebrated author of *Rights of Man,* is even harsher: "Toleration is not the opposite of Intolerance, but is the counterfeit of it. Both are despotisms. The one assumes to itself the right of withholding Liberty of Conscience, and the other of granting it."[11]

Medieval philosophy had adapted the notion to questions of faith. You know the article by Thomas Aquinas, *Utrum ritus infidelium sint tolerandi*, in *Summa Theologica* II.2?[12] Should the rites of infidels be tolerated? The article discusses this question at length. The rites of Jews should be tolerated, but there are certain rites that should not be tolerated. And most important, the heretic must never be tolerated. This is the great distinction made by Christian theology. To understand the evolution of the thinking, the writings of St Augustine are valuable.[13] He begins by saying that faith is a free act. But later, when explaining the words of St Luke, *Compelle intrare* (compel them to enter),[14] Augustine modifies his conception. Henceforth, we find him stating two positions. On the one hand, *Credere nemo potest nisi volens* (No one can believe unless he so chooses), and here we have the young Augustine's *nisi volens*. Later, this *nisi volens* disappears. Aquinas considers these two moments in Augustine's thinking, taken together, to constitute the doctrine of the Church. On the one hand, *Accipere fidem est voluntatis* (To receive the faith is a free act); on the other, *Sed tenere fidem iam acceptam est necessitatis* (But if you have become Christian, you must keep the faith, it is a necessity). You are not permitted to leave, to stop being Christian. If you leave the faith, you become a heretic. No tolerance for that! Aquinas analyzes the rites of the Jews at length. They must be permitted to follow them. But if one of them converts and then wants to leave: no tolerance!

That corresponds to the situation still existing in certain Muslim countries, for example. The presence of people who are not Muslims is tolerated, but he who abjures Islam and embraces another religion is liable to capital punishment. When you are a Muslim, you must remain one.

At the global level, we see two distinctly different attitudes. There are the prophetic religions in which a message is revealed by the prophets, a message constituting the true faith, commanded by God, which one is bound to accept. This is the case not only for Christianity but also for other religions. Judaism today is a religion of great tolerance, but one finds in the Bible certain declarations – even in Jeremiah, even in Isaiah – that sound a very different note. Islam is similar, and if you know Chinese history ... People always think Confucius stood for reason itself. But in the ninth century, Confucians systematically destroyed Buddhist monasteries and others. By contrast – and this is why I spoke of two very different attitudes – Buddhists, and Sufis even more so, believe in a unity of the divine, a fundamental unity that can encompass different paths. The Other – the other religion, the other person – has a different way of approaching the same truth. He does not see it as clearly. The great Sufi poets, who are not highly regarded in today's Arab world, nor in Iran, left us beautiful texts on the subject.

There was a Frenchman, Henri Corbin,[15] who had studied them extensively. I met Corbin at the home of Alexandre Koyré in 1933. We were celebrating the publication of the first volume of *Recherches philosophiques*. Heidegger's work was making its entrance in France. Henri Corbin had translated Heidegger for *Recherches philosophiques*, a seemingly rather innocent Heidegger, an interesting one too, for he was putting forward something that seemed so different. But later, Corbin gave up all that and turned to the study of Islamic philosophy. He became interested in the secret philosophy of Avicenna. A great man, Henri Corbin! For him, there was one truth, but many different ways of approaching that truth.

So we have two utterly different attitudes: prophetism and universalism. Prima facie, for what is called the problem of tolerance, these two approaches are mutually exclusive. In the prophetic world, others must be shown the righteous path for their own good, their salvation. For universalists, truth is not based on prophecy.

Are you saying that, philosophically speaking, the idea of tolerance can readily lead to paradoxes? In Locke or in other authors?

The *Letter Concerning Toleration* was, as we know, written in Latin in 1685.[16] It may have been completed in 1686. It was published in 1689. So there was an interval between when it was written and when it was published. Locke, throughout his life, almost up to the moment of his death, did not want to be acknowledged as the author, since he disliked controversies and attacks. But he knew it was being translated into English. He writes that his Dutch friend had found out that there was an English translation. And this translation was published, also in 1689, very soon after the original. We know for a fact that the translator was a man named William Popple,[17] a highly cultivated merchant and a man of very strong Unitarian conviction, as well as a nephew of the great poet Andrew Marvell. Popple added a preface to his translation. An Italian writer had claimed that Locke had done the translation himself and had inspired the well-known prologue containing the maxim: "Absolute liberty, nothing but liberty. This is what we stand in need of." A great hymn to liberty, no doubt!

But if you have some familiarity with Locke, you know that nothing could be further from what he actually wrote. He was not at all thinking of some kind of absolute liberty. This philosopher, who was anything but a revolutionary, did hold the deep conviction that the state must keep out of certain realms, and this desire for liberty is perfectly clear in the *Letter Concerning Toleration*. Locke begins by marking out the bounds of state and church power. A church is a voluntary association. Within its walls, it can do what it likes; it can exclude people from membership, it has that right. The state, for its part, has the role of preserving public order and enforcing the law, but it has nothing to do with religion. There is therefore a sharp dividing line between state power and the role of the church. Of course, this idea did not originate with Locke. If you study the history of English thought, you find ideas that are not stated with the same clarity but have the same basic thrust; in Milton,[18] for example, long before Locke.

In America as well, there was an important author, Roger Williams,[19] whose works have never been translated into French, I believe, but whom I would like to publish in my series. Williams was a Massachusetts clergyman and lived with the Puritans. He revolted against their dictatorship over matters of faith. These people, who had left England because they did not accept the supremacy of the Anglican Church, were as intolerant as anyone could be. Once settled in Massachusetts, they enjoyed immense power and brooked no opposition in matters of faith. So Williams was forced into exile in Rhode Island. In 1644 he wrote *The Bloudy Tenent of Persecution for Cause of Conscience* against the Puritans, a too-little-known but magisterial work.

In Holland, Locke was close to the Arminians, who believed in universal grace and harmony between God's decrees and human liberty. Locke was attracted by their spirit of moderation and by the credo of Episcopius, *In necessariis unitas, in dubiis libertas, in omnibus caritas* (In necessary things unity; in doubtful things liberty; in all things charity).[20]

His major principle is that the state should impose no religious obligations. But he also conceives of four exceptions to tolerance. First, the state cannot tolerate practices contrary to morality, good moral standards. He does not define what he means by this, but it is a sphere, a domain, in which no tolerance is possible. Second, those who seek to impose their ideas on others must not be tolerated. Third, the Catholics are not to be tolerated. Locke was not the first to believe this; Milton said the same thing. It is not that they found the Catholic credo particularly shocking. But the Catholics were subjects of a foreign prince and thus constituted a threat to the state, to the community. If you know about the wars of religion, if you know that when the Spanish conquered territory they imposed Catholicism by force, you get a glimmer of understanding. Rome was militant. The Catholic princes imposed Catholicism. Whence the reasoning: Catholics are subjects of the pope, who is a foreign prince, so no Catholics!

The fourth exception, equally unacceptable, concerns atheists because, in Locke's thinking, an atheist is someone who may violate his oath, hence cannot be trusted to uphold a contract. Atheists are people bereft of morality.

Godless and lawless?

Exactly. This is a very important limit to toleration in Locke. The exception regarding Catholics is less important because it was temporary, due to the political situation. But the one about atheists is not temporary because it is based on his definition of atheism. Upholding contracts, good morality: these things are tied to religious observance. There is clearly something in Locke that remains problematic. On the one hand, he says that faith in Jesus Christ forms the basis of morality. On the other, he says – especially in the third letter on toleration – that heartfelt belief and the conduct ensuing from it form the basis of religion. These are fascinating developments in which he does not talk of Christ. So there is in Locke something not truly resolved; namely, his belief that God's existence is subject to rational proof, and has been proven. To deny God's existence is to defy intelligence itself, and that is a malevolent act. The atheist is someone who refuses to accept truth. Those who do not want to accept God are either idiotic – in general they are not – or evil. Locke's conception of tolerance, which was so important and still played such a major role in the eighteenth century, is a conception based on an entirely insufficient foundation.

Do you mean that the foundation is not wholly rational?

In one sense, for Locke, it is not the job of the state to interfere in matters of faith. Seen in historical context, this position clearly constitutes a great stride forward. The great principle of *cuius regio, eius religio* (whose realm, his religion) still existed after the Reformation. This was the conclusion of the Peace of Augsburg between the Catholics and the Protestants. Those who did not wish to accept the prince's religion were allowed to emigrate. The state determines religion: if you don't like it, you can go elsewhere. In late-sixteenth-century France, after Henry IV, the Edict of Nantes gave the Huguenots the crucial right to practise their religion. But as every French schoolchild knows, the Edict of Nantes was revoked in 1685 and the Huguenots dispersed to Germany, Holland, England …

And Geneva, taking French clockwork with them!

That's right; Swiss cuckoo clocks come from the persecutions! In 1685 the principle of *cuius regio, eius religio* was restored in France and the monarchy reimposed Catholicism. The supremacy of the state, its right to impose religion, was a political reality in the time of Locke. The *Letter Concerning Toleration* was written in 1685, the year the Edict of Nantes was revoked. It declares that the state does not have the right to interfere in matters of religion. There were already some leanings in this direction, but Locke established it systematically by marking out the role of the state. For him, the state looks after public order. The role of the church is entirely different. So I would say that this was a huge step forward in human affairs and was recognized as such in the eighteenth century. But it can't be denied that the foundation was not truly stable, philosophically speaking, even though this epistle marked a step forward from the standpoint of tolerance.

Yet, in various authors who had dwelt on the issue of tolerance before him, Locke could find texts, conceptions on which to base a broader definition of tolerance, or distinctions that might have lent nuance to his position on atheism.

For atheism, the exception is explained by his own philosophy. He believed that morality is linked to religion, which forms its foundation. In that he differs from Pierre Bayle,[21] who is little known in France despite the work of Élisabeth Labrousse, an excellent historian who also happens to be a good Protestant. For Labrousse, Bayle is the great fideist; he says that religion cannot be established by reason, only by faith. All his arguments are marshalled against a rational basis for faith, and his direct faith is all the greater. If you read Bayle, it's important to take the trouble to read the notes to his *Historical and Critical Dictionary*, which are voluminous. On this, my friend Michel Paradis has done excellent work that states the essence of the question.[22] Nothing can be said against atheism because religion cannot be proven. Each religion is as good as any other. There is no argument from reason: there is only faith. But this faith is personal. So it cannot be said that one religion is better than another, and atheists are full-fledged citizens. This was already evident in *Various Thoughts on the Occasion of a Comet* but it becomes transparently clear in the magnificent *A Philosophical Commentary on These Words of the Gospel, Luke 14:23, "Compel Them to Come In, That My House May Be Full."* This is an imposing work. I would have liked to publish it but it is impossible.[23] Bayle has the failing of writing too much, talking too much. It is hard to condense; still, the ideas are perfectly clear. Tolerance is found here in its clearest sense, but in a radically different form from Locke. They knew, or at least knew of, each other. Did they really meet in Rotterdam? It has not been proven that they did, but they had common acquaintances such as the Quaker merchant Benjamin Furly.[24] They were familiar with each other's work. Bayle spoke of Locke in glowing terms; Locke esteemed Bayle. Yet there was a gulf between them. In Bayle, you really have the fundaments of tolerance today. I would say that we don't give Bayle his due.

When we discussed your Philosophy and World Community series, you explained how your experience coming out of the war led you to think that, for therapeutic purposes in a certain number of authoritarian regimes, the study of Locke could be salutary.

Not just Locke. I saw the need to make important texts that uphold a certain tradition available to professors and students: the tradition of tolerance, let's say, but more fundamentally that of faith in the possibility of discussion based on rational argument – the desire to understand and converse with our fellow human beings as part of a quest for mutual understanding. The first step was to make a list of these texts; Locke had a major role to play, obviously, and Asoka, whom I've mentioned, but also a third author, Sebastian Castellio, who established, *contra* Calvin, the right to heresy.[25] Castellio was French. He is often said to have been a Savoyard, but he came from the department of Ain. He also wrote *Advice to a Desolate France*, an important text offering an initial definition of heresy and establishing the right to doubt. In his book *Concerning Heretics: Whether They Are to Be Persecuted*, he asks, "Who is a heretic?" He answers, "He who thinks differently from us," and goes on to say that neither the church nor the state has the right to persecute him.

Under the communist regime in Poland, this book sold out in six weeks. Poland has a tradition of tolerance dating back to the sixteenth century. The principle of *cuius regio, eius religio* was imposed in Europe but not in Poland. In the sixteenth century, Poland was the great country of tolerance where all sects were allowed, including the Socinians, who rejected the Trinity. That changed later.

The person in charge of the classics series at the government publishing house, Irena Krońska,[26] was a remarkable woman, a poet, married to a philosopher. She came to Oxford, and in 1973, before attending the World Congress of Philosophy in Varna, Bulgaria, I saw her again. She had cancer, unfortunately, and had insisted on returning to Poland to die. She inserted a photocopied page into the Castellio book bearing the inscription "*liber prohibitus.*" The title of the Italian edition was *Faith, Doubt, and Toleration.*

Liber prohibitus? *Do you mean that the book was banned in the seventeenth century and that Krońska reproduced the stamp indicating this? How astute of her.*

It was a clear allusion to the claims of the Church and the regime in the twentieth century. Now that we are at liberty to write the history of the communist regimes of central Europe, we should perhaps acknowledge that on certain matters, in particular the question of classical authors, they always left a great deal of latitude. It is not surprising that it was possible in Poland to publish important things like Locke.

The best evidence is that the Hungarian Academy, during the communist era, requested permission to have a second edition of Locke with my preface; yet it is a text that does not sit well within a communist regime. This second edition dates from 1982; the first had been done a few years earlier. You see, we did manage to sow some seeds in a few countries.

Anthony Collins,[27] who is not well known in France, was also published in the Philosophy and World Community series, but only in English and in Italian and German translations.

Did Cusanus merit a place in the series?

He should be there, but I've been slow in adding a translation to my edition of the Latin text. In *Peace in Faith* (*De pace fidei*),[28] the problem of tolerance comes up again. It is a wonderful text. Do you know the background? In 1453 the West, Italy especially, was in great distress, what with the fall of Constantinople. It was known at the papal court that Ottoman sultan Mehmed the Conqueror was studying maps of Italy every day: an invasion was in the offing. What to do? At the Vatican, the idea of a preventive war arose among the cardinals. It was also around this time that printing was invented, and among the first printed books was a collection of letters, the *Türkenbriefe*, calling on the princes of Europe to do something,[29] to wage preventive war on the Turks. Emissaries were sent to Germany. The cardinal Nicolaus Cusanus, instead of taking part in this agitation for a preventive war, wrote his *De pace fidei*. This book presents the vision of someone reeling from the fall of Constantinople and the cruelties committed in the name of religion. He imagines a gathering

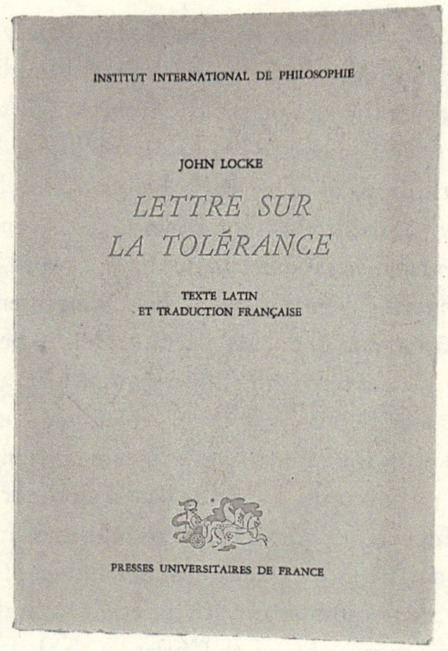

9.2 / John Locke, *Lettre sur la tolérance*, ed. Raymond Klibansky, Paris, 1965. Édition de l'Institut international de Philosophie, Philosophie et communauté mondiale series.

at the centre of the world – that is, Jerusalem – of representatives of the various countries and religions: a Hindu, a Jew, an Arab, a Spaniard, a German, an Englishman, and others, the wise men of the principal countries, the principal religions, under the presidency of the divine word, the Logos. Each of these sages speaks of his own religion. They all want to see if there is a way to put an end to the atrocities committed in the name of religion. And they find that *una est religio in rituum diversitate* (religion is one, with a diversity of rites), and *una veritas in variis signis resplendet* (one truth shines in various forms); in sum, that unity can be attained by following entirely different paths. While rites may differ, all strive for the same goal: reverence and service to the One God. And despite the Jews' objection to the Trinity, all must recognize in the end that God is both one and three. The result is an end to wars of religion.

I also published Cusanus's correspondence with Juan de Segovia,[30] the titular bishop of Caesarea in Palestine, who had opposed the Pope at the Council of Florence (Council of Basel). A cultivated man who sought to withdraw from the world and have nothing further to do with conciliarism and its feuds, he had retired to the hills of Savoy and invited ʿĪsā ibn Jābir (Yça Gidelli), the highly educated religious leader of Segovia's Mudejar community, to join him there. Together, they set about translating the Koran, the one from Arabic to Castilian Spanish and the other from Spanish to Latin: *Alcoran trilingüe.* The goal was to discover what the basis of unity might be. And a lovely correspondence between the two of them has come down to us. It conveys the idea that peace, peace within faith, is established not by the sword but by the spirit and through dicussion. On the one hand, there is an intent to establish peace through persuasion and not arms: Mehmed has to be persuaded. So the pope wrote a letter to Mehmed to convince him, a letter that is extant. One might say: This is great, here is tolerance. But on what basis? Obviously we all want the same thing, a sincere faith in God. We want unity; however, this unity has to be based on the truth of the Christian faith. The important point is that Cusanus says that the choice of religion is secondary. *Una est religio in rituum diversitate,* that is the great maxim. Rites are not important. It's different from the practice of the Church, but this unity is based on Christian truth.

He wants to show that all intelligent people must ultimately admit this principle. You see how this line of thinking is found in Pico della Mirandola in late fifteenth-century Florence.[31] There is a very profound unity. It is presupposed that truth expresses itself particularly in the Christian religion and that it is incomplete in the others. It is admitted that religions all want the same thing and none will be said to be superior to any other. This is a revelation dating back to the ancients and this ancient wisdom is transmitted, manifesting a profound unity in this way. I showed that Cusanus was translated into German during the Thirty Years' War and then used to show that the parties were killing each other with total disregard for unity.

It would be some time before Cusanus's pacifist thought was rediscovered.

That's true: It wasn't until the eighteenth century that Cusanus was rediscovered by Lessing, who wanted to translate *De pace fidei.* It seems surprising that no one had done this before, doesn't it? Lessing was working on his *Nathan the Wise,* which is the great play on tolerance.[32] In this play, representatives of the three great religions have to come to agreement on the idea that, while there is only one truth, we do not know who possesses it. This idea does not really align with the thinking of Cusanus, for whom it went without saying that Christianity represented the truth. You know the story of the three rings. What does it mean from the Church's point of view? At the death of the father, the three rings are identical to one another. Which one is authentic? Impossible to say. Doesn't this open the door to relativism? Which is the true religion? It cannot be known, so the others must be allowed. The fable of the three rings is found earlier, in Boccaccio,[33] and Lessing built his play around it.

There is a statue of Nathan in front of Lessing's house in Wolfenbüttel across from the Herzog August Library, the wonderful library of the dukes of Brunswick, where Lessing succeeded Leibniz in the role of librarian. I go there to work almost every year. The library itself, by virtue of its organization and fabulous holdings, is a researcher's paradise. Its outreach was greatly extended under the impetus of its former director, Paul Raabe.[34] It is complemented by a research program, courses, conferences, and publications, making it a unique institution. The research program was directed by Sabine Solf,[35] a remarkable woman whose cheerful intelligence contributed much to the warm welcome one can expect there.

Is the status of tolerance today different from what it was in the past?

After all these historical considerations and others, it is important to realize that the problem of tolerance and its limits is still relevant today, but that the domain of the debate has shifted. While in some countries, religion is still the domain in which tolerance is or is not exercised, in Western, putatively democratic societies, tolerance covers the vast field of political convictions and social behaviours. A glance at the controversies roiling society is enough to convince one of this. Should abortion be tolerated? Homosexuals in the Navy? The tendentious rewriting of history? Pornography? Free access to drugs?

Is tolerance without limits conceivable? Two considerations must be addressed: it is clear that tolerance cannot extend to intolerance; however, unlimited tolerance is apt to lead to intolerance.

On the one hand, respect for the rights of others implies that rights violations cannot be tolerated. On the other, boundless tolerance, extending to incitement to hatred, for example, can degenerate into violence. In the end, tolerance must become a dialogue within "a reciprocity of human dignity" – this must be stressed – and any discourse on tolerance is pointless if it avoids consideration of the limits of tolerance.

10

THE INTERNATIONAL INSTITUTE OF PHILOSOPHY

Your work at the International Institute of Philosophy extends over nearly forty-five years. Your contributions to the work and publications of the institute represent an effort to involve philosophy in the world of peace-building.

The International Institute of Philosophy[1] was founded at the 9th International Congress of Philosophy (Descartes Congress) in Paris in 1937. Philosophers from every country took part. For France, the Platonist Léon Robin was the principal inspiration. There were other French scholars too, such as Émile Bréhier, and many foreign philosophers gathered in Paris. The modest descriptor "institute" was adopted, rather than academy, although it actually is an academy in that members have to be nominated and elected; membership is not a mere process of registration. The number of members is limited: initially set at 100, it was increased to 115 when the bylaws were changed to make the institute truly international, covering all continents.

The war interrupted the work of the institute, which then consisted of an international bibliography of philosophy as well as chronicles of certain philosophical disciplines. It was only several years later that the work resumed. In 1947 an initial meeting was held in Sweden. The Swedish, in particular the editor of the journal *Theoria*, Åke Petzäll of Gothenburg, did much to animate or revive this enterprise. Bréhier's son-in-law, Raymond Bayer, who wrote on aesthetics, became the secretary. We resumed the bibliography, but it was limited to a bibliography of titles only. In 1953 the institute was placed on a truly international footing. Among the philosophers gathered in Brussels at the very fine Erasmus House, we took pains to choose those who stood out for their interest in international cooperation, and also for the quality of their work and their willingness to discuss it.

At that point, I proposed that the bibliography be changed. A list of titles is of no use to anyone. What were needed were abstracts of each publication, which is much more difficult, and an attempt to establish centres for philosophical bibliography in each country. I took on the responsibility for directing these endeavours and succeeded in having centres founded in over fifty countries. The publication of the quarterly *Bibliography of Philosophy* is supported by UNESCO and has been uninterrupted since the journal's inception.[2]

One might say that the Bibliography of Philosophy, *the analytical bibliography produced by the institute, is particularly useful precisely because the abstracts capture the essence of the papers discussed. Philosophical publication has proliferated and the sheer volume of publication has quickly become unmanageable.*

Yes. Readers can use these intelligently prepared abstracts to determine whether a work is essential to their own academic interests or whether it is only recapitulating things written elsewhere. Obviously, much depends on the analyst, the bibliographer, who has to be able to deliver the essence of each paper.

You created other publications for the institute as well.

The other task was to produce chronicles or, as I put it, a publication that could serve as a *logon didonai*, a stock-taking of the current state of philosophy, including each of its branches and every country in which it is practised: a universal overview. There were, as always in philosophy, rivalries, especially in the areas of mathematical philosophy and logic. The Swiss school had a great master at the Swiss Federal Institute of

Technology in Zürich, Ferdinand Gonseth, who had written important works on the philosophy of geometry; it was in conflict with the Dutch school, represented by the distinguished philosopher of mathematics L.E.J. Brouwer. I had to accept the editor's position because they were willing to cooperate with me, but not with each other!

Philosophy in the Mid-Century,[3] which was to have been published for the International Congress of Philosophy held in Venice in 1958, contains papers of the greatest interest. In particular, the section on the philosophy of science in the first volume is often cited. This volume contains the well-known paper by the Dutch philosopher E.W. Beth on semantic tableaux as well as a summary produced by Niels Bohr, at my request and in response to my questions, titled "Quantum Physics and Philosophy: Causality and Complementarity." The second volume deals with various aspects of philosophy, giving prominence to the philosophy of language; the third is devoted to the history of philosophy; the fourth, to philosophy on the different continents.

Philosophy in China was represented by the renowned philosopher Feng Youlan, whose contribution concerns Marxism-Leninism in China and who presented himself as the spokesperson for Marxism. It was evident that he did not believe in it, but he had to do it. Marxism also made an appearance in the Soviet contribution. We had invited Russian philosophers and it was quite evident to me that these two conceptions of Marxism could not co-exist in the long run without clashing. On this occasion, the philosophers told the diplomats and statesmen that this alliance between China and Russia could not last. The diplomats were disbelieving, but the Russian engineers soon had to leave China and the break occurred. It had been predictable to anyone with the ability to interpret a philosophical text.

These chronicles, published in four volumes under the title *Philosophy in the Mid-Century*, were followed by another four-volume work, *Contemporary Philosophy*, a larger survey published in 1968–71 for the fourteenth edition of the congress held in Vienna. As contributors, I chose competent representatives of philosophy in every country and from all the important schools. The problem of Marxism was posed once again. I asked several important representatives of Marxist thought what Marxism was. Rather than refute it, it was more interesting to ask the Marxists to define it. It became quite clear that it was no longer possible, after this second series, to speak of Marxism, but rather of Marxisms. This is an example of the kind of lesson one can learn from such philosophical compilations.

In 1993 another series of chronicles devoted to the current state of philosophy was published under the title *La Philosophie en Europe*. This work, which I edited and prefaced with David Pears, contains some studies of great interest, of which I will mention two: "Rendre à nouveau raison?" on philosophy in France, by Dominique Janicaud; and "Allemagne," by Reiner Wiehl, on philosophy in Germany. The book sold unexpectedly well, even in Canada, to my surprise, and the success was consolation for a difficult birth. The project had been launched by UNESCO, which, in exchange for financial aid, regrettably took an active part in its material organization. As a result, the production process took years, and all the contributors had to revise manuscripts outdated by the passage of time. But this delay made it possible to compare the manuscripts of the Russian philosophers before and after the collapse of the Soviet Union. The least one can say is that it would be euphemistic to apply the word "evolution" to the modifications made by the authors themselves.

Each year, the institute holds meetings in a different country. When did that begin?

In 1953, with the second founding of the institute. In 1954 we held our meeting in conjunction with that of the Association des sociétés de philosophie de langue française in Grenoble, and in 1955 we were invited to Athens, where the king and queen asked to participate in the sessions. At the opening session, at the Academy of Athens, the queen told me that the only ambassador in attendance was the Canadian ambassador, who was a former university-level history professor. It made something of an impression, since the other ambassadors had sent an attaché. We spoke of dialectic. The meeting had a different theme every year, and the proceedings were published by the academy or philosophical society in the host country.[4] In 1956 we met in Paris; in 1957 in Poland.

This was just after the Polish Spring, when the Eastern-bloc countries first began opening up to the West. It was the first time that philosophers of East and West had met under the aegis of the Polish Academy. The great Polish philosophers were there, most notably our member Tadeusz

Kotarbiński, the hero of the philosophical resistance who had first stood up to the man who had taken power in his own country, Józef Piłsudski, then to Stalin and, during the war, to Hitler. He was the founder of the underground university. There were also well-known logicians such as Kazimierz Adjukiewicz, the great aesthetician Roman Ingarden, and the historian of aesthetics Władysław Tatarkiewicz, as well as many other famous names. Russian and Chinese philosophers were represented. After the end of the meeting, we were hosted in the middle of a forest in the northern part of the country, in one of those little castles once used by the tsar and the emperors of Germany and Austria for hunting, and by important ministers after the war. Goering had stayed there, others as well, and now it was the philosophers' turn! It was once again evident that the Russians and the Chinese stood quite apart. The 1958 meeting was held in conjunction with the International Congress of Philosophy in Venice.

In 1959 the institute was invited to India, where the vice-president, Sarvepalli Radhakrishnan, was one of our members. We were invited by a philosopher who had been the maharaja of Mysore, a philosopher of the absolute, a philosopher of the old school.[5] He had written a book, *Dattatreya,* which is one of the last avatars of the great tradition of Indian mystic thought. In *Philosophy in the Mid-Century,* he wrote about the Indian philosophical tradition and "the way it is lived today."

Was he a real maharaja?

Yes, he was, but above all a remarkable man. After the abolition of the princely states, he was named governor of the state of which he had formerly been the sovereign. The maharaja of Kashmir, who had an interest in Greek philosophy, also attended the meeting and we had absorbing discussions. The following generation of Indians was educated in England and the latest in America. These three generations are represented in volume IV of *Philosophy in the Mid-Century.* Humayun Kabir, who was minister of culture and president of the Indian Philosophical Congress, wrote on Indian philosophy, as did Mr Chari. After the congress, Kabir gave me a car tour of India. So we had interesting discussions with Asian thinkers.

Iranian philosophers had solicited my support for their proposal to the empress for the creation of the Imperial Iranian Academy of Philosophy, and I gave it. The academy was founded and I became a member. It still exists, although it is no longer imperial. Am I still a founding member? I don't know. The institute was then, in 1975, invited to Iran. On that occasion, I recalled that King Khosrow I of Persia had offered hospitality to the Platonic philosophers after Justinian's closing of the academy in Athens, and I brought up the role played by Persia as a crossroads between East and West. The empress invited us to Mashhad, the holy city near the Afghanistan border, and she came and spoke of Plotinus. For her, the history of Persian culture had not begun with the Hejira, and this position favoured dialogue – a dialogue that has, alas, become very difficult today.

Can we say that the institute played a major role during the Cold War by fostering rapprochement between the West and part of the East, and also by helping to internationalize philosophical thought?

The institute always had difficulties with the communist empire. We were asked to accept a member from the Soviet Union and did so, but only as an associate member; he was a senior official in the hierarchy, an official philosopher. He was one of our few associate members. Later, another became a member. Then they tried to force others on us and we refused. But the Russians did collaborate on the bibliography. The Russian bibliographic centre did regular and punctual work. Obviously, there were many changes. Some officials stayed on. We received Russian contributions to *Contemporary Philosophy*, including a noteworthy one from the logician Alexander Zinoviev, who authored well-known books and eventually had to leave Russia. He spoke prudently of the introduction of analytical logic, which, as we know, was due to the influence of mathematicians and physicists but also to that of certain military officers who wanted to put solid foundations in place for technological development. It gradually took its place alongside the dialectical logic that had been the only variety tolerated under Stalin. Zinoviev wrote *Yawning Heights*, a notable satire in which he mimics the language of bureaucrats.[6] In 1987, on the 350th anniversary of *Discourse on the Method*, the institute was hosted by the Swedish Academy in honour of Descartes and perhaps also in memory of his death in Sweden. On that occasion I spoke about the history of the institute.[7] In 1990 we were invited to Prague for a commemoration of the philosopher Jan Patočka, a great figure of our century, of whom I will have more to say.

What, in your view, is the specific role played by the institute today in the dialogue among philosophers?

The institute has members … I wouldn't say in all countries – there are countries in which philosophy is not highly developed – but members belonging to all the major schools, and these schools have to be represented. So it brings together philosophers known for their writings on analytical philosophy with others who are metaphysicians, and the encounter is always fruitful. That is the role of the institute: to promote dialogue and reciprocal understanding among cultures through philosophy.

And also communication among different spiritual traditions, between Asian and Western schools of thought. You knew Raimon Panikkar?[8]

He is a member of the institute. Panikkar is from a prominent Indian family. His father was one of the first to advocate for Indian independence; his uncle, a famous historian. But his mother was Catalan and he was educated in Spain, earning a doctorate in the natural sciences. At the same time, he periodically led the life of a Hindu holy man at Benares. So on the one hand he interprets India, and on the other he is a Catholic philosopher. His thought represents a synthesis of Catholicism and Hinduism. He was a professor of philosophy and religion at Santa Barbara in California. Now that he is retired, he lives at a nice spot in the mountains above Barcelona and writes a great deal. At one point he was a chaplain to students in Rome. That was when I met him, in the 1960s; I was then a guest professor at the University of Rome. Afterward I often met him at events organized by Enrico Castelli,[9] who took on the job of editing several works by Tommaso Campanella published under the aegis of Castelli's Institute of Philosophical Studies. Castelli was another paradoxical figure of the Italian past, a man who derived a degree of arrogance from his origins in Piedmontese nobility while nonetheless being a very great master of dialogue.

You knew other eminent philosophers during this long period. I am thinking, for example, of your encounter with Martin Buber in Israel in 1965.

I met Buber[10] when I was very young. He lived in Germany right near my school, in a small neighbouring town, and he came to visit fairly often. I saw him again later on one of my visits to Israel and he invited me to his home. He had translated the Bible into German with Franz Rosenzweig. His political stance was highly conciliatory toward the Arabs; this pleased me and his work interested me, even though the study of the Jewish tradition was not central to my concerns. His adversary, Gershom Scholem,[11] also lived in Israel but was not a member of the institute. They could not see eye to eye on Hasidism – nor on the past, nor even on the Hebrew present.

What was the main source of the disagreement?

Buber saw, shall we say, the mystical side of Hasidism, whereas Scholem was more interested in its connection to the historical past. He reproached Buber for interpreting it from a far too Western perspective. They also had profound political differences, a different approach to the Arab world. I met Scholem in Hamburg at the Warburg Library long before the advent of Hitler, in 1926, I believe. I saw him later in Jerusalem, and then in Montreal where he came to lecture.

Were Japanese and Chinese philosophers represented?

My contacts with Japanese philosophers date from my years as a student in Heidelberg. I earned a little money by teaching Greek and Latin to Japanese students. It was there that I met my great friend Seizo Ohe,[12] whose memory was honoured at the 1994 meeting of the institute in Kyoto. At my request, he had written about philosophy in Japan for *Philosophy in the Mid-Century* and later for *Contemporary Philosophy*. In this latter article, he introduced the concept of "humanism baptized in Hiroshima," which has been important for recent Japanese philosophy. Another of my students was Chikatsugu Iwasaki, who translated Aristotle's *Metaphysics* into Japanese. There was Toshihiko Izutsu,[13] a great thinker and one of the foremost specialists on all the Eastern schools of thought; we became friends and he too agreed to contribute to *Contemporary Philosophy*. He wrote on Zen philosophy as well as on poetry and philosophy in Japan. In the early 1970s, Ohe and Izutsu arranged for me to come to Japan, where I gave courses at Keio University and the University of Tokyo.

I put their names forward for membership in the institute, and solid and fruitful relations resulted. During my stay in Japan, I met Tomonobu Imamichi,[14] the founder of the Centre for Comparative Philosophy and Aesthetics in Tokyo, which often hosts Western thinkers in Japan. He was elected president of the International Institute of Philosophy in 1996.

In regard to China, however, contact became difficult after the death of Feng Youlan.[15]

Could it be said that the institute has been characterized, among other things, by its dedication to freedom of philosophical endeavour and intercultural communication, or do you think it was only the historical conjuncture that conduced to this goal? Today more than ever, for reasons other than those of the Cold War, we see the need for a rapprochement between cultures and traditions, and you've devoted a lot of effort to this work throughout your life.

The International Institute of Philosophy strives to be more than a mere enabler of discussion. The point of the institute is precisely to bring together the various doctrines, the various ways of thinking. The goal is to allow for their essence to be expressed and to foster their coexistence: to establish a genuine dialogue between them. I won't say that it always succeeds. It is very difficult, because there are of course strict analytical philosophers who speak of soft, weak philosophy and strong philosophy as two different approaches. As you know, there's been a backlash in philosophy against these tendencies, consisting in attempts to canonize "weak thought."

Yes, by our friend Gianni Vattimo.[16]

However, we always succeed in getting a discussion going, even if it does not go into as much depth as one might wish.

It can be said that the institute has always had among its members people like you – such as Jean Wahl and Paul Ricoeur – who insist on philosophical rigour, as their work shows, but who also want to give philosophy a prophetic role, a role of communication and moral injunction.

We do have great philosophers like the logician Jaakko Hintikka and the master of analytical philosophy Willard Van Orman Quine. This is a notable enrichment, as this insistence on rigour is valid, and it's always necessary to ensure that philosophy observes a degree of rigour. It must be more than the intelligent but facile conversation to which it is reduced in certain circles of American philosophy, such as neopragmatism.

Yet a philosophy that stops at rigour, that is reducible to a naturalistic or scientific program, would abandon its critical and prophetic aspect.

Absolutely. There would be no content, no purpose. But if there were only content and no rigour, there would be no possibility of discussion, for discussion demands a basis acknowledged by all, a logos to which everyone submits, as Plato puts it. In this new American tendency, which has adherents in certain universities, philosophers align themselves with that journalistic word "postmodernism." Productive discussion is in peril when rational dialogue is reduced to an expression of sentiments.

Because an ideal of rationality has been abandoned. You knew great philosophers who both did excellent scientific work and possessed great spiritual power, and here I'm thinking of Leszek Kołakowski.[17] *Could you talk about him?*

I first met him in 1957. A certain openness to the West could be glimpsed in Poland. Władysław Gomułka's rise to power engendered great hope. The Academy of Sciences had invited the institute to a meeting of Eastern philosophers, from China, Russia, and other communist countries, alongside philosophers from the West. There I observed a young man whose ascendancy was visible. This was Kołakowski, who, though he had been one of the hopes of the party, had become critical of the regime. He was the spokesperson for an oppositional tendency among youth.

Unfortunately, the opening did not last; the regime took an increasingly hard line and his situation became more and more difficult. At the 14th International Congress of Philosophy, held in Vienna in 1968, Polish colleagues intimated that Kołakowski was in serious danger. Fortunately, I managed to get him invited by my university and he was able to leave Poland in time.

His abundant and outstanding work is founded on three main pillars: religion, a critique of Marxism, and metaphysics. Religion is one of his central concerns, a through line running from *Świadomość religijna i więź kościelna* (1965),[18] on seventeenth-century sectarian movements, to his recent *God Owes Us Nothing*, in which he shows, through an analysis of discussions about Jansenius, how official Church doctrine fundamentally abandoned Augustine and the emphasis on divine grace in favour of the Jesuits' Semi-Pelagianism.[19] And let us not forget his extraordinary *Conversations with the Devil*.[20] The critique of Marxism is the subject of a monumental and premonitory work: *Main Currents of Marxism*.[21] An analysis of problems of metaphysics culminates in his analysis of Damascius in *Metaphysical Horror*.[22]

He is a good example of someone who studied logic with the great Polish masters and at the same time possesses a rich imagination and an understanding of what is important from a human point of view; a man not summed up by reason, who can see human beings in their totality. But he observes them as a philosopher. He sees that logic does not suffice to resolve the most important questions, but that without logic one gets no closer to a solution. He wrote an article on history, "*Fabula mundi* and Cleopatra's Nose," which appeared in the special issue of the *Revue internationale de la philosophie* published in honour of my seventieth birthday, titled "Méthode et philosophie de l'histoire." In this paper, he uses an ostensibly offhand account of a historical incident to demonstrate, in essence, the problem of history. He possesses the art of being able to combine humour with depth. In January 1997 I had the great pleasure of introducing him when he received the Nonino Prize awarded to "a master of our time."[23]

I believe you were awarded that prize yourself.

I had met the extraordinary Nonino family two years earlier when, to my great surprise, I was awarded that distinction. The Nonino prizes for scholarly literature, poetry, and fiction are well known in Italy and are

10.1 / Raymond Klibansky with Chaïm Perelman and Jean Wahl, Montreal, 1962. Private collection.

the work of an exceptional woman, a force of nature, Giannola Nonino, wonderfully assisted by her three beautiful daughters, whose energy, enthusiasm, and human warmth served to bring together a prestigious jury. Over the years, the award has gone to Léopold Senghor, Claude Lévi-Strauss, V.S. Naipaul, and the great Turkish writer Yaşar Kemal.

Among the philosophers you met during this long peregrination through the work of the institute, who are those who stand apart and whom you would like us to know about? Perhaps not so much for their scientific efforts, since this question isn't really about that, but in terms of the charisma one expects of a philosopher in the contemporary world?

I'm thinking of a French philosopher who cannot be accused of being an analytical philosopher: my dear friend Jean Wahl,[24] who came to Montreal, to McGill, and was then invited to the Université de Montréal. He made a big impression on the many young people who took a great interest in his works. He also wrote poetry and told me of his encounters with Henri Bergson. Wahl was a man in the grand tradition, one who wrote on existence without being an existentialist. We tend today to forget that he founded the Collège philosophique, a centre for non-conformist intellectuals, of which he told me a great deal. He introduced me to Maurice Merleau-Ponty and especially to Gabriel Marcel, who came to Montreal and frequently discussed his plays with me.

In terms of personalities, there was also Tadeusz Kotarbiński, who was the philosopher of good work. He introduced praxiology in a systematic way. He was not outwardly charismatic but his character came through. Here was a man who risked his life to live his philosophy, who weathered many political changes and showed young people the way. I'm also thinking of Alexandre Koyré and of Georges Canguilhem, a master of the philosophy of science and the history of biology. It is a great pleasure to see people who live their philosophy gathered together.

Even a lesser-known figure such as Jean Hyppolite inspired many young French students at the École normale supérieure, of which he was the director. I can never mention his name without recalling an anecdote. At the institute's 1967 annual meetings in Liège, we were discussing the theme "Demonstration, Verification, and Justification" when Hippolyte, in the general assembly that I was chairing, interrupted the work to declare that he had just received a telegram informing him that one of his students, Régis Debray,[25] had been arrested in Bolivia and was accused of having aided Che Guevara. He urged the institute to call on the president of Bolivia to intervene on behalf of the prisoner, whose life was in danger. Another French delegate, with pronounced right-leaning political opinions, strongly opposed the measure, arguing that the institute should not get involved in politics. The verbal jousting that ensued was a delight for lovers of rhetoric. I unfortunately had to interrupt it. There was clearly no consensus, and therefore nothing could be done on behalf of the institute. I proposed that a telegram be sent bearing the signatures of all the members who supported the motion – and there were many. This telegram, bearing all the signatures except that of the sole objector, took a hefty bite out of the institute's budget! Although the "journalist in question" was imprisoned, he was fortunately released after a certain time thanks to French diplomatic pressure.

I also remember an eminent Greek philosopher, Ioannis Theodorakopoulos, whom I had known since Heidelberg. He was from Mistra, near

10.2 / Raymond Klibansky with Roberto Almaggia (left) and Alexandre Koyré (right), Florence, 1957. Private collection.

Sparta, where Gemistus Plethon lived in the fifteenth century. Wanting to revive Neoplatonist thought in Greece, he translated Plato into modern Greek and wrote three fine books. He was an inspiration to Greek youth and served as president of the Academy of Athens.

In 1969, at the invitation of Hans-Georg Gadamer, a notable meeting on philosophy and history was held in Heidelberg. There were lively discussions in which my friend Karl Löwith participated. Gadamer represented historical thought, while Löwith put the emphasis on nature in history. He believed that not everything could be reduced to history and language, and that the force of nature must be reckoned with.

Each of these gatherings brought together charismatic individuals espousing clear positions, and the interest of the discussions resided in watching these positions square off.

I would also like to mention one of my dearest friends, the American philosopher Max Black.[26] He wrote on the problems posed by the concept of rationality. Black's most striking trait was his radiant serenity. In 1968,

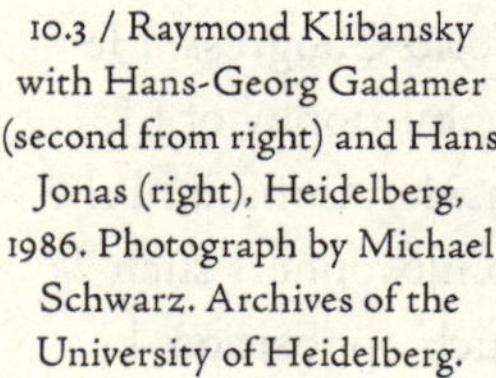

10.3 / Raymond Klibansky with Hans-Georg Gadamer (second from right) and Hans Jonas (right), Heidelberg, 1986. Photograph by Michael Schwarz. Archives of the University of Heidelberg.

during the racial troubles at Cornell University, he was one of the only people to keep a cool head. He was a wise man.

The great risk of the type of enumeration you've requested is that I might leave out someone important. I'm now thinking of figures as diverse as my friends Guido Calogero, Alfred Ayer, Chaim Perelman, and Georg Henrik von Wright, who were successive presidents of the institute. I would also like to mention my dear friend Jeanne Hersch, of whom I spoke in connection with Jaspers and who wrote such interesting things about time.

Finally, I want to mention a philosopher who is not a member of the institute, although he is closely associated with it. Henry Duméry,[27] the author of the excellent *Philosophie de la religion,* which got him put on the Index, has headed up the administration of the institute on a volunteer basis for over forty years. He has been tremendously generous with his time and energy, liaising with the French authorities and working hard to resolve the sporadic crises that will arise in the life of any institution. He has always, with utter disinterestedness, refused to occupy the place among the members of the institute that his philosophical output would have assured him.

Was the Frankfurt School represented in the institute?

Max Horkheimer and Theodor W. Adorno were not members. But we have a very active member in the person of Karl-Otto Apel, an important philosopher, a man of dialogue. The renowned Jürgen Habermas is also a member. He was with us at Brighton for the 1998 World Congress. He spoke of the philosophy of language and critiqued the philosophy of J.L. Austin, the theories derived from purely linguistic considerations, and the whole discussion of speech acts found in the work of philosophers such as John Searle. Abruptly, clearly not having foreseen such opposition, he found himself facing two antagonists, two women. One was Elizabeth Anscombe, Wittgenstein's student, and the other was Ruth Barcan Marcus, the great logician. The questions they asked gave him a fair bit of difficulty! It was a terrific discussion.

Did you know Adorno, whom you've just mentioned?

Fairly well. After 1933 Adorno, as a Jew, had to leave Germany.[28] He came to Oxford and would have liked to obtain an academic position. He went around wearing the knee-length gown of the undergraduate, which was ridiculous. The only talent he was acknowledged to have was his knowledge of music theory. At Oxford he was out of his element. He went to the United States, where he collaborated with the Institute for Social Research. In California, he became Thomas Mann's adviser on music theory for *Doctor Faustus*. With Adorno's help, Mann had one of the characters in this novel whistle a melody in which the name Wiesengrund (Adorno's original surname) appears. He was unhappy about not having been better acknowledged by Mann, and complained of this.

He and his friend Max Horkheimer wrote *Dialectic of Enlightenment*[29] and *The Authoritarian Personality*[30] during their stay in the United States, which made their fame. He returned to Germany, where he and Horkheimer founded the Frankfurt School.

Adorno's writings on music, such as *Philosophy of Modern Music* and *Introduction to the Sociology of Music*, are worthy of note.[31] His thoughts on the foundations of sociology are provocative, and his critical theory of society had a powerful influence on the formation of radical youth in 1960s Germany.

Adorno's legacy is considerable. A great many students are enthusiastic about his aesthetic theory.

He did indeed have many adherents, who cherish his memory. But he was not admired by all. One day I was with Georg Lukacs[32] in Budapest and he asked me what I thought of the Frankfurt School, with which he was engaged in a sharply worded polemic. Lukacs characterized this school as the *Grand Hotel Abgrund*, which translates as the "Grand Hotel Abyss." He regarded the Frankfurt philosophers as people who spoke of the decline of the democratic capitalist world as if contemplating this phenomenon through the window of a large, comfortable hotel teetering on the edge of the abyss: people who enjoyed the benefits of a world they condemned.

It was far from easy to visit Lukacs. He had taken part in the Hungarian national opposition movement and had accepted the national education portfolio in the government of Imre Nagy. During the Russian invasion of 1956 people feared for his life, and members of the International Institute of Philosophy tried to intervene on his behalf. The Soviets stopped at deporting him to Romania. He was later able to return to his country but he was under intense surveillance. In the summer of 1970, I was invited to speak at the Hungarian Academy. Lukacs, who had spent several years in Heidelberg during his youth and had frequented Max Weber's home, had asked to see me. Permission had to be obtained from the secret police. Marianne Weber had often talked about the intense discussions that took place between her husband and the young Lukacs. It was in Heidelberg that he wrote his best book, *Soul and Form*, and prepared his *The Theory of the Novel*, published in 1916.

You did not share Lukacs's opinion of the Frankfurt School, for you knew how much these people had suffered, most of them being Jewish.

On the contrary: I did share Lukacs's opinion, for I saw how Adorno, who was a very intelligent man, made a systematic critique of German democracy, German contemporary society. He showed students the failings of the system without appreciating the consequences. The events of May 1968 also took place in Frankfurt, but in an incomparably less civilized manner than in France. Truly revolting, vulgar things happened there. The rector of Goethe University Frankfurt drew my attention to certain facts. During these riots, Adorno was no longer there, he had disappeared. The students demanded that he show up and Adorno called the police, for which the students would not forgive him. They had not followed the master but the master's teachings! True radicals! Whereas he was a cowardly man. It hasn't been mentioned that he only came back at some point because the students were demanding that he appear. Female students, Valkyries, took their shirts off and fell upon him, bare-breasted. The great aesthetician never got over the shock. He died soon afterward.

Did you know Ernst Bloch?[33]

Not really. I saw him in Vienna and when I met him, he made a bad impression on me. In Vienna in 1968, there was a discussion with the Russian philosophers in which F.V. Konstantinov, their leader, took part. I asked him certain questions. He was struggling to answer when Bloch showed up and started insulting him. Bloch was very anti-Soviet at that time and he preferred attack to dialogue. I never knew him as a youth. His father was, as you know, a railway administrator at Ludwigshafen, near Mannheim, and the young Bloch went to Switzerland during the First World War. He detested militarism and wrote a notable book, *The Spirit of Utopia*. He became a refugee in the United States during the Second World War but was unhappy there. After the war, he returned to Europe and was appointed at Leipzig. He wrote a monumental work, *The Principle of Hope* (*Das Prinzip Hoffnung*). He couldn't stand the German Democratic Republic.

Which was very punctilious with him and kept him under surveillance.

He was then appointed at Tübingen. He was a high-calibre thinker, no doubt, but as a man, at the end – in Vienna, for instance, when I met him – he was embittered and had become incapable of discussion.

When we look at the very diverse philosophers you admired, who were and still are your friends, what do they have in common?

I would say an aptitude for constructive dialogue.

I would now like to address a very different aspect of your work, which is also associated with the International Institute of Philosophy, and that is the International Dictionary of Philosophy.[34]

In philosophy during my university years, I devoted a lot of work to the close connections between thought and language. This concern led me to formulate a plan for a dictionary of key terms in philosophy and political thought. This multilingual work was intended to highlight the importance for philosophical writing of the language in which it is expressed, and would give equivalents for terms in different languages – equivalents, not translations, for it is essential to know that the meanings are never identical. This project was submitted to the 1950 Inter-American Congress of Philosophy in Mexico City and approved. In 1952 I was asked by UNESCO to present it to a group of philosophers from different countries who had been convened in Paris. UNESCO was willing to give a small amount of money, much too little. The Rockefeller Foundation ultimately wanted to support the project, provided that I take full responsibility for it and put it ahead of my other work. I was unable to do that.

The following year, I was elected as a member of the International Institute of Philosophy in Paris, and the institute took up the project again. Since it would have demanded immense resources, we had to content ourselves with choosing a series of terms such as justice, democracy, liberty, right, class, and so on, and making detailed studies of them in different languages; the results were published in philosophy journals. The dictionary is a long-term project. Someone would have to have the time to oversee the work. The institute lacks the necessary resources. It relies on the good graces of the French government, which, it must be acknowledged, has always given its support without asking anything in return, regardless of the government in power. Recognition of the importance of culture is not treated lightly in France.

Later, I thought it would be better to begin with a multilingual glossary of key terms in philosophy. This was published in 1995 under the auspices of the International Institute of Philosophy. The glossary comprises about five hundred basic philosophical terms in French, English, German, Italian, and Spanish along with their equivalents. After this first stage, we will look at extending it to Russian, Arabic, and Japanese. It became necessary for the *Bibliography of Philosophy*, which you've done such a good job of representing for French-speaking Canada, to have keywords that can serve as a basis for the index. The purpose of the glossary is to present the equivalents. With this done, detailed studies can be devoted to illuminating the differences between the closest equivalents in the different languages in question.

This problem of equivalence is particularly well illustrated by the vocabulary of fundamental freedoms. Consider, for example, the translations of the *Universal Declaration of Human Rights*, which pose a crucial problem: can these notions be considered universal, or are they necessarily tied to the presuppositions of certain cultures? In my introduction to the initial project, I discussed the attempts made in the seventeenth century to arrive at a universal language and how they did not lead to unification because the differences are fundamental. The idea is to grasp these differences as the first stage in understanding; too often, people talk to each other without realizing that the fundamental concepts do not mean the same thing in two different languages. What do these differences consist of? There is no yardstick with which to measure them. So I would say that we need the basic terms and their closest equivalents in each language; the differences among these can then be studied and elucidated.

The task of the philosopher and the historian of philosophy is to achieve true understanding; it cannot be reduced to a mechanical understanding of each word and its variants.

Having completed this overview of the activities of the International Institute of Philosophy, how would you summarize the role of the institute?

It is always easier to talk about what an institution *should be*, about an ideal. That way, one can ignore budgetary constraints and human failings. What the institute has been from time to time, and should always be, is first and foremost a locus of dialogue and discussion among different cultures and schools of thought.

A dialogue cannot take place without the members being willing to transcend their big differences. Nor can it take place without a foundation. This means that there must be a tireless effort of publication, dissemination of information. Some people work with extraordinary devotion, of course, but the ideal would be for each member of the institute, each philosopher, in his or her country or university, to feel responsible for the dissemination of their country's philosophical output through the *Bibliography of Philosophy*.

An institution is judged, among other things, by its publications. The institute, which has published many interesting works – such as the one on the foundations of human rights, which I haven't had a chance to mention – must therefore have a program consistent with its mission.

Finally, there are times when the institute must take a position. In totalitarian countries, the plight of philosophers who do not bend to the whims of the regime is precarious, if not dangerous, as was shown by the unfortunate case of our friend Jan Patočka. At the 1968 World Congress of Philosophy in Vienna, I proposed that we send a manifesto in favour of freedom of thought to the ministries of education of each country in order to assist philosophers deprived of their positions. Needless to say, we did not receive an encouraging response, but no matter! The failure of our struggle for freedom is a foregone conclusion unless we devote our undying efforts to it.

11

JAN PATOČKA

I want to dwell for a moment on the figure of Jan Patočka, a great defender of freedom. When did you meet Patočka?

At the 1968 World Congress of Philosophy in Vienna. The conference organizers had planned a symposium on the relationship between philosophy and science. The Austrians had invited selected philosophers from each country and the discussion proved very interesting. Karl Popper represented Britain; Hans-Georg Gadamer, Germany; Chaim Perelman, Belgium. I represented Canada, and Teodor Oizerman[1] the Soviet Union.

The congress opened on the day of the Russian invasion of Czechoslovakia.[2] I saw one participant who was nervous and pale: it was Jan Patočka, who had just learned what had happened in his country. It had dawned on him that the discussion was going to take place in the presence of a Russian philosopher and he could not stand the idea. Still shaken by that encounter, I interrupted the discussion and addressed the Russian philosophers: "Our topic is interesting, but it is first necessary to study the conditions under which it is possible for philosophers to practise philosophy, and I would like to ask my Russian colleague if he believes the practice of philosophy is possible without freedom of thought." Oizerman took refuge in a stereotyped position: "There are revolutionary conditions under which certain freedoms must be suspended." He tried to convince the audience that these conditions existed in Czechoslovakia but did not succeed. This discussion was

11.1 / Jan Patočka, 1971.
Photograph by Jindřich Přibík.
Prague, Archív Jana Patočky.

broadcast in Czechoslovakia. It was much noticed in Poland and other countries.

My friendship with Patočka goes back to that meeting. He greatly appreciated a document that had been sent on behalf of the professors and teachers of Oxford to the University of Prague under equally disastrous circumstances thirty years earlier, in 1938, on the eve of the invasion of Prague by German tanks.[3] That letter, which I had written in Latin, had garnered signatures from all the colleges of Oxford and closed with the following wish: "Assailed and besieged from without though you may be, may you never believe that you are divided from us. We are convinced that your nation has just proven by its acts what it has long proclaimed: Great is the truth and it will prevail. *Pravda vítězí.*"

After the meetings, Patočka returned to his country and bore up under the circumstances of the day. It was hard to stay in touch with him because he was under surveillance. The only solution I found was to ask him to prepare an edition of John Amos Comenius's writings for our Philosophy and World Community series, thus making him an official member of the international editorial committee. An official letter was sent to the Czech ministry in the summer of 1973 asking, in the interests of international cooperation, that it facilitate Patočka's participation in the editorial committee meeting to be held in Varna at the International Congress of Philosophy. To our great surprise, he was permitted to come to Bulgaria. As he later gathered, the request should have been denied, but since he left on a Friday and the ministry bureaucrats did not work on weekends, they took no initiative to detain him. It was the last time he was able to leave the country. When Aachen University awarded him an honorary doctorate, he was not allowed to travel to receive it. Instead, in August 1976, the Institute of Philosophy and Sociology of the Czechoslovakian Academy of Sciences passed a motion expressing surprise that the International Institute of Philosophy still recognized Patočka and Karel

11.2 / Jan Patočka, Edmund Husserl, and Eugen Fink in Leuven, Belgium, 1934.
Husserl Archives Leuven.

Kosik[4] as members, claiming that "they had long since lost their moral right to represent the scholars of Czechoslovakia and lacked the scientific qualifications necessary to do so."

Patočka suffered greatly from the mindset to which such a statement attests and, in particular, from the fact that the only model of philosophy offered in Czechoslovakia was the communist society model, while authentic philosophy remained oppressed.

Can you briefly recount Patočka's intellectual trajectory?

In 1936 he obtained his *Habilitation* in Prague with an essay on the natural world that was particularly indebted to the ideas of Husserl. In this book, *Qu'est-ce que la phénoménologie?*, he developed an entirely new thesis as to what phenomenology should become. In his view, it was neither a doctrine nor a rigid theory, but rather what he sought to designate as an avenue of research. In this way, he succeeded in negating what he considered Husserl's subjectivism, his transcendental stance; for Patočka, that position was just a theory. Philosophy, as he saw it, is not created out of pure theory; philosophy, as he unceasingly stressed at that time, is inseparable from *epimeleia tēs psuchēs*, or care for the soul, as it is often (if very approximately) translated. Care for the soul: for Patočka, that was philosophy.[5]

But the question then becomes: "What is the soul?" The soul is not what is called the psyche; it categorically does not correspond to the *res cogitans*; it is not thought. It is, rather, that which makes a human human. The soul is what reminds human beings of who they are, what gives them their existence. In a phrase, it is the essence of our pains, our effort. Taking existence seriously thus means that philosophy can never be pure theory, pure contemplation, but must always remain tied to concrete action. This link between thought and action is, for Patočka, the decisive factor. Theory must always be more than mere theory; it is bound up with praxis.

This observation represents the impetus that drove him to critique Husserl with such lucidity at the outset, for here indeed is the drama of phenomenology. Husserl was his teacher and he always showed him the greatest consideration; he revered him from their very first encounter when he went to Freiburg as a student in 1933. Husserl received him with these words: "Finally a compatriot comes to see me." He gave him the gift of a lectern that he himself had received fifty years earlier from Thomas Masaryk as a student in Leipzig.

Patočka took this to indicate that he was the heir to a great tradition, for he himself deeply admired Masaryk's love of truth and the courage he had displayed from earliest youth in a number of critical situations. As a young man, Masaryk, the leader of the nationalist movement in Czechoslovakia, found himself confronted with a manuscript, the "Königinhofer-Codex," that purported to imbue Czech literature with a past of medieval poetry as glorious as it was unexpected; it was said to be the equivalent of the German *Niebelungenlied*. Masaryk made short work of demonstrating that the manuscript was nothing but a modern fake, even though that went against the interests of his own party and of Czech nationalism. This episode showed every student the importance of bearing in mind that historical truth must always be respected. That is what Patočka revered in Masaryk. But although Masaryk and Husserl were his role models, he criticized both of them in his own philosophy: Masaryk for his belief in the continuous progress of humanity, of rational thought; Husserl for his subjectivism, his concept that the totality of the objective world is an object dominated by transcendental subjectivity, and hence by the general law affirming that human thought marks reality.

What did Patočka mean by "the real"?

For Patočka, "the real" meant something entirely different. It meant the world of action and of suffering. Not only did he try to extend the concept of *Lebenswelt* as Husserl had set it forth in his great work *The Crisis of European Sciences,*[6] but he also undertook to set it on entirely different foundations.

I would like briefly to sketch out his criticism of Husserl. Husserl speaks of a crisis of European sciences, but for Patočka, the problem is much deeper, more fundamental. It is not just the crisis of European sciences; it is the crisis of European humanity. Whereas for Husserl, *Lebenswelt* represents a pre-scientific world, for Patočka a more fundamental understanding must be sought, since for him it is not so much a pre-scientific world as a pre-historical world. In this world, human beings feel as though they are in a hideaway. They know their environment; they do of course fear external forces, but they know the nature of those forces. It is a world without fundamental problems, in which people are able to distinguish between what is perilous and what is useful. With the rise of historical man, everything becomes problematic for the first time. The *Lebenswelt,* the natural world, is thus identified with the pre-historical world. Patočka wants to show that for Husserl, this world remains unattainable.

How did he go about refuting Husserl?

For Husserl, consciousness is always consciousness of intentionality, a technical term used by Brentano meaning that consciousness is always consciousness *of* something. For Husserl, *Lebenswelt* constitutes "the horizon of horizons," "the last horizon." Doesn't the notion of a horizon, which is in no way reducible to the concept of an object, exclude the essential characteristic of intentionality: consciousness of an object?

According to Patočka's analysis, it appears that the Husserlian conception of *Lebenswelt* cannot be satisfactorily explained in the context of Husserl's own philosophy.

Much more important for Patočka, however, is what he designates as the "problematic character" of contemporary humanity, which leads him to think of moderns as being united by a "solidarity of the shaken." But why and how has humanity been shaken? Here we reach the interesting point of his thought, which finds expression in his renowned *Heretical Essays in the Philosophy of History*.[7] Written in Czech in 1975 and distributed through *samizdat* in Prague, the book was translated into French, Italian, and German. This work contains a dark chapter on war; Patočka speaks of the twentieth century as a century of war, in which the demonic manifests itself once again. Isolated man and the human community are characterized by a solidarity of the shaken. The word "solidarity" is employed here well before its use as a rallying cry in Poland. The philosopher, well before the politicians, had put forward a concept that characterizes the contemporary situation.

How did Patočka conceive of this solidarity?

In this solidarity, the job of the soul is to make people capable of being what they can be. For him, philosophy is care for the soul; it is not pure contemplation, speculation, but always represents a link between theory and practice. Pure theoretical activity is not philosophy; it is cut off from what constitutes human life. This led Patočka to realize that this point not only must be stated but must also be theorized. And on this question he departed from Heidegger, in whose work he had developed considerable interest and whose critique of Husserl seemed greatly important to him. Indeed, rather too much stress is laid on the affinities between Patočka and Heidegger, for he came to characterize Heidegger's thought as a kind of defeatism. In contrast to Heidegger, Patočka does not adopt a contemptuous view of technification and does not see it as constituting a new concept; it is, rather, an act whereby one dives deeply into what stands before oneself and finds, in this human element, the movement toward one's own existence. For Patočka, it is the description of this movement that constitutes the purpose of philosophy, the inquiry into how human beings can find themselves again, how they can produce themselves, starting from themselves. On this level he compares having with being; we want to have and we forget to be. He goes on to discuss this point in detail in an effort to shed light on his concept of human beings as subjects and objects of philosophy.

What do you see as the link between Patočka's philosophy and his interest in Comenius?[38]

Patočka's interest in the works of Comenius arises from the affinity he must have felt with the Czech patriot who watched his people and his faith crushed by enemy forces. He was even more attracted by what he considered the dominant features of Comenius's thought. For Comenius, reason was not "a natural light finding its principles – that is, itself – in the world of explored things." To understand things as they are, reason must first learn that its tendency to measure things by itself can only lead to true results if it opens itself up to something totally different and superior to which it submits. Consequently, Comenius's starting point is not sovereign reason but reason as one force among the forces of the whole soul, "buried in the whole universe, which must first make sure of its true place within the whole and keep itself in that position." According to Patočka, Comenius's effort consists "in an almost stubborn defence of the great trans-subjective whole against the invasion of modern subjectivism."

The notion of the "open soul" comes into its own in Patočka's late philosophy. In his assessment of Comenius as an educator, Patočka emphasizes that Comenius was not thinking of the transmission of specialized knowledge, the preparation of students to practise a profession, but of the goal of education itself. This consisted in nothing less than "showing men the path of humanity," in "rendering man truly human." Comenius's ideas on the worldview around which he centred his concept of education led him to write his most complete work, the *General Consultation on an Improvement of All Things Human.* It consists of several parts, which were discovered at Halle in 1935 and 1940. The last is the draft "Total Reform," the *Panorthosia*. Patočka told me in a letter dated 26 August 1975 of his plan to produce a French translation of the *Panorthosia* for Philosophy and World Community. This translation has not been found. It is possible that the pressing problems he had to face during the too brief time he had left to live monopolized his time to the point of depriving him of the leisure to complete this project.

He died shortly afterward?

In 1977. The culmination of his philosophy took place in the last years of his life, on the occasion of Charter 77, of which he conceived the outline, and which may be considered the application of his philosophical thought to a concrete political situation. Every manual of philosophy should contain the words he wrote then: first the text of Charter 77 and the two appeals he sketched out on his deathbed. They are the expressions of his concept of freedom, which make him a martyr; that is, a privileged witness to our time. He was one of the last martyrs of philosophy. What happened was that he was interrogated by the police for over eleven hours and then taken to hospital, where he was interrogated again, until he suffered a heart attack.

Efforts made by his friends abroad to save him did not avail.

No, they did not. You will recall the visit we made together to the Czech Consulate in Montreal in February 1977 along with Charles Taylor and my friend Vianney Décarie, the Aristotelian philosopher, who came representing the Université de Montréal. We wanted to express our indignation at Patočka's arrest. The consul gave us a glacial reception.

Just before dying, Patočka was able to write those two appeals, which have fortunately been preserved and were distributed through *samizdat* before being translated into English. They are rightly called Patočka's "Political Testament." I found the text in the *Boston Globe* and translated it into French before distributing it along with a petition from the Canadian Philosophical Association.

EPILOGUE

TOLERANCE, LIBERTY, PHILOSOPHY

We are witnesses today to a great worry, a great anxiety on the part of philosophical thought in confrontation with itself. Would you say that philosophy gives in too easily to the relativist argument – one of the most often debated arguments in philosophy – the argument that each thing is worth what it is worth and European culture is worth no more than any other? That the tradition of rationality that has come down to us from ancient Greece is therefore no more valid than other traditions – some violent and archaic, some theocratic and fundamentalist – that we have inherited from other places? Do you share this worry about the fate of the rationality that is represented by the philosophical work to which you have always devoted your efforts?

I would say that the enemies are in the European and North American universities rather than among thinkers from other continents, who – I won't say all, because I don't know them all – generally take rationality very seriously. The really destructive ones are the writers like Richard Rorty[1] and those who would abolish all linguistic, social, and philosophical codes. It is they who promote relativism. The possibility of suprapersonal discussion illuminated by some common standard vanishes. Doesn't it just become the projection of the will of those individuals or social groups who hold power and are able to dictate how others should think? These thinkers surely do not realize the extent to which they are indebted to fashionable ideas with all their talk of "intelligent conversations." What makes a conversation intelligent? We agree because we share certain prejudices, but such agreement is a function of the moment, the whim of fashion. It depends on forces that these thinkers could contradict but do not even want to contradict. They can't see their own conditioning.

Do you think the ideal of rationality can survive all these brutal assaults? Is there despair over the fate of philosophy? Many thinkers say that philosophy was unable to prevent the horrors of our century. It failed to prevent Stalinism, it failed to prevent Auschwitz. Others go so far as to claim that it was the cause of these horrors. In consequence, philosophy is said to be a discipline that should devote itself to specialized tasks such as the epistemology of science and naturalistic research programs but no longer has anything to tell us about fundamental things: ethics, human conduct.

On this specific point, we see that these tendencies betray a lack of intelligent, rational thought. The problem was not philosophy but philosophers, or certain philosophers. Even though philosophy has at times claimed to be able to govern the world as such, it is human beings who govern it. Sadly, philosophy has never managed to make it so that the people who have the power are philosophers. It's an ideal. People laugh at this Platonic ideal. Kings must become philosophers; philosophers must become kings. It's easy to cast a sardonic glance at such proposals. But at the end of the day, what can philosophers do if they are not listened to, or if philosophical arguments are used to establish the supremacy of one ethnic group or political system? All it can do is continue to produce arguments showing that these claims lack merit.

We are witnessing the resurfacing of religious fanaticism, ancestral hatreds, in different parts of the world; the hatred of others by virtue of their religion, ethnicity, or tribe. Do you believe in the power of reason to defend the historic mission of philosophy against all the irrational forces by which we are assailed?

I tend to shy away from talk about "reason." It is an abstraction. There is no reason as such; there are only people who reason. What counts is not my power but the rules I consider valid, regardless of any personal feeling or historical situation – the rules to which I submit and to which I tell myself that my interlocutor must also submit if he wants to be considered a reasonable person. You cannot make an interlocutor submit to the force of

12.1 / Raymond Klibansky receiving a *doctorat honoris causa* with Isaiah Berlin, Bologna, May 1995. Archives of the University of Bologna.

argument. If he does not submit, it becomes a wrestling match, a game of might over right. Logical argument alone will not suffice to secure this submission; it results from a choice, a fundamental choice. That is the essential choice, the choice of sociability, the choice of the community, not that of the individual who makes law because he is the strongest.

So what are these rules? They range from the basic logical principles governing all argument to the linguistically and historically conditioned norms proper to different civilizations. Without getting into the significant problems posed by this diversity, we must not underestimate the great force of all that is irrational: the prejudices we harbour, the collective memories, all the unconscious forces of that kind. Memory comes into play; the memory of what our ancestors endured persists, even if we are oblivious to it. Things we heard, youthful memories, can govern attitudes even if we are unaware of it. The will to agree is, after all, often weaker than the fear of others and the fear of forces beyond our control.

Do I take it, then, that for reason to operate unimpeded and in accordance with what reason dictates, memory must forgive, must forget certain things; and that history shows it is often unable to do so?

Philosophers should believe that reasoning matters, absolutely. They must convey the meaning of rules by illustrating them with striking examples in different domains. But while they must believe that reasoning matters, they must not believe that it wins out over action. That would be naïve! As for believing that reason is a force, all we have to do is look at our own personal lives: which of my acts is exclusively, or even largely, determined by reason? Just look at the lives of the philosophers themselves!

Do I think philosophy is bankrupt? Well, what does that mean? Philosophy is not one thing. There are philosophers who want their lives, and the lives of their communities, to be informed and governed by being set on certain rational foundations, but this enterprise is always imperilled, always in question. The best example is Patočka, whom we have just discussed. He rejected tyranny, fought against intolerance. He did not change the regime; the regime got the better of him. It killed him. But he left us with the conviction that responsible thought must guide philosophers in the quest for spiritual ideals, as his student President Václav Havel reminded us in his opening remarks at the Prague conference of the International Institute of Philosophy in memory of Patočka, held in 1990 on the theme of responsibility.

This notion of tolerance that you evoke, in regard to Jan Patočka for example, has in some sense been emblematic of your work, on both the philosophical and the cultural planes, during these difficult years. You've worked hard to create a rapprochement between cultures isolated by centuries of indifference. I particularly recall your insistence, during the early years of our collaboration on the Bibliography of Philosophy, *on the importance of involving our Chinese and Soviet colleagues in this bibliography so that world philosophy could find an opportunity for dialogue and discussion. It can be said in this regard that you've succeeded, in the face of many obstacles, in living a life reminiscent of the Republic of Letters in the Renaissance, a life like that of Pico della Mirandola. You kept up a kind of universal contact, and one feels an energy in your work; one sees it, for example, in the major projects aimed at chronicling contemporary philosophy of which we have spoken.*

I have always believed in the necessity of dialogue and in the virtue of tolerance. But we must not forget the limits of tolerance. Philosophers must take a stand when freedom is threatened, when fundamental rights – their own or others' – are in danger; ultimately, whenever tolerance is in peril.

You knew the greatest philosophers of our era. I'm thinking of Paul Ricoeur, Hans-Georg Gadamer, and Karl-Otto Apel, of course, but also of Emmanuel Levinas, whose work was very influential in France. In thinking of him in particular, I wonder if it is possible, in our secularized world, to have a philosophical vision of a world cut adrift from religion.

Our openness to the world of Walter Benjamin, for example, comes from that too. He was a thinker who always retained some connection to a form of belief, albeit very secularized – to the idea that basic intuitions as to the nature of humanity and its value are not possible without a leap of faith. We have to believe that the force of humanity does not arise *ex nihilo*, as it were. Or if it does, then we must believe in it because we have no reason to demonstrate it, and philosophers as important as Levinas or Benjamin perhaps appeal to us more by virtue of it. They have more to say to us, at any rate, than more critical philosophers who destroy everything in a sort of analytical suspension, philosophers who, as Charles Taylor says in *Sources of the Self*,[2] avoid theorizing our moral commitment, our basic commitment, our responsibility.

All your philosophical work has been founded on strong convictions about humanism. Would you like to tell us, in closing, about this humanism that has guided you?

It consists of a certain conception of human beings and their role, and this conception has two sources. There is a religious conception, yes, but one that is unconnected to any particular religion. Thus, for example, Judaism is in constant transformation. What the prophets say differs from what is found in the five books of the Pentateuch. The spirit of the Babylonian

12.2 / Raymond Klibansky in Oxford garden. Photograph by Désirée Park, n.d.

and the Jerusalem Talmuds is worlds apart from that of Kabbalah. Each philosopher, from Philo to Maimonides and on to Rosenzweig, offers a distinctly different interpretation. The same goes for the other religions.

As to the notion of humanity, it can be seen to have a religious foundation, but also to have a philosophical foundation. We could not be talking as we are if we hadn't had Greek philosophy and the tradition of Greek and Roman philosophy. The influence of the Latin interpretation of Greek philosophy is greatly underestimated. Cicero, who used to be read in schools, was a popularizer, but one who had a talent for conveying big ideas. When he describes the nature of humans, he distinguishes us from animals by *ratio* and *oratio*: by reason and by the expression of reason in reasoned language. We can see that there is a contribution from Greek philosophy, through the intermediary of Latin thought, which still survives and is part of our roots, the roots of our thought.

Your introduction of this conception of humanism as openness and rootedness directs our thoughts toward the other concepts that have marked your personal philosophical development, chief among them tolerance, followed by that whole period in which you worked on melancholy. Melancholy is a complex feeling that differs from one epoch to another, as you have made clear, but if we think of the melancholy expressed in Dürer's engraving, the melancholy of the angel oppressed by the infinitude of knowledge and by the abyss of our ignorance, I would venture to ask you whether melancholy – the melancholy that relates to knowledge – is a feeling that inhabits you in later life.

To answer that, I would have to write another book on melancholy! But yes, that is my interpretation of Dürer's work. The artist sees the great mission of art and its goal, but realizes at the same time that he is incapable of adequately expressing his inner vision, his image of beauty, his ideas – or, as he puts it, the images in his soul. He wants to transpose these images but realizes that as a man, as an artist, he is incapable of producing something entirely equal to his vision.

Would you propose a transposition to the melancholy of the philosopher who fails to offer a perfect vision of the world?

For the philosopher and also for late-eighteenth-century people, and especially for the nineteenth-century poets, it's something else. Here it is not the artist who is incapable of perfectly expressing what he sees, but the person who suffers. He suffers deeply and wonders what the cause of his suffering could be. He acknowledges that he does not know the cause. Suffering without a cause: now that is true suffering! This shows us once more that we must go back to Plato and Aristotle, because the world is based on a knowledge of causes. We can in fact know the causes, and it is the philosopher's duty to know the causes, even as he or she acknowledges the limits of what can be established with certainty. This conviction, which is so profound in Plato and Aristotle, constitutes the great task of philosophy. People in the nineteenth century knew they were unable, and that was the source of their great suffering. They found themselves in a world whose cause they could not really discern. They did not know why they suffered, and we inherited that situation.

12.3 / Raymond Klibansky in his office at McGill University, Montreal, 1997. Photograph by Anne-Marie Tougas.

But we ourselves, at the end of the twentieth century, are also in a world that knows no cause, experiencing as a result the melancholy that runs through all your work – that is, in some sense, central to your life.

It inhabited me when I saw so many terrible things I could do nothing about. There was no act of will or intelligence on my part that could effect the slightest change. During the war I could observe; I could in some cases suggest an action or appeal to the authorities. But the power of each individual is so limited! We wonder: Why all this? If we identify with the search for the good, why is that search so powerless? We wonder how, in an orderly world, so much unhappiness can be possible. That's the reality. Make no mistake, we need what Nietzsche calls *Wahrhaftigkeit*, veracity, the power to become aware of the state of things.

Lucidity?

Lucidity, yes. But it must not lead to nihilism. The fact that our efforts often have minimal, or even non-existent results does not mean we should not make them. Personal effort, effort enlightened by conviction, does make a difference. Individual action makes a difference. History is full of examples showing that the action of one individual, the personality of one individual, did change something.

NOTES

Foreword

1 *Les Poesies d'Ausiàs March*, ed. Joan Ferraté (Barcelona: Edicions Quaderns Crema, 1979), 72.

Acknowledgments

1 *Erinnerung an ein Jahrhundert Gespräche mit Georges Leroux* (Frankfurt am Main and Leipzig: Insel-Verlag, 2001).

2 *The Notion of Tolerance and Human Rights: Essays in Honour of Raymond Klibansky*, ed. Ethel Groffier and Michel Paradis (Ottawa: Carleton University Press, 1991).

Introduction

1 For the biography of Klibansky, see Georges Leroux, ed., *Raymond Klibansky: la bibliothèque d'un philosophe*, exhibition catalogue (Montreal: Bibliothèque et Archives nationales du Québec, 2013). For additional information, see also a selection of his essays, *Tradition antique et tolérance moderne*, ed. Philippe Despoix and Georges Leroux (Montreal: Presses de l'Université de Montréal, 2016). All references to Klibansky's publications, including biographical documents, essays, articles, and literature on his life and work, can be found in the bibliography at the end of this book.

2 In the Heidelberg cultural milieu, strongly influenced by the *George-Kreis*, the dominant trends were mostly anti-Weimar. When Klibansky alludes to his republican convictions, he refers primarily to the liberal ideals to which he was introduced in the Weber circle, or later in Hamburg, where he met Cassirer and the Warburg scholars. See Walter Laqueur, *Weimar: A Cultural History* (London: Routledge, 2017); Peter E. Gordon and John P. McCormick, eds, *Weimar Thought: A Contested Legacy* (Princeton: Princeton University Press, 2013).

3 A sketch of Heidelberg cultural and political life can be found in the memoirs of the philosopher Hermann Glockner (1896–1979), *Heidelberger Bilderbuch: Erinnerungen* (Bonn: H. Bouvier & Co., 1969). Glockner had studied with Heinrich Rickert, with

whom he had obtained his *Habilitation* in 1924. He edited the "Jubilee" edition of the works of Hegel. His adherence to Nazism in 1934 no doubt explains why Klibansky never mentioned him, even though they were colleagues until Klibansky's departure from Germany in 1933.

4 On Jaspers's presence and influence in Heidelberg, see Wilhelmine Drescher, *Erinnerungen an Karl Jaspers in Heidelberg* (Meisenheim am Glan: Anton Hain, 1975).

5 His monograph on Cusanus, initially to have been included in his *Great Philosophers* (1957), was eventually published separately as *Nikolaus Cusanus* (München: R. Piper, 1964); English version, *Anselm and Nicholas of Cusa: From the Great Philosophers, Volume II*, ed. Hannah Arendt, trans. Ralph Mannheim (New York: Harcourt Brace Jovanovich, 1974). Jaspers refers to Cassirer's book but doesn't elaborate on any possible influence or link to his interpretation. On Jaspers's interpretation of Cusanus's thought, see Pavao Zitko, *Karl Jaspers, lettore di Cusano: Presupposti interpretativi ed esiti teoretici*, PhD diss., University of Zagreb, Faculty of Philosophy, 2017, with major bibliography, in Italian.

6 On these questions, see Edward Skidelsky, *Ernst Cassirer: The Last Philosopher of Culture* (Princeton: Princeton University Press, 2008), and, among recent works, Emily J. Levine, *Dreamland of Humanists: Warburg, Cassirer, Panofsky and the Hamburg School* (Chicago: Chicago University Press, 2013).

7 The bulk of these archives are now housed at the Deutsches Literaturarchiv in Marbach. Some documents remain in the Rare Books and Special Collections Department of McGill University, which also contains Klibansky's library, bequeathed upon his death in 2005. A preliminary inventory of these archives has been completed. To them must be added a set of private archives kept by the family.

8 Charles de Bovelles, *Le livre du sage*, ed. and trans. Pierre Magnard (Paris: J. Vrin, 2010), 91.

9 Kurt Flasch, "Laudatio auf den Preisträger Raymond Klibansky," in *Verleihung des Lessingpreises 1993 an Raymond Klibansky: Reden anlässlich der Preisübergabe* (Hamburg: Freie und Hansestadt Hamburg, 1994), 12–22.

10 See Werner Beierwaltes and Hans Gerhard Senger, eds, *Nicolai de Cusa, Opera Omnia: Symposium zum Abschluss der Heidelberger Akademie-Ausgabe* (Heidelberg: Universitätsverlag Winter, 2006) as well as Morimichi Watanabe, "The Origins of Modern Cusanus Research in Germany and the Establishment of the Heidelberg *Opera Omnia*," in Gerald Christianson and Thomas M. Izbicki, eds, *Nicholas of Cusa in Search of God and Wisdom: Essays in Honor of Morimichi Watanabe by the American Cusanus Society* (Leiden and New York: E.J. Brill, 1991).

11 Gertrud Bing (1892–1964), German art historian; wrote her dissertation on Lessing and Leibniz under Ernst Cassirer; starting in 1921, she worked as a librarian at the Kulturwissenchaftlichen Bibliothek founded by Aby Warburg in Hamburg, then directed by Fritz Saxl. When the library was moved to London, she settled in Britain, where she pursued the study and publication of Warburg's writings. See Gertrud Bing, *Gertrud Bing: Fragments sur Aby Warburg*, ed. Philippe Despoix and Martin Treml,

trans. Diane Meur, Philippe Despoix, and Hervé Joubert-Laurencin (Paris: Institut national d'histoire de l'art, 2019).

12 Aby Warburg, "Pagan-Antique Prophecy in Words and Images in the Age of Luther," in *The Renewal of Pagan Antiquity: Contributions to the Cultural History of the European Renaissance*, trans. David Britt (Los Angeles: Getty Research Institute for the History of Art and the Humanities, 1999), 645.

13 Aby Warburg, "Pagan-Antique Prophecy," 650, quoted in Ernst Cassirer, *The Individual and the Cosmos in the Renaissance* (New York: Harper & Row, 1964), 169, and in Raymond Klibansky, "Regagner Athènes à partir d'Alexandrie?"

14 Karl Mannheim (1893–1947) studied under the supervision of Alfred Weber from 1922 to 1925 and was a *Privatdozent* in Heidelberg.

15 For the history of this book, and for Klibansky's role at the Warburg Institute, see Philippe Despoix and Jillian Tomm, eds (with the collaboration of Eric Méchoulan and Georges Leroux), *Raymond Klibansky and the Warburg Library Network: Intellectual Peregrinations from Hamburg to London and Montreal* (Montreal and Kingston: McGill-Queen's University Press, 2018).

16 On the Warburg family, see Ron Chernow, *The Warburgs: The Twentieth Century Odyssey of a Remarkable Jewish Family* (New York: Random House, 1993).

17 Aristotle, *The Works of Aristotle*, vol. 7, *Problemata*, ed. W.D. Ross, trans. E.S. Forster (Oxford: Clarendon Press, 1927), 953a. The importance of this text had already been stressed by Panofsky and Saxl in their 1923 book, where it was placed in an appendix.

18 It was rechristened in 1938 the Society for the Protection of Science and Learning, a name that would persist until 1997, when it officially became the Council for Assisting Academic Refugees.

19 Einstein's letters to Klibansky are kept in his private archives along with the memorandum written by Klibansky at Einstein's request.

20 At Klibansky's death, his library was bequeathed to the Rare Books and Special Collections department of the McGill University library system. An inventory of the library has been completed and is available online. See also Jillian Tomm, "The Imprint of the Scholar: An Analysis of the Printed Books of McGill University's Raymond Klibansky Collection," PhD diss., McGill University, 2012; Jillian Tomm and Georges Leroux, "La collection Raymond Klibansky conservée à l'Université McGill: présentation de la bibliothèque d'un humaniste montréalais," *Mémoires du livre/Studies in Book Culture* 5, no. 1 (fall 2013); https://www.mcgill.ca/library/branches/rarebooks/special-collections/klibansky/. The Raymond Klibansky Collection was the subject of an exhibition held in 2012–13 at the Grande Bibliothèque in Montreal. Organized by Bibliothèque et Archives nationales du Québec and prepared by Georges Leroux, this exhibition gave rise to the publication of an illustrated catalogue accompanied by a sizable bibliography: Georges Leroux, ed., *Raymond Klibansky, 1905–2005: la bibliothèque d'un philosophe* (Montreal: Bibliothèque et Archives nationales du Québec, 2013).

21 *Raymond Klibansky: From Philosophy to Life*, directed by Anne Marie Tougas (National Film Board of Canada, 2002), 51 minutes, online at https://www.onf.ca/film/raymond_klibansky_from_philosophy_to_life/.

22 Sir William Osler (1849–1919), Regius Professor of Medicine at Oxford from 1905 until his death, had bequeathed his medical history library to McGill University, his alma mater (1872), including an impressive collection on these subjects.

23 The *International Bibliography of Philosophy*, begun in 1937 after the Descartes Congress in Paris, was supported by UNESCO and published quarterly by Librairie philosophique J. Vrin until 2010 (publications for the year 2005), the last year it was printed. Since then, this wide-ranging analytical project has entered a phase of transition and reconstruction on a virtual platform.

24 *The Edicts of Asoka*, ed. and trans. N.A. Nikam and R.P. McKeon (Chicago: University of Chicago Press, 1959).

25 This prize, awarded annually by the City of Hamburg, was given to him in 1993; see Kurt Flasch, "Laudatio," followed by an address given by Raymond Klibansky, pp. 23–32. I would note that the first recipient of this prize, in 1930, was none other than Friedrich Gundolf.

26 Raymond Klibansky first quoted this phrase in the preface to *Philosophy and History* (Oxford: Clarendon Press, 1936), the *Festschrift* he published with H.J. Paton in tribute to Ernst Cassirer. While it is not found anywhere in the works of Cusanus, it may derive from an alteration of a passage in *De ludo globi* that reads as follows: "*quodque una veritas in variis signis varie materiam determinat. Non enim possunt esse plura signa, nisi concomitetur pluralitatem varietas, nec potest veritas un variis signis nisi varie materiam determinare.*" It comes in the context of a discussion of currency, the relationship between the form and materiality of the sign. Ernst Cassirer commented on this passage in "Ficino's Place in Intellectual History," *Journal of the History of Ideas* 6 (1945): 483–501, likening it to similar doctrines in Ficino and Pico della Mirandola. On these questions, see Kurt Flasch, "Ernst Cassirer, interprète de Nicolas de Cues," *Revue germanique internationale* 15 (2012): 9–19. In the edition of the *De pace fidei* that he prepared with Hildebrand Bascour, Klibansky cites an annotation by Cusanus on a manuscript of the Latin version of the Qur'an prepared by Pierre le Vénérable and published as *Lex sive doctrina Mahumeti*, which reads: "*Fides una, ritus diversus*" (*Codex cusanus 108*, folio 25 verso); see Nicolaus Cusanus, *De pace fidei*, ed. Hildebrand Bascour and Raymond Klibansky, xxxix. On these issues, see Pim Valkenberg, "*Una Religio in Rituum Varietate*: Religious Pluralism, the Qur'an, and Nicholas of Cusa," in Ian Christopher Levy, Rita George-Tvrtković, and Donald F. Duclow, eds, *Nicholas of Cusa and Islam: Polemic and Dialogue in the Late Middle Ages* (Leiden & Boston: Brill, 2014), 30–48.

Chapter One

1 Hermann Klibansky, native of Frankfurt, married Rosa Scheidt; they had two children, Raymond and Sonia (d. 1994).

2 Lazarus Goldschmidt (1871–1950), first German translator of the "uncensored text" of the Babylonian Talmud, which was first published in Leipzig (1897–1909). The translation was completed in London in 1935, and a more recent edition was published as

Der Babylonische Talmud (Frankfurt am Main: Jüdischer Verlag im Suhrkamp Verlag, 1996).

3 Raymond Poincaré (1860–1934), president of France from 1913 to 1920; cousin of mathematician Henri Poincaré (1854–1912).

4 Pinkus Klibansky, paternal uncle of Raymond Klibansky; ran a boarding school for Jewish children in Frankfurt, the great majority of them children of Polish background. Most of these children returned to Poland at the start of the war. See Tim Grady, *A Deadly Legacy: German Jews and the Great War* (New Haven: Yale University Press, 2017), 61.

5 Hans Bethe (1906–2005), Nobel Prize laureate in physics for 1957, author of major works in nuclear physics such as *Intermediate Quantum Mechanics* (Menlo Park, CA: Benjamin-Cumming, 1986) and director of the Los Alamos laboratory, where the first atomic bomb was made. Memoir, *The Road to Los Alamos* (New York: American Institute of Physics, 1991).

6 Felix Bölte (1863–1943), German philologist who taught at the Goethe Gymnasium in Frankfurt. In addition to his numerous articles in the Pauly-Wissowa Encyclopedia, he published a major study on Julius Caesar's *The Gallic Wars*.

7 The Odenwald School was founded in 1910 by Paul Geheeb (1870–1961) and his wife, Edith Cassirer-Geheeb (1885–1982). Forced to leave Germany in 1934, they emigrated to Switzerland, where they founded a new school under the name École d'Humanité, which was directed by Geheeb until his death, and still exists. The Odenwald School, which had continued operating after the war, was shut down in 2015 following reports of sexual abuse. See Martin Näf, *Paul Geheeb: Seine Entwicklung bis zur Gründung der Odenwaldschule* (Weinheim: Beltz, 1998) and *Paul und Edith Geheeb Cassirer: Gründer der Odenwaldschule und der École d'Humanité; Deustche, Schweizerische Reform Pädagogik 1910–1961* (Weinheim: Beltz, 2006). See also Dennis Shirley, *The Politics of Progressive Education: The Odenwaldschule in Nazi Germany* (Cambridge, MA: Harvard University Press, 1992).

8 Otto Braun, *The Diary of Otto Braun, with Selections from his Letters and Poems*, ed. Julie Vogelstein, trans. Ella Winter and F.W. Stella Browne (New York: Alfred Knopf, 1924; reprint, Literary Licensing, 2011).

9 Walter Solmitz (1905–1962) was a student at the Odenwald School and later at Heidelberg and Hamburg, where he did doctoral studies under Ernst Cassirer. Interned in Dachau after Kristallnacht, he was able to leave Germany and reach London thanks to the efforts of Fritz Saxl and Gertrud Bing. He then emigrated to the United States, where he completed his studies at Harvard. He died by suicide in 1962. See Joist Grolle, *Bericht von einem schwierigen Leben: Walter Solmitz (1905 bis 1962); Schüler von Aby Warburg und Ernst Cassirer* (Berlin/Hamburg: Dietrich Reimer, 1994). This book contains a selection of texts by Solmitz, including his essay on Paul Geheeb and his tribute to Aby Warburg. In his introduction, the author reminds us of the importance of Geheeb's pedagogy to Solmitz and confirms his friendship with Raymond Klibansky.

10 Alwine von Keller (1878–1965), teacher at the Odenwald School starting in 1916; translated the writings of Sri Aurobindo; trained as a psychoanalyst with Carl Jung.

11 Klaus Mann (1906–1949), German writer, among the foremost figures of dissidence in the time of Nazism. In addition to his important literary oeuvre, he left an autobiography, *The Turning Point: Thirty-Five Years in This Century* (New York: L.B. Fischer, 1942), and a book on Gide, *André Gide and the Crisis of Modern Thought* (New York: Creative Age Press, 1943); see also the biography by Frederic Spotts, *Cursed Legacy: The Tragic Life of Klaus Mann* (New Haven: Yale University Press, 2016).

12 Golo Mann (1909–1994) completed a doctorate in philosophy on Hegel's thought with Karl Jaspers in Heidelberg. He published a number of historical works and a memoir, *Reminiscences and Reflections: A Youth in Germany* (New York: W.W. Norton and Co., 1990).

13 Friedrich Hölderlin, "Heidelberg," trans. Christopher Middleton, in *Hyperion and Selected Poems*, ed. Eric L. Santner (New York: Continuum, 1990), 144–5.

14 A richly illustrated commemorative work on the city of Heidelberg provides the historical and cultural background to its storied reputation: Elmar Mittler, ed., *Heidelberg: Geschichte und Gestalt* (Heidelberg: Universitätsverlag C. Winter, 1996), containing Raymond Klibansky's contribution evoking his memories of the city, "Aus dem Heidelberger Geistesleben: Autobiographische Anmerkungen," 270–83. That article is the German translation of a speech given on 24 April 1991 on the occasion of an honorary award given to him at the Université du Québec à Montréal, also published in the original French as "L'université allemande dans les années trente: notes autobiographiques," *Philosophiques* 18 (1991): 139–57.

15 Ludwig Curtius (1874–1954), archaeologist and historian of ancient art; directed the German Archaeological Institute in Rome from 1928 to 1937.

16 Heinrich Rickert (1863–1936), central figure of Neo-Kantianism; a major work is *The Limits of Concept Formation in Natural Science: A Logical Introduction to the Historical Sciences*, ed. and trans. Guy Oakes (Cambridge & London: Cambridge University Press, [1902] 1986).

17 Karl Jaspers (1883–1969) was initially trained as a physician and a psychiatrist. Considered the founder of existential philosophy, his philosophical influence was immense. See Chris Thornhill and Ronny Miron, "Karl Jaspers," *The Stanford Encyclopedia of Philosophy* (Spring 2020), ed. Edward N. Zalta, online at https://plato.stanford.edu/archives/spr2020/entries/jaspers/; Jean-Claude Gens, *Karl Jaspers: biographie* (Paris: Bayard, 2003).

18 Karl Jaspers, *General Psychopathology* (Manchester: Manchester University Press, 1962); Jaspers, *Psychologie der Weltanschauungen* (Berlin: Springer, 1919).

19 See Karl Jaspers, *Die geistige Situation der Zeit* (Berlin: Walter de Gruyter, 1931); translated as *Man in the Modern Age*, trans. E. Paul and C. Paul (London: Routledge, 1933).

20 Max Weber, *The Vocation Lectures*, eds David Owen and Tracy B. Strong, trans. Rodney Livingstone (Indianapolis: Hackett Publishing Company, 2004), 6, 16.

21 Oswald Spengler (1880–1936) left a considerable historical and political oeuvre but is best known for his two-volume work *The Decline of the West: Form and Actuality*, trans. Charles Francis Atkinson (New York: Alfred A. Knopf, 1932).

22 This thesis was central to his great three-volume work *Philosophie* (Berlin: J. Springer, 1932), translated into English by E.B. Ashton as *Philosophy* (Chicago: University of Chicago Press, 1969–71). See also Hannah Arendt and Karl Jaspers, *Correspondence 1926–1969*, trans. Robert Kimber and Rita Kimber (New York: Harcourt Brace Jovanovich, 1992).

23 Jeanne Hersch (1910–2000), Swiss philosopher and student of Karl Jaspers, to whom she devoted an important work, *Karl Jaspers* (Lausanne: L'âge d'homme, 1979); also authored a history of philosophy, *L'étonnement philosophique: une histoire de la philosophie* (Paris: Gallimard, 1993).

24 Walter Biemel and Hans Saner, eds, *The Heidegger-Jaspers Correspondence (1920–1963)*, trans. Gary E. Aylesworth (New York: Humanity Books, 2003).

25 I was unable to identify this individual.

26 Ferdinand Tönnies (1855–1936) is considered the co-founder, with Max Weber, of German sociology. He is mainly known for his great work *Community and Society* (1887), ed. and trans. Charles P. Loomis (New York: Dover, 2002). See Werner J. Cahnman, *Weber and Tönnies: Comparative Sociology in Historical Perspective* (New Brunswick: Transaction, 1995).

27 Harry Clemens Ulrich Graf von Kessler (1868–1937), scion of a noble family; took part in many artistic and political activities, and left a voluminous diary in two volumes, *Journey into the Abyss: The Diaries of Count Harry Kessler (1880–1918)*, ed. and trans. Laird M. Easton (New York: Alfred A. Knopf, 2011), and *Berlin in Lights: The Diaries of Count Harry Kessler, 1918–1937*, ed. and trans. Charles Kessler (New York: Grove Press, 2000).

28 Ulrich von Wilamowitz-Moellendorf (1848–1931) produced an immense philological oeuvre, mainly devoted to Homer and Plato; memoir, *Erinnerungen 1848–1914* (Leipzig: Koehler, 1928).

29 Heinrich (Heinz) Cassirer (1903–1979) fled Germany with his family and settled in Glasgow, where he studied the works of Immanuel Kant. He published a commentary on the *Critique of Pure Reason* as well as a study on St Paul and Kant, *Grace and Law: St Paul, Kant and the Hebrew Prophets* (Edinburgh: Hansel Press, 1988).

30 Ernst Cassirer (1874–1945) studied philosophy with Hermann Cohen. The early part of his career was devoted to the Neo-Kantian project of renewing the theory of knowledge. In later years, his work was devoted to the philosophy of culture and symbolic forms. See Michael Friedman, "Ernst Cassirer," *The Stanford Encyclopedia of Philosophy* (Fall 2018 edition), Edward N. Zalta, ed., online at https://plato.stanford.edu/archives/fall2018/entries/cassirer/; Ernst Cassirer, *The Philosophy of Symbolic Forms*, 3 vols., trans. Steve G. Lofts (London & New York: Routledge, [1923–29] 2021). Cassirer married his cousin Antonia (Toni) Bondy in 1902 and the couple had three children. Toni Cassirer's memoirs were published in 1948 as *Mein Leben mit Ernst Cassirer* (Leipzig: F. Meiner, 2018); see also her *Ernst Cassirer in America* (Turin: Edizioni di "Filosofia," 1955). With

his colleague H.J. Paton, Raymond Klibansky published a Festschrift in honour of Cassirer under the title *Philosophy and History: Essays Presented to Ernst Cassirer* (New York: Oxford University Press, 1936), and he also published his own recollections of Cassirer, most notably in an interview with Patrick Conley, "Die Grenzen des akademischen Lebens sprengen: Ein Gespräch über Ernst Cassirer und die Bibliothek Warburg," *Merkur* 50 (1996): 274–7. Cassirer's influence over twentieth-century philosophy was immense; see the special issue of the *Journal of Transcendental Philosophy* titled "Cassirer's Children," vol. 2, no. 1 (2021).

31 See Raymond Klibansky, interview with Thomas Göller, "Erinnerungen an Ernst Cassirer: Raymond Klibansky im Gespräch mit Thomas Göller," *Internationale Zeitschrift für Philosophie* 2 (1999): 275–88.

32 Carlotta (Lotte) Labowsky (1905–1991) was a Hamburg native who completed her doctorate in Heidelberg in 1932, published two years later as *Die Ethik des Panaitios: Untersuchungen zur Geschichte des Decorum bei Cicero und Horaz* (Leipzig: Meiner, 1934). She went into exile at Oxford, where she was appointed a Somerville Fellow and worked closely with Raymond Klibansky on the Warburg Institute's projects dealing with the *Corpus Platonicum Medii Aevi*. See Regina Weber, *Lotte Labowsky (1905–1991) – Schülerin Aby Warburgs, Kollegin Raymond Klibanskys: Eine Wissenschaftlerin zwischen Fremd- und Selbstbestimmung im englischen Exil* (Berlin/Hamburg: Dietrich Reimer, 2012).

33 Eva Cassirer (1920–2009) was Ernst Cassirer's niece. She was educated in the philosophy of science, the discipline to which she devoted her entire career. See also her correspondence with Rainer Maria Rilke, *Briefwechsel* (Göttingen: Wallstein, 2009). On the Cassirer family, see Sigrid Bauschinger, *Die Cassirers, Unternehmer, Kunsthändler, Philosophen: Biografie einer Familie* (München: H. Beck, 2015), 55–128.

34 A key source on Raymond Klibansky's relationship to the Warburg Library is Philippe Despoix and Jillian Tomm, eds (with the collaboration of Éric Méchoulan and Georges Leroux), *Raymond Klibansky and the Warburg Library Network: Intellectual Peregrinations from Hamburg to London and Montreal* (Montreal and Kingston: McGill-Queen's University Press, 2018).

35 Fritz Saxl (1890–1948) was born in Vienna where he completed a dissertation on Rembrandt under the supervision of Max Dvorak. After a research stay with Heinrich Wölfflin in Berlin, and another in Italy studying astrological manuscripts, he joined the Warburg Library in Hamburg in 1912. After Warburg's death in 1929, he became its director and was instrumental in transferring it to London, where he took refuge. He devoted the rest of his life to the library, which became part of the University of London in 1944.

36 Erwin Panofsky (1892–1968) was born into a German Jewish family in Hanover and was educated mainly in Berlin, where he studied philosophy, philology, and art history. He taught at the University of Hamburg from 1920 to 1933, the date of his emigration to the United States. His work is considered the most important development in the discipline of iconology, founded by Aby Warburg and Fritz Saxl in Hamburg. See

Sylvia Ferretti, *Cassirer, Panofsky, Warburg: Symbol, Art and History*, trans. Richard Pierce (New Haven: Yale University Press, 1989).

37 Erwin Panofsky and Fritz Saxl, *Dürers "Melencolia I": Eine quellen- und typengeschichtliche Untersuchung* (Berlin and Leipzig: Teubner, 1923). On the history of this research and Klibansky's contribution, see Despoix and Tomm, *Raymond Klibansky*.

38 Ernst Gombrich, *Aby Warburg: An Intellectual Biography, with a Memoir on the History of the Library by F. Saxl* (London: Warburg Institute, 1970).

39 Edgar Wind (1900–1971) was Erwin Panofsky's first student, and his contribution to art history bears the stamp of the Warburg method. Notable books by him are *Pagan Mysteries in the Renaissance* (New York: W.W. Norton, 1968) and *The Eloquence of Symbols: Studies in Humanist Art*, ed. J. Anderson, with an appendix on a biography of Warburg (Oxford: Clarendon Press, 1983).

40 For an early and important statement of Gentile's ideas, see *The Theory of Mind as Pure Act*, trans. from the 3rd rev. ed. by H. Wildon Carr (London: Macmillan, [1912] 1922).

Chapter Two

1 Ernst Robert Curtius (1886–1956) devoted his research to the interpretation of European humanism, primarily in the medieval and Renaissance tradition. He presented his work as a form of resistance to totalitarianism. One of his great works was *European Literature and the Latin Middle Ages*, trans. Willard R. Trask (Princeton: Princeton University Press, 1990).

2 Thomas Mann, *Reflections of a Nonpolitical Man*, 1st English ed., trans. Walter D. Morris (New York: F. Ungar, 1982).

3 Alfred Weber (1868–1958), economist and sociologist, younger brother of Max Weber; for a notable work see *Theory of the Location of Industries*, trans. C.J. Friedrich (Chicago: University of Chicago Press, 1929).

4 Max Weber (1864–1920), *Wirtschaft und Gesellschaft* (1922). The English translation was published as *Economy and Society: An Outline of Interpretive Sociology*, 2 vols., eds Guenther Roth and Claus Wittich, trans. Ephraim Fischoff et al. (Berkeley: University of California Press, 1978).

5 Karl Mannheim, *Ideology and Utopia: An Introduction to the Sociology of Knowledge* (New York: Harcourt, Brace, 1954).

6 Pierre Viénot (1897–1944), French statesman, ambassador to London during the liberation; published his thoughts after spending six years in Germany as the representative of the Franco-German Study Committee as *Is Germany Finished?* (New York: Macmillan, 1932; reprint, Cambridge: Cambridge University Press, 2013). His ideas on the crisis of German culture impressed Klibansky, who had great admiration for him.

7 Else von Richthofen Jaffé (1874–1973) was one of a small number of women studying at Heidelberg University, where she completed a doctorate in economics in 1901. Her husband, Edgar Jaffé (1865–1921), co-edited the journal *Archiv für Sozialwissenschaft und Sozialpolitik* with Max Weber and Werner Sombart. See Guenther Roth, "Edgar Jaffé

and Else von Richthofen in the Mirror of Newly Found Letters," *Max Weber Studies* 10, no. 2: 151–88 (2010).

8 Marie Baum (1874–1964) held a PhD in chemistry and also specialized in sociology of the family. A militant feminist, she was elected in 1919 to the Weimar National Assembly. She was also an intimate friend of Ricarda Huch (1864–1947), the great specialist of European history and German romanticism and the author of a considerable literary oeuvre; see Marie Baum, *Leuchtende Spur: Das Leben Ricarda Huchs* (Tübingen: Wunderlich, 1950).

9 In contrast to her research on Cardinal Bessarion's library (*Bessarion's Library and the Biblioteca Marciana: Six Early Inventories* [Rome: Edizioni di Storia e Letteratura, 1979]), Labowsky's published thesis, *Die Ethik des Panaitios: Untersuchungen zur Geschichte des Decorum bei Cicero und Horaz* (Leipzig: F. Meiner, 1934), was never translated.

10 Heinrich Zimmer (1890–1943) held the chair of Indian studies at Heidelberg University from 1924 to 1938. He was forced out by the Nazi regime and emigrated to England, where he taught at Oxford. His major work was *Myths and Symbols in Indian Art and Civilization*, ed. Joseph Campbell (Princeton: Princeton University Press, 1946).

11 Friedrich Gundolf (1880–1931) joined the circle of Stefan George in 1899 and they remained friends until 1926. Gundolf left an imposing oeuvre in the fields of history and literary criticism, including *Shakespeare und der deutsche Geist* (Berlin: Bondi, 1927) and *Goethe*, 13th ed. (Berlin: Bondi, 1930). He also published a book on George's work titled *George* (Berlin: Bondi, 1920). Their correspondence, too, has been published, as *Briefwechsel*, ed. Robert Boehringer and Georg Peter Landmann (München and Düsseldorf: Helmut Kupper, 1962).

12 Friedrich Gundolf, *The Mantle of Caesar*, trans. Jacob Wittmer Hartmann (New York: Macy-Masius, Vanguard Press, 1928).

13 August Wilhelm von Schlegel and Friedrich von Schlegel, *Athenaeum: Eine Zeitschrift*, 3 vols. (Darmstadt: Wissenschaftliche Buchgesellschaft, 1983).

14 Emil Julius Gumbel (1891–1966), professor of mathematics at Heidelberg University. A courageous critic of Nazism, whose hate crimes he analyzed, he was forced to emigrate to France, later settling in the United States. His archives, containing documents of his fight against Nazism, were compiled at the Leo Baeck Institute in New York; see Arthur D. Brenner, *Emil J. Gumbel, Weimar German Pacifist and Professor* (Leiden: Brill Academic Publishers, 2001).

15 Karl Wolfskehl (1869–1948), member of the *George-Kreis*, close friend of Rainer Maria Rilke, Thomas Mann, and many other writers and artists; fled Germany for Italy in 1933 but was forced by Italian fascism to emigrate to New Zealand. He left a major poetic oeuvre and numerous translations. His and his wife Hanna's correspondence with George was published as *Von Menschen und Mächten: Stefan George – Karl und Hanna Wolfskehl; der Briefwechsel, 1892–1933*, ed. Birgit Bägenbaur and Ute Oelman (München: C.H. Beck, 2015); his letters from exile as *Poetry and Exile: Letters from New Zealand, 1938–1948*, ed. and trans. Nelson Wattie (Lyttelton: Cold Hub Press, 2017).

16 Stefan George (1868–1933), author of a large poetic oeuvre, whose influence on Weimar culture was considerable. The "Circle" that he gathered around him has been the subject of numerous studies, due to its proximity to the development of National Socialism; see, e.g., Robert E. Norton, *Secret Germany: Stefan George and His Circle* (Ithaca: Cornell University Press, 2002).

17 Friedrich Gundolf, *George* (Berlin: Bondi, 1920), 31.

18 Stefan George, "The Star of the Covenant," in *The Works of Stefan George*, 2nd rev. and enl. ed., trans. Olga Marx and Ernst Morwitz (Chapel Hill: University of North Carolina Press, 1974), 338.

19 Ibid., 300.

20 Albert Saint-Paul, *Les Encensoirs: poésies* (Paris: Librairie des Bibliophiles, 1885).

21 Stefan George, "Frankish Lands," section of "The Seventh Ring," in *The Works*, 222.

22 Stéphane Mallarmé, "Théodore de Banville," in *Divagations*, trans. Barbara Johnson (Cambridge: The Belknap Press of Harvard University, 2007), 94.

23 This letter, written in French, is in the George archives housed at the State Library of Württemberg in Stuttgart. See also Stuart Merrill, *The White Tomb: Selected Writings* (Jersey City, NJ: Talisman House, 1999).

24 Ernst Kantorowicz (1895–1963), historian specializing in the political history of the Middle Ages; student of Eberhard Gothein at Heidelberg, where he became involved in the *George-Kreis*. On their relationship, see Robert E. Lerner, *Ernst Kantorowicz: A Life* (Princeton: Princeton University Press, 2017). Kantorowicz is best known for his biography *Frederick the Second, 1194–1250*, trans. E.O. Lorimer (New York: F. Ungar, [1967]), as well as *The King's Two Bodies: A Study in Mediaeval Political Theology* (Princeton: Princeton University Press, 1957).

25 A copy of Stefan George, *Maximin: Ein Gedenkbuch* (Berlin: Blaetter für die Kunst, 1907), written in memory of Maximilian Kronberger, was in Klibansky's library.

26 Ida Coblenz (1870–1942) was an intimate of Stefan George in the 1890s but instead married Leopold Auerbach, and later Richard Dehmel, who died young in 1920 from the consequences of a war wound. Confined to Hamburg at the height of the deportations, she died by suicide in 1942.

27 Edith Landmann (1877–1951) devoted several works to George's thought: notably *Georgika: Das Wesen des Dichters; Stefan George, Umriss seines Werkes; Stefan George, Umriss seiner Wirkung* (Heidelberg: Weiss'sche Universitäts Buchhandlung, 1920) and *Stefan George und die Griechen: Idee einer neuen Ethik*, ed. Michael Landmann (Amsterdam: Castrum Peregrini Presse, 1971). A book of conversations with George, *Gespräche mit Stefan George, 1902–1931*, ed. Berthold Vallentin (Dusseldorf: Kupper Bondi, 1963), was published posthumously. Her son Michael Landmann published a memoir, *Erinnerungen an Stefan George: Seine Freundschaft mit Julius und Edith Landmann* (Amsterdam: Castrum Peregrini Presse, 1980).

28 Friedrich Wolters (1876–1930) met Stefan George in 1909. He was involved in promoting the ideals of the *George-Kreis* and founded a journal, *Jahrbuch für die geistige Bewegung*, that was edited by Friedrich Gundolf. He later became a militant National Socialist. His correspondence with George was published as *Briefwechsel, 1904–1930*

(Amsterdam: Castrum Peregrini Presse, 1998). See also his politico-philosophical manifesto *Herrschaft und Dienst* (Berlin: Georg Bondi, 1920) and his *Stefan George und die Blätter für die Kunst: Deutsche Geistesgeschichte seit 1890* (Berlin: Georg Bondi, 1929).

29 Max Kommerell (1902–1944) was a member of the *George-Kreis* until he left it in 1930, and a student of Friedrich Gundolf. His study on the role of the poet as "Führer" in German literature, *Der Dichter als Führer in der deutschen Klassik: Klopstock, Herder, Goethe, Schiller, Jean Paul, Hölderlin*, 2nd ed. (Frankfurt am Main: Klostermann, 1929) played a major role in the ideology of the *George-Kreis*. A conservative thinker, he became a member of the National Socialist party in 1941: Norton, *Secret Germany*, 731.

30 Claus von Stauffenberg (1907–1944), German officer, prominent figure in the German resistance to the Nazi regime; executed after the failed plot of 20 July 1944 to assassinate Hitler. See Peter Hoffmann, *Stauffenberg: A Family History, 1905–1944* (Montreal and Kingston: McGill-Queen's University Press, 2003).

31 Edith Landmann, *Gespräche mit Stefan George* (Düsseldorf: Küpper, 1963).

32 Peter Hoffmann, *Stauffenberg: A Family History, 1905–1944* (Montreal and Kingston: McGill-Queen's University Press, 2003), 312.

33 Ibid.

34 Karl Wolfskehl, "Mare Nostrum or The Five Windows," in *Three Worlds: Selected Poems*, translated and edited by Andrew Paul Wood and Friedrich Voit (Lyttleton, NZ: Cold Hub Press, 2016), 153, 155.

35 Wolfskehl, "To the Germans," in Wood and Voit, eds, *Three Worlds*, 191.

Chapter Three

1 The edition of Charles de Bovelles's *Liber de Sapiente* prepared by Klibansky was published, at the invitation of Ernst Cassirer, as an appendix to Cassirer's *Individuum und Kosmos in der Philosophie der Renaissance* (Leipzig: Teubner, 1927; reprint, Darmstadt: Wissenschaftliche Buchgesellschaft, 1963). The English translation, *The Individual and the Cosmos in Renaissance Philosophy*, trans. Mario Domandi (New York: Harper & Row, 1963), does not contain the appendix. This book was published by Cassirer in homage to Aby Warburg on the occasion of his sixtieth birthday. Klibansky drew upon the Renaissance editions of the treatise, in particular that of Henri Estienne (Stephanus), published in Paris in 1510, in a compilation of works by Charles de Bovelles. On this point, see Cassirer, *Individuum und Kosmos*, 299. Several notes in the Warburg Institute archives document Klibansky's work on the proofs of the 1927 edition, including discussions with Gertrud Bing and Fritz Saxl. See, for example, Klibansky's letter, dated 18 July 1927 after his return to Heidelberg, thanking Fritz Saxl for his proofreading help (WIA GC/18830). For more on Bovelles's treatise, see *Charles de Bovelles, Liber de sapiente or Book of the Wise*, ed. Michel Ferrari and Tamara Albertini, special issue of *Intellectual History Review* 21, vol. 3: 257–394 (2011). For notes on the modern publication history of this treatise, see the comments of its French editor and translator in Pierre Magnard, "L'homme délivré de son ombre," introduction to Charles de Bovelles, *Le Livre du sage* (Paris: J. Vrin, 1982).

2 Valentin Weigel (1533–1588), *Theologia Weigelii* (Newstatt: Knuber, 1618). This edition of Weigel's writings is in the Raymond Klibansky Collection, housed in the Rare Books and Special Collections Department of McGill University.

3 Hermann Cohen (1842–1918), founder of the Marburg school of philosophy and foremost avatar of Neo-Kantianism; see, for example, *Kommentar zu Immanuel Kants Kritik der reinen Vernunft* (Hildesheim: Olms, [1907] 1978). The influence of Cohen's thought on Cassirer is inestimable, as Klibansky always maintained. See Kirstin Zeyer, *Cusanus in Marburg: Hermann Cohens und Ernst Cassirers produktive Form der Philosophiegeschichtsaneignung* (Münster: Aschendorf, 2015).

4 Ernst Hoffmann (1880–1952), director of the Heidelberg Academy's Nicolaus Cusanus publication program; studied under Ulrich von Wilamowitz and Hermann Diels and became a renowned Hellenist; supervised Klibansky's thesis on Proclus, defended in 1928 and published in 1929 (see bibliography). For a collection of his works, see "Platonismus und Mittelalter," in *Vorträge der Bibliothek Warburg* 3 (1923–24): 17–82 (Leipzig: B.G. Teubner, 1926); *Das Universum des Nikolaus von Cues* (Heidelberg: C. Winter, 1930); "Platonism in Augustine's Philosophy of History," in R. Klibansky and H.J. Paton, eds, *Philosophy and History: Essays Presented to Ernst Cassirer* (Oxford: Clarendon Press, 1936), 173–90. Hoffmann had to give up his university chair during National Socialism because of his part-Jewish heritage but enjoyed the protection of influential figures and did not lose his professorship. In 1945, despite his advanced age, he regained his chair and resumed teaching. His successor was Karl Löwith, whom Hans-Georg Gadamer had persuaded to return to Germany. After Hoffmann's death, Klibansky arranged for his library to be acquired by the Université de Montréal, where it is now included in the catalogue as the "Hoffmann Collection." This precious library of over three thousand titles comprises numerous rare editions of ancient and modern authors studied by Hoffmann.

5 Giovanni Andrea Bussi (1417–1475), Renaissance humanist and close friend and collaborator of Nicolaus Cusanus, for whom he served as secretary in Rome, as well as of Cardinal Bessarion.

6 Jean Trouillard (1907–1984), French Neoplatonist. See Joseph Combès, "Néoplatonisme aujourd'hui: la vie et l'œuvre de Jean Trouillard," in *Études néoplatoniciennes*, 2nd revised and augmented ed. (Grenoble: Jérôme Millon, 1996), 354–65, for an homage to him.

7 See Plotinus, *Traité sur la liberté et la volonte de l'Un*, introduction, Greek text, translation, and commentary by Georges Leroux (Paris: Librairie Philosophique Vrin, 1990); English translation, *The Six Enneads*, trans. Stephen MacKenna and B.S. Page (Chicago: Encyclopædia Britannica, [1955]).

8 Cusanus discusses this canvas by the Flemish painter Rogier van der Weyden in *De visione dei*, I, 2 as an illustration of the concept of total and reciprocal vision between God and man, which he calls "omnivoyance." He situates the canvas at Brussels City Hall. The whereabouts of this painting, like many others by this artist, is unknown.

9 Cusanusstift, charitable institution located in Kues, where it was founded by Nicolaus Cusanus in 1458; contains a large library where Klibansky had an opportunity to work on Cusanus's manuscripts.

10 Nicolaus Cusanus, *De visione dei*, IV, 12. See Jasper Hopkins, *Nicholas of Cusa's Dialectical Mysticism: Text, Translation and Interpretive Study of* De visione dei (Minneapolis: Arthur J. Banning Press, 1985), 685.

11 *De visione dei*, VII, 26–7: "Immo quomodo dabis tu te mihi si etiam me ipsum non dederis mihi? Et cum sic in silentio contemplationis quiesco tu Domine intra praecordia mea respondes dicens: sis tu tuus et ego ero tuus. O Domine, suavitas omnis dulcedinis posuisti in libertate mea, ut sim, si voluero mei ipsius."

12 Nicholas of Cusa, *Dialogus De ludo globi* (1463), ed. Hans Gerhard Senger, vol. 9 of *Opera Omnia* (Hamburg: Meiner, 1998); English version, "The Bowling-Game," in *Complete Philosophical and Theological Treatises of Nicholas of Cusa*, trans. Jasper Hopkins (Minneapolis: Arthur J. Banning Press, 2001), 2: 1179–1274. See Sarah Powrie, "Nicholas of Cusa's Dialogue with Augustine: The Measure of the Soul's Greatness in *De ludo globi*," *Renaissance and Reformation* 38, no. 2 (2015): 15–25.

13 Brethren of the Common Life (*Fratres vitae communis*), Christian pietist movement founded by Gerard Groote (1340–1384); Cusanus attended their school at Deventer.

14 Franz von Baader (1765–1841), German philosopher and Catholic theologian whose work developed into a form of theosophy. His general interest in mysticism and tendency toward esotericism included study of Meister Eckhart and Jakob Böhme.

15 Alfred Rosenberg (1893–1946), one of the principal ideologues of Nazism. His book, first published in Münich in 1930, reprinted numerous times, and translated into English as *The Myth of the Twentieth Century*, contains the fundamental theses of National Socialism, which he helped spread throughout Germany and around the world.

16 Meister Eckhart, *Opera latina*, ed. Raymond Klibansky, vol. 1, *Super oratione dominica*; see also Eckhart, *Meister Eckhart: A Modern Translation*, trans. Raymond Bernard Blakney (New York: Harper Torchbooks, [1941] 2004); Eckhart, *The Essential Sermons, Commentaries, Treatises and Defense*, trans. Edmund Colledge and Bernard McGinn (Mahwah, NJ: Paulist Press International, 1981).

17 Brethren of the Free Spirit, a heretical sect that spread throughout northern Europe, mainly Germany and Holland, starting in the thirteenth century; see Bernard McGinn, *The Harvest of Mysticism in Medieval Germany* (New York: Crossroad, 2005).

Chapter Four

1 Friedrich Endemann (1857–1936), eminent jurist, professor of law, and member of the Heidelberg Academy of Sciences. Although he did sign the election proclamation, thus swearing allegiance to Hitler, he was never a Nazi Party member. The initial three hundred academics who signed were joined by six hundred more at the second signing in Leipzig on 11 November 1933, among them Martin Heidegger, then rector of the University of Freiburg, and Hans-Georg Gadamer.

2 Eugen Fehrle (1880–1957), professor of classics and history of religions at Heidelberg University from 1909 onward. In 1923, after a trip to Italy, he endorsed the National Socialist platform, and in 1931 became a party member. His role in the Nazification (*Gleichschaltung*) of German universities was considerable. He served in the SS in 1939. The double entendre implicit in Klibansky's use of the term *extraordinarius* (professor without chair) is no doubt intended as an expression of amazement at this fellow classicist's devotion to the Nazi regime.

3 August Faust (1895–1945), student and assistant of Heinrich Rickert in Heidelberg, historian of philosophy; enrolled in the Hitler Youth and later became a Nazi party member; died by suicide in 1945.

4 Jakob Burckhardt (1818–1897), Swiss art historian specializing in the Renaissance. See *Reflections on History*, trans. Mary D. Hottinger (Indianapolis: Liberty Fund, [1999]); *The Civilization of the Renaissance in Italy*, translated from the first German edition (1860) by S.G.C. Middlemore (London: C. Kegan Paul, 1878). The third edition is considered the standard text: *Geschichte der Renaissance in Italien*, ed. Heinrich Holtzinger, vol. 3, (Stuttgart: Ebner und Seubert, 1891).

5 See Eike Volgast, "Die Universität Heidelberg: Historische Entwicklung," in Elmar Mittler, ed., *Heidelberg: Geschichte und Gestalt* (Heidelberg: Universitätsverlag C. Winter, 1996), 284–7, as well as the remarks of Raymond Klibansky, "Aus dem Heidelberger Geisterleben: Autobiographischen Anmerkungen," ibid., 270–82. This latter text was published in a slightly different earlier version: "L'Université allemande dans les années trente (Notes autobiographiques)," *Philosophiques* 18, no. 2: 139–57 (1992). See also Birgit Vézina, *"Die Gleichschaltung" der Universität Heidelberg im Zuge der nationalsozialistischen Machtergreifung* (Heidelberg: C. Winter, 1982), as well as Dorothee Mussgnug, *Die vertriebenen Heidelberger Dozenten: zur Geschichte der Ruprecht-Karls-Universität nach 1933* (Heidelberg: C. Winter, 1988).

6 Heinrich Rickert, prolific author and indubitably major figure in German philosophy; appears to have opted for public silence during the rise of fascism. These important issues are discussed in Christian Tilitzki, *Die deutsche Universitätsphilosophie in der Weimarer Republik und im Dritten Reich*, 2 vols. (Berlin: Akademie Verlag, 2002; reprint, 2014).

7 Eduard Spranger (1882–1963), philosopher and psychologist; studied with Wilhelm Dilthey.

8 Raymond Klibansky, "L'Université allemande dans les années trente (Notes autobiographiques)," *Philosophiques* 18, no. 2: 151–3 (1992).

9 Klibansky's rejection of Heidegger's ideas was unconditional. Although he did express great esteem for certain French thinkers such as Dominique Janicaud (1937–2002), with whom he was able to discuss these issues, he remained steadfast in his rejection of Heidegger throughout his life. On Heidegger's reception in France, see Dominique Janicaud, *Heidegger in France*, trans. François Raffoul and David Pettigrew (Bloomington: Indiana University Press, 2015).

10 Karl Löwith (1897–1973), philosopher who studied with Husserl and Heidegger; memoir, *My Life in Germany, before and after 1933: A Report* (Urbana: University of Illinois Press, 1994).

11 See Walter Biemel and Hans Saner, eds, *The Heidegger-Jaspers Correspondence (1920–1963)*, trans. Gary E. Aylesworth (New York: Humanity Books, 2003), and also David Farrell Rell, "The Jaspers-Heidegger Relationship," *Journal of the British Society of Phenomenology* 9, no. 2: 126–9 (1978).

12 Jacques Pirenne (1891–1972), Belgian jurist and historian; co-organized a peace conference with King Leopold III just before the war. With the invasion of Belgium in May 1940, he left for France, going on to Geneva a year later after falling afoul of the Vichy regime.

13 Klibansky's role in saving the library was acknowledged by Fritz Saxl in his appendix to Ernst Gombrich, *Aby Warburg: An Intellectual Biography* (London: Warburg Institute, 1970), 336. On this point, see Martin Treml, "The Warburg Library within German Judaism: Raymond Klibansky in His Letters to Fritz Saxl and Gertrud Bing," in Philippe Despoix and Jillian Tomm, eds, *Raymond Klibansky and the Warburg Library Network: Intellectual Peregrinations from Hamburg to London and Montreal* (Montreal and Kingston: McGill-Queen's University Press, 2018), 65ff.

14 Marcel Cachin (1869–1958), French parliamentarian who began his career as a socialist and then became, as of 1920, a Communist Party militant; directed the journal *L'Humanité* from 1918 until his death. His notebooks were published as *Carnets 1906–1947: Marcel Cachin* (Paris: Éditions du CNRS, 1993–97).

15 Charles Du Bos, *Le Dialogue avec André Gide* (Paris: Au Sans Pareil, 1929). See also Du Bos, *Approximations: Série 4* (Paris: Corrêa, 1929).

16 See Ernst Robert Curtius, *Deutsch-Französische Gespräche 1920–1950: La correspondance de Ernst Robert Curtius avec André Gide, Charles Du Bos et Valéry Larbaud*, ed. H. and J. Dieckmann (Frankfurt am Main: Vittorio Klostermann, 1980).

17 See ch. 1, note 27.

18 Alexandre Koyré (1892–1964), philosopher and historian of science. A native of Russia, he went to Germany to study with Husserl and then to France, where he defended his theses in 1922 and 1929. He held a chair at the École pratique des hautes études until 1962.

19 Étienne Gilson (1884–1978), philosopher and historian of medieval thought. See Florian Michel, *Étienne Gilson: Une biographie intellectuelle et politique* (Paris: Vrin, 2018). This letter is kept in the Klibansky file of the Academic Assistance Council archives in New Bodley.

20 Jacques Benoist Méchin (1901–1983), historian, journalist, and author of the voluminous *Histoire de l'armée allemande*, 5 vols. (Paris: Albin Michel, 1965; many reprints); indicted for collaboration with the Nazi occupation and condemned to death in 1947, then pardoned; memoir, *À l'épreuve du temps*, ed. Éric Roussel (Paris: Perrin, 2019).

Chapter Five

1 William Beveridge (1878–1963), British parliamentarian instrumental in forming the Academic Assistance Council in 1933 (renamed the Society for the Protection of Science and Learning in 1936). The original mission of the society, to help academics exiled for racial or political reasons, was expanded in 1999 and 2014 to encompass support for

academic freedom, under the new name, Council for At-Risk Academics. See William Beveridge, *A Defence of Free Learning* (New York: Oxford University Press, 1959).

2 Albert Einstein, "Science and Civilization," address given 3 October 1933, in *Out of My Later Years* (Totowa, NJ: Littlefield, Adams, 1967), 139–41.

3 Jenny de Margerie (née Fabre-Luce, 1896–1991), wife of Roland Jacquin de Margerie (1899–1990).

4 Charles Corbin (1881–1970), French diplomat, ambassador to Britain in the lead-up to the Second World War.

5 Jacques de Lacretelle (1888–1985), French writer and member of the Académie française.

6 Nikolai Berdyaev (1894–1948), philosopher, native of Russia who settled in France in 1924.

7 Née Edmée Frisch de Fels (1875–1991).

8 Henry de Montherlant (1895–1972) was a French writer who was critical of French policy as the German threat mounted after 1931. However, his public comment became increasingly marked by ambiguity, earning him the reputation of a collaborator; see Jean-Louis Garet, "Montherlant sous l'occupation," *Vingtième siècle: Revue d'histoire* 31 (1991): 65–74.

9 Political Warfare Executive, propaganda body created in 1941 and connected to the Foreign Office.

10 Bletchley Park, where Alan Turing worked, used a machine known as the Bombe to decode many lines of messages; see F.H. Hinsley and Alan Stripp, *Codebreakers: The Inside Story of Bletchley Park* (Oxford: Oxford University Press, 1993).

11 Erich Klibansky (1900–42), son of Pinkus Klibansky (see ch. 1, note 4) and first cousin of Raymond Klibansky; attended the Goethe Gymnasium in Frankfurt. After his doctoral studies, in 1929, he was appointed principal of the Jawne Gymnasium in Köln, where he helped save many Jewish students by arranging for them to leave for England. He was deported with his family on 21 July 1942 to a camp near Minsk, where they were murdered by an *Einsatzkommando* on 24 July 1942. A November 1990 exhibition in Köln, including a rich iconography, was devoted to him; see the catalogue, *Die Jawne zu Köln: Zur Geschichte der ersten jüdischen Gymnasiums im Rheinland und zum Gedächtnis an Erich Klibansky, 1900–1942* (Köln, Scriba Verlag 1990). On 28 November 1990, the city of Köln named a square in his memory. For a notable testimonial to the work of Erich Klibansky, see Ernie Meyer, "My Teacher, My Saviour," *Jerusalem Post International*, 4 June 1988, 17.

12 See, for example, Erich Klibansky, *Gerichtsszene und Prozessform in erzählenden deutschen Dichtungen des 12.–14. Jahrhunderts* (Berlin: E. Ebering, 1925; reprint, Nendeln, Liechtenstein: Kraus, 1967).

13 The White Rose was a group of students at the University of Munich who resisted Nazism. The group, including Sophie Scholl and her brother Hans as well as Alexander Schmorell and numerous students, carried on its activities by distributing pamphlets anonymously in several cities. After the arrest of the Scholls in Munich, several of the group's members were tried, convicted, and executed. See Alexandra Lloyd, ed., *The White Rose: Reading, Writing, Resistance* (Oxford: Taylor Institution Library, 2019), and Harald Steffahn, *Die Weisse Rose* (Hamburg: Rowohlt Taschenbuch, 1992).

14 Bernard Groethuysen (1880–1946), Dutch-born French writer, essayist, and author of important philosophical work; studied at the University of Munich and settled in Paris in 1904.

15 Walter Hübner (1884–1970), Anglicist; see *Die englische Dichtung in der Schule* (Leipzig: Quelle & Meyer, 1934). Hübner was a fervent adherent of Friedrich Gundolf's program as stated in *Shakespeare und der deutsche Geist* (Berlin: Bondi, 1911) and echoes the argument laid out by Ernst Krieck for the Nazification of the English dramatist in *Nationalpolitische Erziehung* (Leipzig: Armanen, 1932).

16 Kurt Von Fritz (1900–1975), German philologist and historian of Greek thought; emigrated to England in 1936, where he taught the history of science at Oxford; later taught in the United States but moved back to Germany in 1954.

17 Dietrich Bonhoeffer (1906–1945), Lutheran pastor, author of important theological and ethical works, major figure in the German resistance; arrested by the Gestapo in April 1943 and executed on 9 April 1945. See Eric Metaxas, *Bonhoeffer: Pastor, Martyr, Prophet, Spy* (London: Thomas Nelson, 2011).

18 Klaus Fuchs (1911–1988), German physicist; worked for the Manhattan Project while spying for the Soviet Union, and was convicted in 1950. See Robert Chadwell Williams, *Klaus Fuchs: Atom Spy* (Cambridge, MA: Harvard University Press, 1987).

19 Leo Szilard (1898–1964), nuclear physicist; played an important role in the discovery of nuclear fission. See William Lanouette and Bela Silard, *Genius in the Shadows: A Biography of Leo Szilard, the Man Behind the Bomb* (New York: Skyhorse Publishing, 1992). See also Leo Szilard, *The Voice of the Dolphins and Other Stories* (New York: Simon and Schuster, 1961).

20 Francis Simon (1893–1956), German physicist, exiled in England in the early 1930s on account of the racial laws; became a professor of thermodynamics at Oxford.

21 Constance Babington Smith (1912–2000), RAF officer during the war, author of *Air Spy: The Story of Photo Intelligence during World War II* (New York: Harper and Brothers, 1957).

22 The first bombardment of Peenemünde, a German base on the island of Usedom in the Baltic Sea, took place on the night of 17–18 August 1943.

23 Lise Meitner (1878–1968), Austro-Swedish nuclear physicist whose work in collaboration with her nephew Otto Frisch led to the discovery of nuclear fission. She worked closely with Otto Hahn (1879–1968), who won the Nobel Prize in chemistry. Hahn worked in Montreal with Ernest Rutherford. See Otto Hahn, *A Scientific Autobiography*, trans. Willy Ley (New York: Scribner, 1966); Lise Meitner and Dietrich Hahn, *Erinnerungen an Otto Hahn* (Stuttgart: S. Hirzel, 2005). See also Otto Frisch, "Lise Meitner, 1878–1968," *Biographical Memoirs of Fellows of the Royal Society* 16 (1970): 405–20.

24 Otto Robert Frisch (1904–1979), Austria-born British nuclear physicist; memoir, *What Little I Remember* (Cambridge: Cambridge University Press, 1979); see also Otto Frisch, ed., *Trends in Atomic Physics: Essays Dedicated to Lise Meitner, Otto Hahn, Max von Laue on the Occasion of their 80th Birthday* (New York: Interscience Publishers, 1959).

25 Mark Oliphant (1901–2000), Australian physicist, author of *The Atomic Age* (London: Allen and Unwin, 1949).

26 Richard Rhodes, *The Making of the Atomic Bomb* (New York: Simon and Schuster, 1986).

27 The Pugwash Conferences on Science and World Affairs were founded by Joseph Rotblat and Bertrand Russell following the publication of a manifesto signed by Russell and Albert Einstein calling for a conference on the dangers of nuclear weapons. The first meeting was held in Pugwash, Nova Scotia (Canada).

28 Abraham Shalom Yahuda (1877–1951), linguist specializing in the exegetical traditions of the Bible. His book *The Accuracy of the Bible* (London: Heinemann, 1934), a further meditation on the themes discussed in his previous book *The Language of the Pentateuch in Its Relation to Egyptian, with a Hieroglyphic Appendix* (London: Oxford University Press, 1933), aroused considerable controversy.

29 Philipp Lenard (1862–1947), German physicist of Hungarian heritage, 1905 Nobel laureate in physics. A professeur at Heidelberg until 1931, when he retired, he gave his support to the Nazi regime, calling the work of Einstein "Jewish physics." Mark Walker, *Nazi Science: Myth, Truth and the German Atomic Bomb* (New York: Plenum Press, 1995). His conflict with Einstein is discussed in Bruce J. Hillman, *The Man Who Stalked Einstein: How Nazi Scientist Philipp Lenard Changed the Course of History* (London: Rowman and Litlefield, 2015).

30 *The Born-Einstein Letters, 1916–1955: Friendship, Politics and Physics in Uncertain Times* (London: Palgrave Macmillan, 2004).

31 Rabbi Judah Leon Magnes (1877–1948), eminent representative of reform Judaism, first chancellor of Hebrew University of Jerusalem (1925), of which he later served as president (1935–1948); see his *Addresses by the Chancellor of the Hebrew University* (Jerusalem: n.p., 1936); Norman Bentwich, *For Zion's Sake: A Biography of Judah L. Magnes, First Chancellor and First President of the Hebrew University of Jerusalem* (Philadelphia: Jewish Publication Society of America, 1954).

32 Tullio Levi-Civita (1873–1941), Italian mathematician.

33 Jacques Hadamard (1865–1963), French mathematician, successor to Henri Poincaré in the Académie des sciences. Because of his Jewish lineage, he was forced to emigrate to the United States in 1941, moving later to England.

34 This memorandum, with other material pertaining to the founding of the Hebrew University, is in the Klibansky family's personal archive.

35 Unpublished text of this letter:

Lieber Herr Klibansky,

Ich habe Ihr so rasch ausgefertigtes Memorandum sorgfältig gelesen und bis auf einige Einzelheiten recht gut und zweckmäßig befunden.

Es wäre nun gut, wenn Sie einige unserer besten Leute aufsuchten und sie über die wahre Lage der Universität instruirten. Sagen Sie dann mir, dass Sie es auf meinen ausdrücklichen Wunsch thun.

In der Hoffnung auf künftiges gemeinsames Wirken bin ich mit herzlichen Grüßen.

Ihr,

A. Einstein

Dies ist am 7. X auf der Fahrt zum Dampfer geschrieben. Verzeihen Sie das hässliche Papier.

Dear Mr Klibansky:
I have carefully read the memorandum which you so promptly prepared and, save for a few details, I found it very good and very useful.
It would be good for you to go and visit some of our best elements to inform them of the University's real situation. Tell them you are doing so at my express request.
In the hope of future joint work, I remain yours truly, A. Einstein.
Written on 7 October [1933] en route to the steamship. Please excuse the horrible paper.

This letter, among several others from Albert Einstein, is in the family archive; together with Raymond Klibansky's letters, they are currently being prepared for publication.

36 General Bernard Montgomery (1887–1976), senior British army officer, military hero of the two world wars; see his *Memoirs of Field Marshal Montgomery* (Cleveland: World Publishing Company, 1958).

37 John Simon Gabriel Simmons (1915–2005), scholar of Slavonics, librarian at Birmingham and Oxford.

38 Werner Heisenberg (1901–1976), German physicist, renowned for his work on quantum physics; winner of the Nobel Prize in 1932; autobiography, *Physics and Beyond: Encounters and Conversations*, trans. A.J. Pomerans (New York: Harper and Row, 1971).

39 In Operation Epsilon, an Allied program to determine how far Germany had progressed on building an atomic bomb, ten German scientists, among them Werner Heisenberg, Otto Hahn, and Kurt Diebner, were detained in a bugged house in England from July 1945 to January 1946. Their conversations were transcribed and published as Charles Frank, *Operation Epsilon: The Farm Hall Transcripts* (Berkeley: University of California Press, 1993).

40 Albert Speer (1905–1981), *Inside the Third Reich* (New York: Avon, 1970).

41 Hendrik Anthony Kramers (1894–1952), Dutch physicist, collaborator of Niels Bohr; biography, Max Dresden, *H.A. Kramers: Between Tradition and Revolution* (Berlin: Springer, 1987).

42 Niels Bohr (1885–1962), Danish nuclear physicist, Nobel laureate in 1922, forced into exile in Sweden in 1943 by the Nazi regime. He went on to Britain, making several trips from there to the United States during the war.

43 Richard Crossman (1907–1974), British parliamentarian, member of the Political Warfare Executive. See Richard Crossman and Daniel Lerner, *Psychological Warfare against Nazi Germany: The Sykewar Campaign, D-Day to V*-Day (Cambridge, MA: MIT Press, 1971); Victoria Honeyman, *Richard Crossman: A Reforming Radical of the Labour Party* (London: I.B. Tauris, 2006).

44 Denis Sefton Delmer (1904–1979), British journalist of Australian heritage, born in Germany. As of 1940 he worked for the Political Warfare Executive, where he was responsible for the black propaganda campaign against Germany. Memoir, *An Autobiography*, 2 vols. (London: Secker & Warburg, 1961–62).

45 Benedetto Croce (1866–1952), Italian philosopher; selected essays published as *My Philosophy, and Other Essays on the Moral and Political Problems of Our Time*, ed. Raymond Klibansky, trans. E.F. Carritt (London: Allen and Unwin, 1949).

46 Giovanni Gentile, "The Transcending of Time in History," in Raymond Klibansky and H.J. Paton, eds, *Philosophy and History: Essays Presented to Ernst Cassirer* (New York: Oxford University Press, 1936), 91–105.

47 Richard William Hunt (1908–1979), paleographer and medieval historian; worked closely with Klibansky on editing the *Medieval and Renaissance Studies* collection, published under the auspices of the Warburg Institute, with nine volumes and three supplements appearing between 1941 and 1968.

48 Benito Mussolini, *Memoirs 1942–1943, with Documents Relating to the Period*, ed. Raymond Klibansky (London: Weidenfeld and Nicholson, 1949).

49 Francesco Maugeri (1898–1978), Italian admiral, head of the naval intelligence service during the war; memoir, *From the Ashes of Disgrace* (New York: Reynal and Hitchcock, 1948).

50 Maurice Dejean (1899–1982), French diplomat, close to General de Gaulle in London; represented France at the Inter-Allied Conferences.

Chapter Six

1 This major research and publishing program was launched at the Warburg Library; see Raymond Klibansky, *The Continuity of the Platonic Tradition during the Middle Ages: Outlines of a* Corpus Platonicum Medii Aevi (London: Warburg Library, 1939; reprinted with a new preface and additional material, München: Kraus International Publications, 1982). See also Georges Leroux, "Raymond Klibansky and the *Corpus Platonicum Medii Aevi*: A Discussion of the Plato Latinus Series," in Philippe Despoix and Jillian Tomm, eds, *Raymond Klibansky and the Warburg Library Network: Intellectual Peregrinations from Hamburg to London and Montreal* (Montreal and Kingston: McGill-Queen's University Press, 2018), 260–81.

2 For the history of *Saturn and Melancholy*, see Philippe Despoix, "The Long and Complex History of a Warburgian Project," afterword to Raymond Klibansky, Erwin Panofsky, and Fritz Saxl, *Saturn and Melancholy: Studies in the History of Natural Philosophy, Religion, and Art*, ed. Philippe Despoix and Georges Leroux (Montreal and Kingston: McGill-Queen's University Press, (1964) 2019), 449–65.

3 Ludwig Binswanger (1881–1966), Swiss psychiatrist, close friend of Freud; produced a considerable oeuvre in the fields of existential psychoanalysis and anthropology. In 1923 he treated Aby Warburg at his sanatorium in Kreuzlingen. See Ludwig Binswanger, *Die unendliche Heilung: Aby Warburgs Krankengeschichte*, ed. Davide Stimilli (Vienna and Paris: Diaphanes, 2007), and its French translation, *La guérison infinie: histoire clinique d'Aby Warburg*, trans. Maël Renouard and Martin Rueff (Paris: Rivages, 2011). In addition to Warburg's letters and autobiographical fragments, the book contains notes on his stay at Kreuzlingen by Fritz Saxl.

4 Fritz Saxl, *Verzeichnis astrologischer und mythologischer illustrierter Handschriften des lateinischen Mittelalters*, vol. 1 (Heidelberg: C. Winter, 1915); vol. 2 (Heidelberg: C. Winter, 1927); vol. 3, *Manuscripts in English Libraries*, ed. Hans Meier and Harry Bober (London: Warburg Institute, 1953); vol. 4, Patrick McGurk, *Astrological Manuscripts in Italian Libraries (Other than Rome)* (London: Warburg Institute, 1966).

5 Erwin Panofsky, *The Life and Art of Albrecht Dürer*, rev. ed. (Princeton: Princeton University Press, [1943] 2005).

6 Horace, *Ars Poetica*, 60–2: *Ut sylvæ foliis pronos mutantur in annos, / Prima cadunt: ita verborum vetus interit ætas, / Et juvenum ritu florent modo nata, vigentque.*

7 See Georges Leroux, "Addendum: On the Text History of [Ps-] Aristotle, *Problem XXX, 1*," in Klibansky, Panofsky, and Saxl, *Saturn and Melancholy*, 443–7.

8 Hildegard of Bingen, *Liber divinorum operum*, translated by Nathaniel M. Campbell as *The Book of Divine Works* (Washington, DC: Catholic University of America Press, [1163–73/74] 2018); see also *Causæ et curæ*, translated by Priscilla Throop as *Causes and Cures: The Complete English Translation of Hildegardis* Causæ et Curæ Libri *VI* (Charlotte, VT: MedievalMS, 2006).

9 Giovanni Boccaccio, "Trattatello in laude di Dante," ed. P.G. Ricci, in *Tutte le opere di Giovanni Boccaccio*, ed. V. Branca, vol. 3 (Milano: A. Mondadori, 1974), para. 68–79.

10 Arnau de Vilanova (1240–1311), *Opera medica omnia*, 16 vols. (Barcelona: Edicions de la Universitat de Barcelona, 1975–2014); see in particular vol. 3, *De amore heroico*.

11 Marsilio Ficino (1433–1499), *De vita libri tres*; English version, *Three Books on Life*, trans. Carol V. Kaske and John R. Clarke (Tempe, AZ: Renaissance Society of America, (1489) 2002).

12 Giovanni Manardo (1462–1536), *Epistolarum medicinalium libri XX* (Lugduni: Ex officina Godefridi & Marcelli Beringorum fratrum, 1549). There is no modern edition of this text.

13 Pico della Mirandola (1463–1494), *Oration on the Dignity of Man: A New Translation and Commentary*, ed. Francesco Borghesi, Michael Papio, and Massimo Riva (Cambridge: Cambridge University Press, 2012).

14 Robert Burton (1577–1640), *The Anatomy of Melancholy: What It Is, with All the Kinds, Causes, Symptomes, Prognostics, and Several Cures of It* (Oxford: Thorntons, [1651] 1997). The first edition is dated 1621 and it went through five subsequent editions, incorporating substantial modifications. New edition, *The Anatomy of Melancholy*, ed. Angus Gowland (London: Penguin Classics, 2021).

15 Joseph Addison (1672–1719), English essayist; see *Cato: A Tragedy, and Selected Essays*, ed. Christine Dunn Henderson and Mark E. Yellin (Indianapolis: Liberty Fund, 2004).

16 Richard Steele (1672–1729), Irish essayist, close friend and collaborator of Joseph Addison, with whom he founded the magazine *The Spectator*.

17 Immanuel Kant (1724–1809), "Observations on the Feeling of the Beautiful and Sublime," trans. Paul Guyer, in *Observations on the Feeling of the Beautiful and Sublime and Other Writings*, ed. Patrick Frierson (New York: Cambridge University Press, 2011), 28.

18 Giacomo Leopardi, *I Canti: con una scelta da le Operette morali, i Pensieri, gli Appunti, lo Zibaldone*, 16th ed. (Milan: Edizioni scolastiche Mondadori, 1966).

19 Søren Kierkegaard, *Kierkegaard's Writings IV: Either/Or Part II*, ed. and trans. Howard V. Hong and Edna H. Hong (Princeton: Princeton University Press, 2013), 189.

20 Carlo Michelstaedter (1887–1910) is best remembered for his doctoral thesis, published in 1913 after his death: *Persuasion and Rhetoric*, trans. with an introduction and commentary by Russell Scott Valentino, Cinzia Sarti Blum, and David J. Depew (New Haven: Yale University Press, 2004); for this citation, see "La melanconia," 75–6, in *La melodia del giovane divino: Pensieri, racconti, critiche*, ed. S. Campailla (Milano: Adelphi, 2010), 75–82, with comments in *Carlo Michaelstaedter: Kunst, Poesie, Philosophie*, ed. Yvonne Hütter (Tübingen: Narr Verlag, 2014), 51.

Chapter Seven

1 Nicolas Nabokov (1903–1978), musician of Russian heritage, cousin of the writer Vladimir Nabokov. In 1928 he wrote a ballet titled *Ode* for Serge Diaghilev's Ballets Russes company, and in 1945 he worked for the United States Strategic Bombing Survey; biography, Vincent Giroux, *Nicolas Nabokov: A Life in Freedom and Music* (Oxford: Oxford University Press, 2015).

2 Wilhelm Furtwängler (1886–1954), German conductor; biographies, Fred K. Prieberg, *Trial of Strength: Wilhelm Furtwängler in the Third Reich* (Boston: Northeastern University Press, 1994) and Sam H. Shirakawa, *The Devil's Music Master: The Controversial Life and Career of Wilhelm Furtwängler* (Oxford: Oxford University Press, 1992).

3 Friedrich von Bodelschwingh (1877–1946), theologian and son of the founder of the Bethel asylum for epileptics; opponent of the Nazi euthanasia program.

4 Cassirer acknowledges Wolff alongside Ernst Hoffmann in the preface to *Philosophy of Symbolic Forms*, trans. Ralph Manheim, vol. 1, *Language* (London: Routledge, 2021), lxxxiii.

5 Irma Grese (1923–1945), guard at several concentration camps, nicknamed the "Hyena of Auschwitz"; executed 13 December 1945 at the Hamelin prison.

6 Paul-Heinz Koesters, *Deutschland deine Denker: Geschichten von Philosophen und Ideen, die unsere Welt bewegen* (Hamburg: Gruner und Jahr, 1980).

7 Vittorio Ambrosio (1879–1956), Italian general active during the war; took part in the surrender negotiations with the Allies.

8 Stephen Gaselee (1882–1943), British diplomat, librarian at Cambridge and the Foreign Office, renowned bibliophile.

9 Sir Llewellyn Woodward (1890–1971), British historian; memoir, *Short Journey* (London: Faber and Faber, 1942).

10 The Conférences Albert-le-Grand were held annually at the Institut d'études médiévales of the Université de Montréal. The proceedings were published by the Institut d'études médiévales, and some volumes were also published in Paris by Librairie philosophique J. Vrin. Publishing rights to portions of this collection were acquired by the Pontifical Institute of Medieval Studies in Toronto, and the books were distributed by Brepols. Raymond Klibansky gave the fall 1957 address, but the text was not published.

11 The Thomas More Institute for Adult Education was founded in 1945 and is still active today. Father Eric O'Connor (1907–1980) was a Jesuit who taught mathematics at Loyola College from 1941 to 1974 and a co-founder of the institute, with Charlotte Tansey and others. The institute offers a liberal arts education to adults wanting to pursue university studies.

12 Daniel Oduber Quirós (1921–1991), Costa Rican statesman, philosopher, and writer; studied philosophy at McGill from 1945 to 1948, pursuing his studies in France. President of Costa Rica, 1974–78.

13 Robert Lee Vesco was an American financier who, in the early 1970s, gave a large sum of money to a company started by then president of Costa Rica José Figueres, reportedly in exchange for passage of a law protecting him from extradition.

14 Herbert Marcuse (1898–1979), celebrated American philosopher of German heritage.

15 Monseigneur Joseph Charbonneau (1892–1959), archbishop of Montreal from 1940 to 1950. His support for the Asbestos miners' strike earned him the hostility of Premier Maurice Duplessis. Despite the support of the intellectual elite, he was forced to resign by virtue of holding social views deemed too favourable to the labour movement.

16 Hubert Aquin (1929–1977), Quebec writer.

17 Noël Mailloux (1909–1997), Dominican father, psychologist, professor of psychology and psychoanalysis at the Université de Montréal.

18 Camille Bérubé (1909–2007), Capuchin monk and historian of medieval philosophy, in particular the work of Duns Scotus; professor at the Institut d'études médiévales from 1947 to 1967.

19 Henri-Irénée Marrou (1904–1977), French historian, patristician, specialist in early Christian thought, and visiting professor at the Institut d'études médiévales for many years; biography, Pierre Riché, *Henri-Irénée Marrou, historien engagé* (Paris: Éditions du Cerf, 2003).

20 Paul Vignaux (1904–1987), French philosopher, specialist in medieval thought, militant trade unionist, visiting professor at the Institut d'études médiévales. During the Second World War he fled to the United States, where he was active in supporting refugees. On this period and on his time in Canada, see Laurent Jeanpierre, "Paul Vignaux, inspirateur de la 'Deuxième gauche': récits d'un exil français aux États-Unis pendant la Seconde Guerre mondiale," *Matériaux pour l'histoire de notre temps*, no. 60 (September–December 2000): 48–56.

21 Mario Bunge (1919–2020), Canadian philosopher of Argentine heritage, author of major works in the philosophy of science; professor at McGill University starting in 1966, and close friend of Raymond Klibansky; memoir, *Between Two Worlds: Memoirs of a Philosopher-Scientist* (New York: Springer, 2016).

22 Harry McFarland Bracken (1926–2011), American philosopher, Berkeley and Descartes specialist, professor at McGill University from 1966 to 1991.

23 Leszek Kołakowski (1927–2009), Polish philosopher and historian of ideas, critic of Marxism and the communist regime; left Poland in 1968 and came to McGill as a visiting professor, going on to Oxford (All Souls College), where he spent the rest of his career. "*Fabula mundi* and Cleopatra's Nose," ch. 22 of *Modernity on Endless Trial*,

trans. Stefan Czerniawski, Wolfgang Freis, and Agnieszka Kolakowska (Chicago: University of Chicago Press, 1990).

24 Raymond Klibansky, "The Philosophical Character of History," in *Philosophy and History: Essays Presented to Ernst Cassirer*, ed. R. Klibansky and H.J. Paton (Oxford: Clarendon Press, 1936), 323–7; 2nd edition with new bibliography, New York: Harper and Row, 1963. On the history of this text, first presented in German as an inaugural lecture on 9 July 1932 for the status of *Privatdozent*, see my note to the French translation, "Le caractère philosophique de l'histoire," in Raymond Klibansky, *Tradition antique et tolérance moderne*, ed. Philippe Despoix and Georges Leroux (Montreal: Presses de l'Université de Montréal, 2016), 47–67.

25 See "Méthode et philosophie de l'histoire," special issue of *Revue internationale de philosophie*, no. 111–12 (1975), with contributions by Antonio d'Andrea, Nathan Rotenstreich, Leszek Kołakowski, and Raimon Panikkar, among others, and a bibliography of Klibansky's writings prepared by Michael J. Whalley and Désirée Park, pp. 167–74.

26 See Raymond Klibansky and Ernest C. Mossner, eds, *New Letters of David Hume* (Oxford: Oxford University Press, 1954; reprint, New York: Garland, 1983).

27 See Raymond Klibansky, "Hidden Treasures at McGill: A Survey of Manuscripts and Historical Documents," in *Fontanus: From the Collections of McGill University* 2 (1989): 65–96.

28 Countess de Boufflers (1725–1800); biography, P.E. Schazmann, *La Comtesse de Boufflers* (Paris: Fernand Roche, 1933).

29 The countess had met Horace Walpole (1717–1797) on a trip to London in 1763. Klibansky quotes here a letter to Thomas Gray dated 25 January 1766; see *Lettres d'Horace Walpole écrites à ses amis durant ses voyages en France (1739–1775)*, trans. Comte de Baillon, 2nd ed. (Paris: Librairie Académique Didier, 1875), 125; *The Letters of Horace Walpole, Earl of Orford: Including Numerous Letters First Published from the Original Manuscripts*, vol. 3, *1759–1769* (Philadelphia: Lea and Blanchard, 1842), 461.

30 Hume to Countess de Boufflers, 20 August 1776, *The Letters of David Hume*, ed. J.Y.T. Greig, vol. 2 (Oxford: Clarendon Press, 1969), 335.

31 See Klibansky, "Hidden Treasures."

32 Marcus Tullii Ciceronis, *Opera cum delectu commentariorum*, ed. Pierre Joseph Thoulier Olivet (1682–1768), 9 vols. (Paris: 1741–42, bearing the *ex libris* of David Hume).

33 David Fate Norton (1937–2014), eminent Hume specialist, professor at McGill University until his retirement in 1997; major works include *The Cambridge Companion to Hume* (Cambridge: Cambridge University Press, 1993) and *The David Hume Library* (Edinburgh: Edinburgh Bibliographical Society in association with the National Library of Scotland, 1996).

34 In 1992 Heidelberg University officially restored all honours and privileges to the professors who had been excluded by the Nazi regime. Raymond Klibansky went to Heidelberg on this occasion, where he was named an honorary senator.

Chapter Eight

1 This research program was first presented at the Warburg Institute and was reprinted in Raymond Klibansky, *The Continuity of the Platonic Tradition during the Middle Ages*, ix–xxxi, a new edition of which appeared in 1981. The edition of the Corpus Platonicum was the subject of regular reports by Klibansky, as well as scholarly accounts in scientific journals between 1940 and 1965, among others by Paul-Oskar Kristeller, who had also studied under Ernst Hoffmann. See Georges Leroux, "Raymond Klibansky and the *Corpus Platonicum Medii Aevi*: A Discussion of the Plato Latinus Series," in Philippe Despoix and Jillian Tomm, eds, *Raymond Klibansky and the Warburg Library Network: Intellectual Peregrinations from Hamburg to London and Montreal* (Montreal and Kingston: McGill-Queen's University Press, 2018), 260–81.

2 See Klibansky, *Ein Proklos-Fund*. The thesis was accepted 19 February 1929. For a general overview of Proclus's influence on Cusanus, see Hans G. Senger's helpful introduction to Nicolaus Cusanus, *Cusanus-Texte. III, Marginalien. 2, Proclus latinus: Die Exzerpte und Randnoten des Nikolaus von Kues zu den lateinischen Übersetzungen der Proclus-Schriften, 2.1, Theologia Platonis, Elementatio theologica*, ed. Hans G. Senger (Heidelberg: Winter, 1986); *Expositio in Parmenidem Platonis*, ed. Karl Bormann (Heidelberg: Winter, 1986), 1:5–41. Tim. 37b–38d; Proclus, *Commentaire sur le "Parménide" de Platon*, ed. Carlos Steel, trans. Guillaume de Moerbeke, 2 vols. (Leuven: "Ancient and Medieval Philosophy, De Wulf-Mansion Centre," vol. 1, bks. III–IV, 1982–85). The Greek text and the French translation have now been completed: *Commentaire sur le "Parménide" de Platon*, ed. Concetta Luna and Alain-Philippe Segonds (Paris: Les Belles Lettres, 7 vols., 2007–21). See also the Greek text of books I to III: *Procli in Platonis Parmenidem commentaria. T. 1: Libros I–III continens*, ed. Carlos Steel, Caroline Macé, and Pieter d'Hoine (Oxford: Clarendon Press, 2007). In the general introduction to their edition (pp. viii, cdlx), Luna and Segonds pay tribute to Klibansky's work.

3 Proclus, *Proclus' Commentary on Plato's "Parmenides,"* trans. Glenn R. Morrow and John M. Dillon (Princeton: Princeton University Press, 1992).

4 Giordano Bruno (1548–1600), Italian philosopher and Dominican friar, accused of heresy by the Inquisition and, after a multi-year trial, burned at the stake on the Campo de' Fiori on 17 February 1600. On a personal note, I wish to emphasize that on the 400th anniversary of Bruno's death, Klibansky held an informal gathering at his home to commemorate the man whom he considered a martyr to intolerance and a model of freedom of thought. He read aloud a passage from Bruno's *The Ash Wednesday Supper* on that occasion and often cited *Giordano Bruno and the Hermetic Tradition* (Chicago: University of Chicago Press, 1964) by Frances Yates, whose work he held in high esteem.

5 The edition of Chalcidius's commentary on the *Timaeus* in the Plato Latinus series was edited by H.J. Waszink and published in 1975. Its English translation appeared as *On Plato's "Timaeus,"* ed. and trans. John Magee (Cambridge, MA: Harvard University Press, 2016).

6 Klibansky had presented an annotated anthology of texts by members of the School of Chartres, Thierry and Bernard, for his *Habilitation*. This work was never published and is found in the Klibansky archives in Marbach. See also his study published subsequently, "The School of Chartres," in *Twelfth-Century Europe and the Foundations of Modern Society*, ed. M. Clagett, G. Post, and R. Reynolds (Madison: University of Wisconsin Press, 1966), 3–14.

7 See Raymond Klibansky, "Standing on the Shoulders of Giants," *Isis* 26 (1936): 147–9. The attribution of this phrase to Bernard de Chartres is due to Jean de Salisbury (*Metalogicon*, III, 217r).

8 Newton to Robert Hooke, 5 February 1676, in *The Correspondence of Isaac Newton: 1661–1675*, vol. 1 (London: Published for the Royal Society at the University Press, 1959), 416.

9 Charles de Bovelles, *De Intellectu* (Paris: Henri Estienne, 1511; this edition contains several treatises by Charles de Bovelles). On this text, of which there is no modern edition, see Emmanuel Faye, "Les premières pensées métaphysiques de Bovelles, en 1504, annonciatrices du *Livre du Sage*," *Revue de métaphysique et de morale* 78 (2013): 146–65.

10 Klibansky and Regen, *Die Handschriften*.

11 See Raymond Klibansky, "La découverte d'un texte platonicien inconnu de l'antiquité classique," in *Reflections on the Humanities*, ed. Louise Marcil and Shirley Neuman (Ottawa: Canadian Federation for the Humanities, 1993), 41–52; reprinted in Raymond Klibansky, *Tradition antique et tolérance moderne*, ed. Philippe Despoix and Georges Leroux (Montreal: Presses de l'Université de Montréal, 2016), 85–99. On Klibansky's death, his widow, Ethel Groffier, sent me the file compiled on this text. I presented the state of his research to my colleagues in the Budé collection (Paris, Les Belles Lettres), who agreed to include it in their publishing program for the Latin series. Meanwhile, without contacting us or citing Klibansky's published work on this manuscript, Justin A. Stover, a young British scholar specializing in lexical computing, published the text: Apuleius, *A New Work by Apuleius: The Lost Third Book of the De Platone*, ed. and trans. Justin A. Stover (Oxford: Oxford University Press, 2016). See my note on this subject in "Raymond Klibansky and the *Corpus Platonicum Medii Aevi*," in Despoix and Tomm, *Raymond Klibansky and the Warburg Library Network*, 280–1.

12 Klibansky, "Regagner Athènes."

13 Plato, *Timaeus*, trans. Benjamin Jowett (New York: Liberal Arts Press, 1949), 90 ff.

Chapter Nine

1 See Martin Luther (1483–1546), "On Secular Authority" (*Von Weltlicher Obrigkeit*, 1523), in *Selections from His Writings*, ed. John Dillenberger (New York: Anchor Books, 1958), 367 ff, the treatise in which he presented his doctrine of the two kingdoms.

2 G.W.F. Hegel, "Introduction to the Philosophy of History," in *The Philosophy of World History*, ed. and trans. John Sibree (New York: Dover, 1956).

3 Kuno Fischer (1824–1907), philosopher and historian of philosophy; taught in the philosophy department at Heidelberg.

4 Voltaire, *Treatise on Tolerance*, ed. Simon Harvey, trans. Simon Harvey and Brian Masters (Cambridge: Cambridge University Press, [1763] 2000). The aim of this text was to rehabilitate the Protestant Jean Calas, accused of and executed for a crime he had not committed. Voltaire presents an epochal plea for tolerance.

5 Spinoza, *Spinoza on Freedom of Thought: Selections from* Tractatus theologico-politicus *and* Tractatus politicus, ed. T.E. Jessop (Montreal: Casalini, 1962). This series was published under the patronage of the International Institute of Philosophy. See John Locke, *Epistola de tolerantia: A Letter on Toleration*, ed. Raymond Klibansky, trans. J.W. Gough (Oxford: Clarendon Press, 1968). The list of all the texts published in this series is available on the International Institute of Philosophy website at https://www.i-i-p.org/publications.

6 Asoka (–238 BCE), Indian emperor of the Maurya dynasty, author of the Edicts of Asoka and disseminator of the Buddhist ideals of peace; see *The Edicts of Asoka*, ed. and trans. N.A. Nikam and R.P. McKeon (Chicago: University of Chicago Press, 1959).

7 Raymond Klibansky, "Le Trésor de Kandahar," *Revue de la société suisse des bibliophiles/Zeitschrift der schweizerische Bibliophilen Gesellschaft* 1 (2002): 38–40; reprinted in Raymond Klibansky, *Tradition antique et tolérance moderne*, ed. Philippe Despoix and Georges Leroux (Montreal: Presses de l'Université de Montréal, 2016), 279–82.

8 Cicero, *Ad familiares*, bk. 4, letter 6; see also Cicero, *Tusculan Disputations*, 3.1.2–3, trans. J.E. King (Cambridge, MA: Harvard University Press, 1966).

9 [Louis de Jaucourt], "Tolérer," in Denis Diderot and d'Alembert, *Encyclopédie* (1751). Diderot et d'Alembert, article "Tolérer," *Encyclopédie* (1751).

10 Comte de Mirabeau (1749–1791), "Suite de la discussion du projet relatif à la Déclaration des droits, lors de la séance du 22 août 1789," *Archives parlementaires de 1787 à 1860*, 1st ser. (1787–99), vol. 8, *Du 5 mai 1789 au 15 septembre 1789* (Paris: Librairie Administrative P. Dupont, 1875), 472–3.

11 Thomas Paine (1737–1809), *Rights of Man, Being an Answer to Mr Burke's Attack on the French Revolution* (New York: G.P. Putnam, [1791] 1895), 74.

12 Thomas Aquinas (1225–1274), *Summa Theologica*, II.2, question 11, article 3.

13 See, for all the relevant texts, P.R.L. Brown, "St Augustine's Attitude to Religious Coercion," *Journal of Roman Studies* 54 (1964): 107–16.

14 *Luke* 14: 16–24.

15 Henri Corbin (1903–1978), philosopher specializing in Islamic philosophy and theology, professor at the École pratique des hautes études in Paris.

16 See Raymond Klibansky, preface to his edition of John Locke, *Lettre sur la tolérance*, ix–xxxi; English edition, with translation by J.W. Gough, Oxford: Clarendon Press, 1968.

17 William Popple (1638–1708), friend of John Locke and first translator of the *Epistola de Tolerantia* (1689).

18 See John Milton (1608–1674), English poet and political thinker, *A Treatise of Civil Power in Ecclesiastical Causes*, 1659, in *Complete Prose Works of John Milton*, ed. Don Wolfe, vol. 7 (New Haven: Yale University Press, 1974).

19 Roger Williams (1603–1683), theologian and Protestant clergyman, defender of freedom of conscience and rights, author of *The Bloudy Tenent of Persecution, for Cause of Conscience, Discussed, in A Conference betweene Truth and Peace* (1644); see James

Calvin Davis, ed., *On Religious Liberty: Selections from the Works of Roger Williams* (Cambridge, MA: Harvard University Press, 2008).

20 Arminianism, a branch of Protestantism named after Dutch reformed theologian Jacobus Arminius (1560–1609). His ideas embraced the teachings of Bishop Simon Episcopius (1583–1643), Dutch theologian, Remonstrant, and author of the Remonstrant Confession (1621), published after the Synod of Dort.

21 Pierre Bayle (1647–1706), French philosopher and lexicographer, author of *Dictionnaire historique et critique* (1697), which was partially translated into English as *An Historical and Critical Dictionary, Selected and Abridged, with a Life of Pierre Bayle*, 4 vols. (London: Hunt and Clarke, 1826). For a modern biography, see Élisabeth Labrousse (1914–2000), *Bayle*, trans. Denys Potts (Oxford: Oxford University Press, 1983).

22 Michel Paradis, "Les fondements de la tolérance universelle chez Bayle: la séparation de l'Église et de l'État," in Ethel Groffier and Michel Paradis, eds, *The Notion of Tolerance and Human Rights: Essays in Honour of Raymond Klibansky* (Ottawa: Carleton University Press, 1991), 25–35.

23 Pierre Bayle, *A Philosophical Commentary on These Words of the Gospel, Luke 14:23, "Compel Them to Come In, That My House May Be Full": A Modern Translation and Critical Interpretation*, trans. Amie Godman Tannenbaum (New York: Peter Lang, 1987). This translation omits part 3 and the supplement.

24 Benjamin Furly (1636–1714), English Quaker merchant, friend of John Locke in Rotterdam and of his pupil Anthony Ashley Cooper, 3rd Earl of Shaftesbury.

25 Sebastian Castellio (1515–1563), French theologian and preacher, advocate of freedom of conscience; works include *Advice to a Desolate France*, ed. Marius F. Valkhoff, trans. Wouter Valkhoff (Shepherdstown, WV: Patmos Press, 1975), and *Concerning Heretics: Whether They Are to Be Persecuted*, ed. and trans. R. Bainton (New York: Columbia University Press, [1554] 1935). See also Stefan Zweig, *The Right to Heresy: Castellio against Calvin* (New York: Viking Press, 1936).

26 Irena Krońska (1915–1974), Polish philologist and philosopher; her correspondence with the philosopher Jan Patočka is discussed in Wojciech Starzyński, "The correspondence of Irena Krońska with Jan Patočka as an important evidence of the Czech-Polish 'family' philosophical life," *Filozofia* 68 (2013): 71–80.

27 Anthony Collins (1676–1729), English philosopher, author of *A Discourse of Freethinking, Occasioned by the Rise and Growth of a Sect Called Freethinkers* (1713), and *Discourse of the Grounds and Reasons of the Christian Religion, in Two Parts, to Which Is Affixed an Apology for Free Debate and Liberty of Writing* (1724).

28 Nicolaus Cusanus, *De pace fidei*; see the bibliography for the edition produced by Klibansky.

29 On this group of letters and, in general, the Christian reaction to the fall of Constantinople, see Marios Philippides and Walter K. Hanak, *The Siege and the Fall of Constantinople in 1453: Historiography, Topography, and Military Studies* (London: Routledge, 2020), 10–46. See also, more specifically on the *Türkenbriefe*, published in 1598–1600 by Nicolaus Reusner (1545–1602), and possibly the first printed text, Walther Ludwig, "Türkisches und persisches Latein? Sultan Murad III. und Schah Mohammed

Khodabanda als Autoren in Reusners *Epistolae Turcicae*," in *Studien zu Geschichte, Theologie und Wissenschaftsgeschichte*, ed. Akademie der Wissenschaften zu Göttingen (Berlin: de Gruyter, 2012), 8. The origin of the collection could well be Sebastian Brant (1458–1521, 1498 citation), author of the *Ship of Fools* (1494). Several letters written by Western diplomats in the Ottoman Empire, most notably Ogier Ghiselin de Busbecq (1522–1592) and Lady Mary Wortley Montagu (1689–1762), were added.

30 Juan de Segovia (1395–1458), Castilian ecclesiastic and theologian, present at the Council of Florence (Basel); corresponded with Cusanus and advocated peaceful dialogue with the Muslims. He commissioned a Spanish translation of the Koran, which he then translated into Latin. Klibansky's edition of Cusanus, published as *De pace fidei: cum epistula ad Ioannem de Segobia*, ediderunt, commentariisque illustraverunt Raymundus Klibansky et Hildebrandus Bascour, O.S.B. (Hamburg: in Aedibus Felicis Meiner, 1959), contains a translation of Cusanus's letter to Juan de Segovia (93 ff). See also Anne Marie Wolf, *Juan de Segovia and the Fight for Peace: Christians and Muslims in the Fifteenth Century* (Notre Dame, IN: University of Notre Dame Press, 2014).

31 Pico della Mirandola (1463–1494), *Oration on the Dignity of Man: A New Translation and Commentary*, ed. Francesco Borghesi, Michael Papio, and Massimo Riva (Cambridge: Cambridge University Press, 2012).

32 Gotthold Ephraim Lessing (1729–1781), philosopher, writer, and art critic. His play *Nathan the Wise*, published in 1779, was not performed during his lifetime but met with great success after his death. It contains the Parable of the Ring, narrated by the protagonist Nathan, who is said to be modeled on Lessing's friend the philosopher Moses Mendelsohn. *Nathan the Wise: A Drama in Five Acts, in Modern American Prose*, ed. M.J. Levy, trans. C.G. Trump (New York: McGraw-Hill, 1996). Morgan's translation was subsequently collected in *Nathan the Wise, Minna von Barnhelm, and Other Plays and Writings*, ed. Peter Demetz, foreword by Hannah Arendt (New York: Continuum, 1991).

33 See Boccaccio, *Decameron*, I, 3; Pamela D. Stewart, "A Note on Boccaccio, Lessing and the Parable of the Three Rings," in Groffier and Paradis, eds, *The Notion of Tolerance*, 37–45.

34 Paul Raabe (1927–2013), German historian of literature, librarian at Wolfenbüttel (1968–1992); wrote extensively on the Herzog August Library. See *Paul Raabe zum 80. Geburtstag. Ein Lebenswerk in Büchern. Katalog zur Ausstellung 22.2. bis 14.4.2007 in der Landesbibliothek Oldenburg* (Oldenburg: Isensee, 2007).

35 Sabine Solf, research librarian at Wolfenbüttel; see Georg Ruppelt and Sabine Solf, eds, *Lexikon zur Geschichte und Gegenwart der Herzog August Bibliothek Wolfenbüttel* (Wiesbaden: Harrassowitz, 1992).

Chapter Ten

1 For more information, including statutes, list of current members, and future activities, see https://www.i-i-p.org/EN/history.

2 The *Bibliography of Philosophy* has been published by the IIP since 1937 and became analytical in 1954. The last printed volume, containing abstracts for the year 2005, was published in 2010. Since then, the activities of the *Bibliography* have been on hold.

3 For Klibansky's publications in this field, see the bibliography appended to the present book. His interest in the mission and history of the institute is well documented; see Raymond Klibansky with Ethel Groffier, *Idées sans frontières: histoire et structures de l'Institut international de philosophie* (Paris: Les Belles Lettres, 2005).

4 A full list of past meetings of the International Institute of Philosophy, from 1938 to 2011, with reference to the proceedings, is available on the website. For the last published proceedings, see Ilkka Niiniluoto and Sami Pihlström, eds, *Normativity: The 2019 Entretiens of the International Institute of Philosophy* (Helsinki: Societas Philosophica Fennica, 2020), 96. The 2020 meeting was postponed because of the COVID-19 pandemic, as was the last one, originally scheduled to take place in Krakow, Poland, in November 2021 on the theme of scientific knowledge.

5 Jayachamarajendra Wadiyar Bahadur, Maharaja of Mysore, *Dattatreya: The Way and the Goal* (London: Allen and Unwin, 1957).

6 Alexander Zinoviev (1922–2006), Russian writer and philosopher, specialist of logic, vocal critic of the Soviet regime; see his *Yawning Heights*, trans. Gordon Clough (London: Bodley Head, 1978).

7 Raymond Klibansky, commemoration speech given at the IIP meetings in Stockholm, 29 August–2 September 1987, under the theme "Descartes and Contemporary Philosophy of Mind"; for partial proceedings, see *Synthese* (Dordrecht: Kluwer Academic Publishers) 106, no. 1 (1996).

8 Raimon Panikkar (1918–2010), Spanish Catholic priest, author of numerous works on religion (mainly Hinduism and Buddhism) and interfaith dialogue, including *Myths, Faith, and Hermeneutics: Cross-Cultural Studies* (New York: Paulist Press, 1979); *The Silence of God: The Answer of the Buddha*, trans. Robert R. Parr (Maryknoll, NY: Orbitz Books, 1989); *The Unknown Christ of Hinduism: Towards an Ecumenical Christophany* (Maryknoll, NY: Orbitz Books, 1981); and *The Intrareligious Dialogue* (New York: Paulist Press, 1999). On his thought, see Peter C. Phan and Young-chan Ro, eds, *Raimon Panikkar: A Companion to His Life and Thought* (New York: Paulist Press, 2018).

9 Enrico Castelli Gattinara di Zubiena (1900–1977), Italian philosopher, professor at the University of Rome, founder of the journal *Archivio di Filosofia*; organized a series of philosophical conferences in Rome on themes pertaining to religion and dialogue.

10 Martin Buber (1878–1965), Jewish philosopher and religious thinker, born in Vienna; active in Germany (Heppenheim), where he lived before settling in Jerusalem in 1938. Specializing in the Hassidic tradition, he put forward a religious interpretation of Zionism, conceived of as a form of "Hebrew humanism" distinct from the mainstream, secular version of the ideology and compatible with a binational solution to the conflict between Israel and the Palestinians.

11 Gershom Scholem (1897–1982), German-born Israeli philosopher specializing in the Kabbalah and Jewish mysticism. See Amir Engel, *Gershom Scholem: An Intellectual Biography* (Chicago: University of Chicago Press, 2017).

12 Seizo Ohe (–1993), Japanese philosopher specializing in epistemology; professor of philosophy at Nihon University in Tokyo; editor of the journal *Philosophical Studies of Japan*, which published from 1958 to 1975. See his "Japan in a World-Historical Perspective," in *Revue internationale de philosophie*, nos. 107–8 (1974): 24–35.

13 Toshihiko Izutsu (1914–1993), Japanese philosopher, Islamologist focusing on Sufism, professor at the Institute of Islamic Studies of McGill University (1968–1975); translated the Q'ran into Japanese.

14 Tomonobu Imamichi (1922–2012), Japanese philosopher, past president of the International Institute of Philosophy; memoir, *In Search of Wisdom: One Philosopher's Journey*, trans. Mary E. Foster (Tokyo: LCTB International Library Foundation, 2004); on Klibansky, see pp. 167 ff.

15 Feng Youlan (1895–1990), Chinese philosopher; author of *A History of Chinese Philosophy*, 2 vols., trans. Derk Bodde (Princeton: Princeton University Press, 1983); and *The Spirit of Chinese Philosophy*, trans. E.R. Hughes (London: Kegan Paul, 1947).

16 Gianni Vattimo (1936–), Italian philosopher, studied at Heidelberg with Karl Löwith and Hans-Georg Gadamer. Klibansky refers here to Gianni Vattimo and Pier Aldo Rovatti, eds, *Il pensiero debole* (Milano: Feltrinelli, 1983), translated by Peter Carravetta as *Weak Thought* (Albany, NY: State University of New York Press, 2012). See also Santiago Zabala, ed., *Weakening Philosophy: Essays in Honor of Gianni Vattimo*, with contributions from Umberto Eco, Charles Taylor, Richard Rorty, Jean-Luc Nancy, Fernando Savater, and others (Montreal: McGill-Queen's University Press, 2007).

17 *Metaphysical Horror*, rev. ed. (Chicago: University of Chicago Press, 2001).

18 Leszek Kołakowski (1927–2009), *Chrétiens sans église: la conscience religieuse et le lien confessionnel au XVII siècle*, trans. Anna Posner (Paris: Gallimard, 1969).

19 Kołakowski, *God Owes Us Nothing: A Brief Remark on Pascal's Religion and on the Spirit of Jansenism* (Chicago: University of Chicago Press, 1995).

20 Kołakowski, *The Key to Heaven and Conversations with the Devil*, trans. Salvator Attanasio and Celina Wieniewska (New York: Grove Press, 1972).

21 Kołakowski, *Main Currents of Marxism*, 3 vols., trans. P.S. Falla (Oxford: Clarendon, 1978).

22 Kołakowski, *Metaphysical Horror*, rev. ed., ed. A. Kolakowska (Chicago: University of Chicago Press, 2001).

23 The Nonino Prize, awarded since 1990 to "a master of our time," is one of the four prizes awarded annually by the Nonino family. Klibansky was the laureate in 1995, Kołakowski in 1997. See https://it.wikipedia.org/wiki/Premio_Nonino.

24 Jean Wahl (1888–1974), French philosopher.

25 Régis Debray (1940–), French philosopher and journalist.

26 Max Black (1909–1988), British-American philosopher specializing in the philosophy of language.

27 Henri Duméry (1920–2012), French philosopher who specialized in the philosophy of religion and close friend of Klibansky. See his remarkable portrait of Klibansky, "Un philosophe des humanités," introduction to Helmut Kohlenberger, ed., *Reason, Action*

and Experience: Essays in Honor of Raymond Klibansky (Hamburg: Felix Meiner, 1979), 3–11.

28 Theodor W. Adorno (1903–1969), German philosopher, founding member of the Frankfurt School of critical theory. The Institute for Social Research was founded in Frankfurt in 1923, and Adorno's close friend Max Horkheimer was its director starting in 1930. In 1933 the institute relocated to New York, where it was affiliated with Columbia University, before returning to Frankfurt in 1951.

29 Max Horkheimer and Theodor W. Adorno, *Dialectic of Enlightenment*, trans. John Cumming (New York: Herder and Herder, 1972).

30 Theodor W. Adorno et al., *The Authoritarian Personality* (New York: Harper, 1950).

31 Theodor W. Adorno, *Philosophy of Modern Music*, trans. A.G. Mitchell and W.V. Blomster (New York: Seabury Press, 1973); Adorno, *Introduction to the Sociology of Music*, trans. E.B. Ashton (New York: Seabury Press, 1976).

32 Georg Lukacs (1885–1971), Hungarian philosopher, author of numerous works in aesthetics, Marxist theory, and literary criticism. See his essay collection *Soul and Form*, ed. John T. Sanders and Katie Terezakis, trans. Anna Bostock (New York: Columbia University Press, 2010); and *The Theory of the Novel: A Historico-philosophical Essay on the Forms of Great Epic Literature*, trans. Anna Bostock (Boston: MIT Press, 1961).

33 Ernst Bloch (1885–1977), German Marxist philosopher; while his doctoral dissertation was on Rickert's theory of knowledge, he subsequently worked primarily in the tradition of Hegel and Marx on issues in the philosophy of history. His major writings include *The Principle of Hope*, 3 vols., trans. Neville Plaice, Stephen Plaice, and Paul Knight (Oxford: Basil Blackwell, 1986), and *The Spirit of Utopia*, trans. Anthony Nassar (Stanford: Stanford University Press, 2000).

34 For more about the International Dictionary of Philosophy, see *Glossaire/Glossary*, supplement to *Bibliographie de la philosophie/Bibliography of Philosophy* (1996).

Chapter Eleven

1 Teodor Oizerman (1914–2017), Russian philosopher, member of the Russian Academy of Sciences; see Marina F. Bhykova, "In memoriam of Teodor I. Oizerman," *Russian Studies in Philosophy* 55 (2017): 85–8.

2 The invasion by the Warsaw Pact forces took place on 20–21 August 1968.

3 Jan Patočka (1907–1977), Czech philosopher, pupil of Edmund Husserl and Martin Heidegger; banned from university teaching after 1972 for his participation in the 1968 pro-democracy protests; later became a spokesperson for the dissident "Charter 77" human rights movement, named for the manifesto he co-wrote with other intellectuals.

4 Karel Kosík (1926–2003), Czech philosopher and former student of Jan Patočka; upheld a particular interpretation of Marxism influenced by Heidegger's phenomenology; see his *Dialectics of the Concrete: A Study on Problems of Man and World* (Dordrecht & Boston: D. Reidel, 1976). A supporter of the 1968 democratization movement, he was forced to give up his university teaching post in 1970.

5 See Edward F. Findlay, *Caring for the Soul in a Postmodern Age: Politics and Phenomenology in the Thought of Jan Patočka* (Albany, NY: State University of New York Press, 2002); see also Georges Leroux, "Jan Patočka, lecteur de Platon: le platonisme négatif," *Contrejour: Cahiers littéraires* 4 (2003): 28–41. With the radio producer François Ismert, Georges Leroux prepared a two-hour program for the Radio-Canada cultural channel titled *Jan Patočka 1907–1977: Une vie en vérité*, with the participation of Raymond Klibansky, Paul Ricœur, Jan Sokol, and Étienne Tassin, among others; it aired on 22 October 1995.

6 Edmund Husserl, *The Crisis of European Sciences and Transcendental Phenomenology: An Introduction to Phenomenological Philosophy* (Evanston: Northwestern University Press, 1976).

7 *Heretical Essays in the Philosophy of History*, ed. James Dodd, trans. Erazim Kohák (Chicago: Open Court, 1996); *Philosophy and Selected Writings*, ed. Erazim Kohak (Chicago: University of Chicago Press, 1989).

8 John Amos Comenius (1592–1670), philosopher, theologian, educator, and native of Moravia (Bohemia). His great treatise on education reform (*De rerum humanorum emendatione consultatio catholica*, 1662) inspired numerous modern thinkers in the field of education. The last part of the work was translated by A.M.O. Dobbie as *Panorthosia or Universal Reform: Chapters 19 to 26* (Sheffield: Sheffield Academic Press, 1993); there is also a complete translation into French: *La Grande Didactique ou L'Art universel de tout enseigner à tous* (1627–32), 2nd rev. ed., trans. Marie-Françoise Bosquet-Frigout, Dominique Saget, and Bernard Jolibert (Paris: Klincksieck, 2002).

Epilogue

1 Richard Rorty (1931–2007), American philosopher; see, e.g., *Objectivity, Relativism and Truth* (Cambridge: Cambridge University Press, 1991).

2 Charles Taylor (1931–), Canadian philosopher, professor emeritus at McGill University in Montreal, long-time colleague and close friend of Raymond Klibansky in the Department of Philosophy; see, e.g., *Sources of the Self: The Making of the Modern Identity* (Cambridge, MA: Harvard University Press, 1989).

WORKS BY AND ABOUT RAYMOND KLIBANSKY

Main Works (chronological)

Carolus Bovillus [Charles de Bovelles]. *Liber de sapiente.* Edited by Raymond Klibansky. In Ernst Cassirer, *Individuum und Kosmos in der Philosophie der Renaissance,* 299–458. *Studien der Bibliothek Warburg* 10. Leipzig and Berlin: Teubner, 1927.

Ein Proklos-Fund und seine Bedeutung. Sitzungsberichte der Heidelberger Akademie der Wissenschaften 1928–29, Philosophisch-Historische Klasse 5. Abhandlung. Heidelberg: Winter, 1929.

Nicolai de Cusa [Nicholas of Cusa]. *Opera omnia (issu et auctoritate Academiae Litterarum Heidelbergensis edita).* Leipzig: Meiner, 1932–83.

1932. Vol. I, *De docta ignorantia.* Edited by Raymond Klibansky with Ernst Hoffmann.

1934. Vol. II, *Apologia doctae ignorantiae.* Edited by Raymond Klibansky.

1959. Vol. VII, *De pace fidei.* Edited by Raymond Klibansky with Hildebrandus (Hildebrand) Bascour OSB. Second edition, 1970. First published in London by the Warburg Institute, 1956. Reprint of Warburg edition: Nendeln, Liechtenstein: Kraus International, 1977.

1982. Vol. XII, *De venatione sapientiae. De apice theoriae.* Edited by Raymond Klibansky and G.H. Senger.

1983. Vol. V, *Idiota de sapientia. Idiota de mente.* Edited by R. Steiger. With two appendices by Raymond Klibansky: I: *De memoria librorum Idiotae.* II: *De dialogis De vera sapientia Francisco Petrarcae addictis.* Hamburg: Meiner, 1983.

Magistri Eckardi [Meister Eckhart]. *Opera Latina (auspiciis Instituti S. Sabinae in Urbe ad codicum fidem edita).* Fasc. I: *Super oratione dominica,* editit Raymundus Klibansky. Leipzig: Meiner, 1934.

Magistri Eckardi. *Opera Latina (auspiciis Instituti S. Sabinae in Urbe ad codicum fidem edita).* Fasc. XIII: *Quaestiones Parisienses,* edidit Antonius Dondaine OP; *Commentariolum de Eckardi Magisterio,* adiunxit Raymundus Klibansky. Leipzig: Meiner, 1936.

Philosophy and History: Essays Presented to Ernst Cassirer. Edited by R. Klibansky and H.J. Paton. Oxford: Clarendon Press, 1936. Reprint, Gloucester, MA: Peter Smith, 1975.

The Continuity of the Platonic Tradition during the Middle Ages: Outlines of a "Corpus Platonicum Medii Aevi." London: Warburg Institute, 1939. Reprint, London: Warburg

Institute, 1950. Reprinted … *with a New Preface and Four Supplementary Chapters, Together with Plato's "Parmenides" in the Middle Ages and the Renaissance*. Munich: Kraus International, 1981. Reprint, Millwood, NY: Kraus International, 1982.

Corpus Platonicum Medii Ævi. Auspiciis Academiæ Britannicæ. Edidit Raymundus Klibansky. London: Warburg Institute, 1940–62.

Volumes published:

1940. *Plato Latinus I: "Meno," Interprete Henrico Aristippo*. Ed. V. Kordeuder. Recognovit et praefatione instruxit Carlotta Labowsky.

1943. *Plato Arabus II: Alfarabius de Platonis Philosophia*. Ed. Franciscus Rosenthal et Richardus Walzer.

1950. *Plato Latinus II: "Phaedo," Interprete Henrico Aristippo*. Ed. et praefatione instruxit Laurentius Minio-Paluello.

1951. *Plato Arabus I: Galeni Compendium "Timaei" Platonis*. Ed. Paulus Kraus et Richardus Walzer.

1952. *Plato Arabus III: Alfarabius Compendium "Legum" Platonis*. Ed. Franciscus Gabrieli.

1953. *Plato Latinus III: Platonis "Parmenides" nec non Procli Commentarium in Parmenidem, pars adhuc inedita*. Ediderunt, praefatione adnotationibusque illustraverunt Raymundus Klibansky et Carlotta Labowsky.

1962. *Plato Latinus IV: "Timaeus," a Calcidio translatus commentarioque instructus*. Ed. Jan Hendrick Waszink.

Reprint of *Plato Latinus I–III and Plato Arabus I–III*. Nendeln, Liechtenstein: Kraus-Thomson, 1973. Second edition of *Plato Latinus IV*. Leiden: Brill, 1975.

Mediaeval and Renaissance Studies. Edited by Raymond Klibansky and Richard Hunt. 1941–1943–1968. 6 vols. + 3 supplements. Vols. 4–6 (1959–68) also co-edited by Carlotta (Lotte) Labowsky). (Vols. 1–3, and supplements 1 and 3 reprinted, Nendeln, Liechtenstein: Kraus Reprint, 1970–77).

Mussolini, Benito. *Memoirs: 1942–1943, with Documents Relating to the Period*. Edited with commentary by R. Klibansky. Translated by Frances Lobb. London: Weidenfeld and Nicolson, 1949. Reprint, New York: Fertig, 1975.

Croce, Benedetto. *My Philosophy and Other Essays on the Moral and Political Problems of Our Time*. Edited by R. Klibansky. Translated by E.F. Carritt. London: George Allen and Unwin, 1949.

New Letters of David Hume. Edited by Raymond Klibansky and E.C. Mossner. Oxford: Clarendon Press, 1954. Reprint, Oxford, 1969. Reprint, New York: Garland, 1983. Paperback ed., Oxford, 2011.

Plato. *"Philebus" and "Epinomis."* Edited by Raymond Klibansky with the cooperation of Guido Calogero and A.C. Lloyd. Translation and introduction by A.E. Taylor. London: Nelson, 1956.

Philosophy in the Mid-Century/La Philosophie au milieu du vingtième siècle. 4 vols. Edited by Raymond Klibansky. Florence: La Nuova Italia, 1958–59. Reprint, Nendeln, Liechtenstein: Kraus International, 1967–76.

Locke, John. *Lettera sulla tolleranza, testo latino e versione italiana*. Latin text, edited with a preface by Raymond Klibansky. Philosophy and World Community series. Florence:

La Nuova Italia, 1961. This is the first publication of Klibansky's edition of the Latin text, which was subsequently printed in several bilingual editions.

– *Lettre sur la tolérance: texte latin et traduction française*. Critical edition and preface by Raymond Klibansky. Translation and introduction by Raymond Polin. Montreal: Casalini, 1964. Also published in Paris: Presses universitaires de France, 1965; 2nd ed., Paris: Presses universitaires de France, 1967.

– *Epistola de tolerantia: A Letter on Toleration*. Latin text edited with a preface by Raymond Klibansky. English translation with an introduction and notes by J.W. Gough. Oxford: Clarendon Press, 1968.

Plato. *The Sophist and the Statesman*. Edited by Raymond Klibansky and Elizabeth Anscombe. Translation and introduction by A.E. Taylor. London: Nelson, 1961.

Saturn and Melancholy: Studies in the History of Religion, Art, and Natural Philosophy. Co-authored with Erwin Panofsky and Fritz Saxl. London: Nelson; New York: Basic Books, 1964. Reprint, Nendeln, Liechtenstein: Kraus International, 1979. Subsequent editions:

Saturno e la melanconia. Studi di storia della filosofia naturale, religione e arte. Translated by Renzo Federici. Torino: Einaudi, 1983.

Saturne et la mélancolie. Études historiques et philosophiques: nature, religion, médecine et art. Translated by Fabienne Durand-Bogaert and Louis Évrard. Augmented edition with an introduction by Raymond Klibansky. Collection Bibliothèque illustrée des histoires. Paris: Gallimard, 1989.

Saturn und Melancholie. Studien zur Geschichte der Naturphilosophie und Medizin, der Religion und der Kunst. Translated by Christa Buschendorf. Frankfurt: Suhrkamp, 1990.

Translated into Spanish (1991), Japanese (1991), Romanian (2002), Polish (2009), Slovenian (2013).

Contemporary Philosophy. 4 vols. Edited by Raymond Klibansky. Florence: La Nuova Italia, 1968–71.

Philosophy and Science in the Middle Ages. Vol. 6 of *Contemporary Philosophy: A New Survey*. Edited by G. Floistad and R. Klibansky. 2 pts. Dordrecht: Kluwer, 1990.

Die Handschriften der philosophischen Werke des Apuleius. Ein Beitrag zur Überlieferungsgeschichte. Co-authored with Frank Regen. Göttingen: Vandenhoeck & Ruprecht, 1993.

La Philosophie en Europe. Edited by Raymond Klibansky and David Pears. Paris: Gallimard, 1993.

La Pensée philosophique d'expression française au Canada: le rayonnement du Québec. Edited by Raymond Klibansky and Josiane Boulad-Ayoub. Quebec: Presses de l'Université Laval, 1998.

Le Philosophe et la mémoire du siècle: tolérance, liberté et philosophie. Entretiens avec Georges Leroux. Paris: Belles Lettres, 1998; also published in Montreal: Boréal, 2000. Translations:

El filósofo y la memoria del siglo: Tolerancia, libertad, filosofía. Conversaciones con Georges Leroux. Barcelona: Península, 1999.

Erinnerung an ein Jahrhundert. Gespräche mit Georges Leroux. Translated from the French by Petra Willim. Frankfurt: Insel, 2001.

Idées sans frontières: histoire et structures de l'Institut international de philosophie. With the collaboration of Ethel Groffier. Paris: Belles Lettres, 2005.

[posthumous]

Tradition antique et tolérance moderne. Texts selected and introduced by Philippe Despoix and Georges Leroux. Montreal: Presses de l'Université de Montréal, 2016.

Saturn and Melancholy: Studies in the History of Religion, Art, and Natural Philosophy. Co-authored with Erwin Panofsky and Fritz Saxl. New edition by Philippe Despoix and Georges Leroux. With a foreword by Bill Sherman. Montreal and Kingston: McGill-Queen's University Press, 2019.

Articles and Notes (selected list)

"Niccolò da Cusa (Cusano)." In Istituto della Enciclopedia italiana, *Enciclopedia italiana di scienze, lettere ed arti*, ed. Giovanni Treccani, vol. 24, *Mu-Nove*, 761–3. Rome: Istituto della Enciclopedia italiana, 1929–39; 2nd ed., 1949–52.

"Notes and Correspondence. Answer to Query no. 53: Standing on the Shoulders of Giants." *Isis* 26, no. 1 (December 1936): 147–56.

"The Philosophical Character of History." In R. Klibansky and H.J. Paton, eds, *Philosophy and History: Essays Presented to Ernst Cassirer*, 323–37. Oxford: Clarendon Press, 1936.

"Leibniz's Unknown Correspondence with English Scholars and Men of Letters." *Mediaeval and Renaissance Studies* 1 (1941–43): 133–49.

"Plato's Parmenides in the Middle Ages and the Renaissance." *Mediaeval and Renaissance Studies* 1, no. 2 (1943): 281–330.

"The Rock of Parmenides: Mediaeval Accounts of the Origins of Dialectic." *Mediaeval and Renaissance Studies* 1, no. 2 (1943): 171–86.

"L'épître de Bérenger de Poitiers contre les Chartreux." *Revue du Moyen Âge latin* 2 (1946): 314–16.

"Copernic et Nicolas de Cues." In Centre national de la recherche scientifique, *Léonard de Vinci et l'expérience scientifique au seizième siècle*, 225–35. Paris: Presses universitaires de France, 1953.

"Introduction." In International Institute of Philosophy, *Bibliographie de la philosophie/ Bibliography of Philosophy* 1: 9–12. Paris: Librairie Philosophique J. Vrin, 1954.

"The School of Chartres." In M. Clagett, G. Post, and R. Reynolds, eds, *Twelfth-Century Europe and the Foundations of Modern Society*, 3–14. Madison: University of Wisconsin Press, 1961; paperback ed., 1966.

"Peter Abailard and Bernard of Clairvaux: A Letter by Abailard." *Mediaeval and Renaissance Studies* 5 (1961): 1–27.

"Bibliography of Ernst Cassirer's Writings" (with W. Solmitz). In R. Klibansky and H.J. Paton, eds, *Philosophy and History*, 339–46. New York: Harper & Row, 1963.

"The Foundation of Rights." In International Institute of Philosophy, *Le fondement des droits de l'homme: actes des entretiens de l'Aquila*, 204–6. Florence: La Nuova Italia, 1966.

"Opening Address." In *Démonstration, Vérification et Justification: entretiens de l'Institut international de philosophie, Liège, septembre 1967*, 5–13. Louvain & Paris: Nauwelaerts, 1968.

"Il pensiero contemporaneo." *Il sedicesimo*, nos. 14–15 (1968): 1–3.
"La filosofia contemporanea." *Il sedicesemo*, no. 19 (1969): 22–3.
"Oratio in initio conventus Societatis Internationalis Studiis Philosophiæ Medii Ævi Promovendis die V mensis Sept. anni MCMLXXII Matriti habita." *Bulletin de philosophie médiévale* (Louvain) 14 (1972): 186–8.
"Allocution d'ouverture." In Helmut Kohlenberger, ed., *Die Wirkungsgeschichte Anselms von Canterbury, Akten d. 1. Internat. Anselm-Tagung Bad Wimpfen*, 19–22. Frankfurt/Main: Minerva, 1975.
"Nicolas de Cues, Charles de Bovelles et la cycloïde." In C. de Waard and A. Beaulieu, eds, *Correspondance du P. Marin Mersenne, religieux Minime*, 14: 358–62. Paris: Éditions du CNRS, 1980.
"Neoplatonism and Christianity." *Archivio di filosofia*, no. 52 (1984): 591–4.
"Die Wirkungsgeschichte des Dialogs *De pace fidei*." In Rudolf Haubst, ed., *Der Friede unter den Religionen nach Nikolaus von Kues*, 113–25. Mainz: Matthias-Grünewald, 1984.
"Cultures and Values in Historical Perspective." In *Philosophy and Culture: Proceedings of the XVIIth World Congress of Philosophy* 1: 89–92. Montreal: Éditions du Beffroi & Éditions Montmorency, 1986.
"Hidden Treasures at McGill: A Survey of Manuscripts and Historical Documents." *Fontanus* (Montreal): 11 (1989): 65–96.
"Jan Patočka." In P. Horak and J. Zumr, eds, *La Responsabilité/Responsibility: entretiens de Prague, Institut international de philosophie 1990*, 17–35. Prague: Institut de philosophie de l'Académie tchécoslovaque des sciences, 1992.
"Zur fünfzigsten Wiederkehr der Pogromnacht." In *Trumah, Zeitschrift der Hochschule für jüdische Studien* 3: 1–13. Heidelberg: Heidelberg Universitätsverl. Winter, 1992.
"La découverte d'un texte inconnu de l'antiquité classique." In Shirley Neuman and Louise Marcil, eds, *Témoignages: Reflections on the Humanities*, 41–58. Ottawa: Canadian Federation for the Humanities, 1993.
"Patočka" (Czech translation). *Filozoficky časopis* 42 (1994): 543–59.
"Rede zum Lessingpreis der Stadt Hamburg." In *Verleihung des Lessingpreises 1993 an Raymond Klibansky: Reden anlässlich der Preisübergabe* [Kurt Flasch *et al.*], 23–32. Hamburg: Freie und Hansestadt Hamburg, 1994.
"Le avventure della malinconia." *Dianoia* (Bologna) 1 (1996): 11–27.
"Préface." In Paul Dumouchel and Bjarne Melkevik, eds, *Tolérance, pluralisme et histoire*, 9–13. Paris: L'Harmattan, 1998.
"La notion de Kulturwissenschaft." RACAR (*Revue d'art canadienne/Canadian Art Review*) 27, nos. 1–2 (2000): 144–6.
"Le trésor de Kandahar." *Librarium, Revue de la Société suisse des bibliophiles-Zeitschrift der schweizerischen Bibliophilen-Gesellschaft* 1 (2002): 38–40.
"Adam (Adam the Welshman) (c. 1130–1181)." In H.C.G. Matthew and Brian Harrison, eds, *Oxford Dictionary of National Biography*, 1: 191–2. Oxford & New York: Oxford University Press, 2004.

"Balsham, Adam of, called De Parvo Ponte (c. 1100–1157/69?)." In H.C.G. Matthew and Brian Harrison, eds, *Oxford Dictionary of National Biography*, 3: 615–16. Oxford & New York: Oxford University Press, 2004.

Interviews and Biographical Notes

"Raymond Klibansky, philosophe et historien: entretien avec Yves Hersant et Alain de Libera." *Préfaces: Les idées et les sciences dans la bibliographie de la France* 13 (1989): 132–42.

"L'Université allemande dans les années trente (notes autobiographiques)." *Philosophiques* 18 (1991): 139–57.

"Regagner Athènes par Alexandrie: entretien de Christian Jacob avec Raymond Klibansky." In Christian Jacob and François de Polignac, eds, *Alexandrie IIIe siècle av. J.-C.: Tous les savoirs du monde ou le rêve d'universalité des Ptolémées*, 231–45. Paris: Autrement (1992).

"Conversazione con Raymond Klibansky, a cura di Francesco Barocelli." In Graziella Federici Vescovini, ed., *Filosofia, scienza e astrologia nel Trecento europeo*, 7–18. Padova: Il Poligrafo, 1992.

"Rencontres avec Benoît Lacroix." In Giselle Huot, ed., *Dits et gestes de Benoît Lacroix: prophète de l'amour et de l'esprit*, 143–5. Saint-Hyppolyte, QC: Éditions du Noroît; Montreal: Fondation Albert-le-Grand, 1995.

"Aus dem Heidelberger Geistleben." In Elmar Mittler, ed., *Heidelberg Geschichte und Gestalt*, 270–82. Heidelberg: Universitätsverlag C. Winter, 1996.

"Erinnerungen an Ernst Cassirer: Raymond Klibansky im Gespräch mit Thomas Göller." *Internationale Zeitschrift für Philosophie* 2 (1999): 275–88.

"Des bibliothèques privées aux institutions publiques: un parcours dans l'histoire des bibliothèques." Interview with Georges Leroux, with the collaboration of Steve Maskaleut. *L'Action nationale* 89, no. 7 (1999): 57–74.

"Raymond Klibansky, 15 mai 1994." Interview with Michael Buselmeier. In *Erlebte Geschichte erzählt 1994–1997*, 8–29. Heidelberg: Wunderhorn, 2000.

"… Verzweifeln an der Welt. Und Raymond Klibansky kannte sie alle. Ein Plädoyer für die Melancholie." Interview with Raymond Klibansky by André Behr and Lars Reichardt. *Süddeutsche Zeitung Magazin*, no. 114 (18 May 2001): 18–23.

"Die Grenzen des Akademischen Lebens sprengen. Ein Gespräch über Ernst Cassirer und die Bibliothek Warburg." Interview with Patrick Conley. *Merkur* 50, no. 3 (1996): 274–7.

Literature in Honour of Raymond Klibansky

Méthode et Philosophie de l'histoire. Special issue, *Revue internationale de philosophie* 29, no. 111–12 (1975).

Groffier, Ethel, and Michel Paradis, eds. *The Notion of Tolerance and Human Rights: Essays in Honour of Raymond Klibansky*. Ottawa: Carleton University Press, 1991.

Kohlenberger, Helmut, ed. *Reason, Action, and Experience: Essays in Honour of Raymond Klibansky*. Hamburg: Felix Meiner, 1979.

Leroux, Georges. "De Nicolas de Cues aux enfants de Saturne: présentation de l'oeuvre de Raymond Klibansky." In *Hommage à Raymond Klibansky*, 4–9. Université du Québec à Montreal, Département de philosophie, 1991.

Melkevik, Bjarne, and Jean-Marc Narbonne, eds. *Une philosophie dans l'histoire: hommages à Raymond Klibansky*. Quebec: Presses de l'Université Laval, 2000.

Literature about Klibansky (in alphabetical order)

The bibliography on the life and thought of Raymond Klibansky is voluminous; the following is an alphabetical list of selected references.

Cooper, R.M., ed. *Refugee Scholars: Conversations with Tess Simpson*. Leeds: Moorland Books, 1992.

Cristaldi, Rosario V. "Un saggio di Raymond Klibansky." *Memorie e Rendiconti dell'Accademia di Scienze, Lettere et Belle Arti degli Zelanti e dei Dafnici di Acireale*, ser. III, 6 (1986): 469–77.

De Monticelli, Roberta. "Della nobilità dello spirito: Ricordo di Raymond Klibansky." *Rivista di estetica* 40, no. 3 (2000): 230–2.

Despoix, Philippe, and Jillian Tomm, with the collaboration of Éric Méchoulan and Georges Leroux, eds. *Raymond Klibansky and the Warburg Library Network: Intellectual Peregrinations from Hamburg to London and Montreal*. Montreal and Kingston: McGill-Queen's University Press, 2018.

Falk, Barbara. *"Caught in a Snare": Hitler's Refugee Academics, 1933–1949*. Melbourne: University of Melbourne, History Department, 1998.

Flasch, Kurt. "Laudatio auf den Preisträger Raymond Klibansky." In *Verleihung des Lessingpreises 1993 an Raymond Klibansky: Reden anlässlich der Preisübergabe*, 12–22. Hamburg: City of Hamburg, 1994.

Groffier, Ethel. "Raymond Klibansky et la quête de l'objectivité." In Tomonobu Imamichi and Hans Lenk, eds, *Aesthetics in Contemporary Philosophy: Proceedings of the International Institute of Philosophy Conference, Tokyo 2006*, 259–73. Vienna: LIT Verlag, 2009.

Grolle, Joist. *Bericht von einem schwierigen Leben: Walter Solmitz (1905 bis 1962); Schüler von Aby Warburg und Ernst Cassirer*. Berlin and Hamburg: Dietrich Reimer, 1994.

Halfwassen, Jens. "Raymond Klibansky: Erinnerungen an ein Jahrhundert." *Ruperto Carola* 3 (2005): 30–6.

Kuhnekath, Klaus. "Internationalisierung der Philosophie und politisches Engagement aus der Erfahrung der Emigration: Der Fall Raymond Klibansky." In Marion Heinz and Goran Gretic, eds, *Philosophie und Zeitgeist im Nationalsozialismus*, 163–91. Würzburg: Königshausen und Neumann, 2006. Reprinted, *Sozialwissenschaftliche Literaturrundschau* 2 (2004): 46–68.

Le Doeuff, Michèle. "Raymond Klibansky. Périple d'un philosophe illustre." *Préfaces: Les idées et les sciences dans la bibliographie de la France* 13 (May–June 1989): 125–31. Reprinted in Melkevik and Narbonne, *Une philosophie dans l'histoire*; Italian trans.,

Rivista di estetica, new series, no. 15 (2000): 222–9; English trans., *Angelaki* 8, no. 1 (2003): 163–9.

Leroux, Georges. "Raymond Klibansky (1905–2005)." In *Universalia 2006: la politique, les connaissances, la culture en 2005*, 450–1. Paris: Encyclopaedia universalis, 2006.

Leroux, Georges, ed. *Raymond Klibansky (1905–2005): la bibliothèque d'un philosophe; catalogue de l'exposition produite par Bibliothèque et Archives nationales du Québec.* Montreal: Bibliothèque et Archives nationales du Québec, 2013.

Mussgnug, Dorothee. *Die vertriebenen Heidelberger Dozenten: Zur Geschichte der Ruprecht-Karls-Universität nach 1933*. Heidelberg: Carl Winter, 1988.

Senger, Hans Gerhard. "Raymond Klibansky, 1905–2005: Skizze einer philosophischen Biographie." *Mitteilungen und Forschungsbeiträge der Cusanus-Gesellschaft* 30 (2005): xi–xxviii.

– "In Memoriam Raymond Klibansky." *Bulletin de philosophie médiévale* 47 (2005): viii–xv.

Shirley, Dennis. *The Politics of Progressive Education: The Odenwaldschule in Nazi Germany.* Cambridge, MA: Harvard University Press, 1992.

Thimann, Michael. *Caesars Schatten: Die Bibliothek von Friedrich Gundolf; Rekonstruktion und Wissenschaftsgeschichte*. Heidelberg: Manutius, 2003.

Thurner, Martin. "Raymond Klibansky: A Medievalist Keeping His Finger on the Pulse of the Century." *American Cusanus Newsletter* 21, no. 2 (2004): 17–32. Reprinted as "Raymond Klibansky (1905)" in Jaume Aurell and Francisco Crosas, eds, *Rewriting the Middle Ages in the Twentieth Century*, 255–70. Turnhout: Brepols, 2005. Italian trans., "Un medievalista con il polso del suo secolo," *Studia Patavina* 51 (2005): 187–214.

Tomm, Jillian, and Georges Leroux. "La collection Raymond Klibansky conservée à l'Université McGill: présentation de la bibliothèque d'un humaniste montréalais." *Mémoires du livre/Studies in Book Culture* 5, no. 1. https://doi.org/10.7202/1020226ar.

Tomm, Jillian, and Richard Virr, eds. *Meetings with Books: Special Collections in the 21st Century; with a Tribute to Raymond Klibansky & Illustrated Survey of Special Collections at McGill University Library and Archives.* Montreal: McGill University Library and Archives, 2014.

Uzel, Jean Philippe. "Raymond Klibansky et l'histoire de l'art du XXe siècle." RACAR: *Revue d'art canadienne/Canadian Art Review* 27, nos. 1–2 (2003): 138–42.

Vanderveken, Daniel. "In memoriam Raymond Klibansky: hommage à un grand maître." *Philosophiques* 33, no. 2 (2006): 463–75.

Watanabe, Morimichi. "The Origins of Modern Cusanus Research in Germany and the Establishment of the Heidelberg 'Opera omnia.'" In Gerald Christianson and Thomas M. Izbicki, eds, *Nicholas of Cusa in Search of God and Wisdom: Essays in Honor of Morimichi Watanabe by the American Cusanus Society*, 17–42. Leiden & New York: E.J. Brill, 1991.

Weber, Regina. "Aktivitäten der Warburg-Bibliothek, gespiegelt im Marbacher Nachlass Raymond Klibansky." In Claus-Dieter Krohn and Lutz Winckler, eds, *Bibliotheken und Sammlungen im Exil*, 100–14. München: Edition text + kritik, "Exilforschung, Band 29," 2011.

– "Raymond Klibansky, 1905–2005." In John M. Spalek, Konrad Feilchenfeldt, and Sandra H. Hawrylchak, eds, *Deutschsprachige Exilliteratur seit 1933: Band 3 Supplement 1, USA*, 93–124. Berlin: De Gruyter Saur, 2010.

– "Der Philosophiehistoriker Raymond Klibansky (1905–2005) und die 'Internationalisierung' der Philosophe: Das Nachleben der Antike in der 'Philosophie des Dialogs.'" *Amsterdamer Beiträge zur neueren Germanistik* 76 (2010): 79–98.

– *Lotte Labowsky: Schülerin Aby Warburg's, Kollegin Raymond Klibansky's; Eine Wissenschaftlerin zwischen Fremd- und Selbstbestimmung im englischen Exil*. Berlin and Hamburg: Dietrich Reimer, "Hamburger Beiträge zur Wissenschaftsgeschichte, Bd. 21," 2012.

Films

Boutang, Pierre-André, and Annie Chevallay, directors. *Raymond Klibansky*. Documentary presented on the *Metropolis* cultural program on the ARTE network. Production ARTE, 2000. 36 min.

Tougas, Anne-Marie, director. *Raymond Klibansky: From Philosophy to Life*. National Film Board, 2002. 51 min. https://www.nfb.ca/film/raymond_klibansky_from_philosophy_to_life/.

Bibliographical Sources

A complete, regularly updated bibliography is available on the site devoted to Raymond Klibansky: raymondklibanskywebpage.org/bibliography

Other bibliographies:

Groffier, Ethel and Michel Paradis, eds. *The Notion of Tolerance and Human Rights: Essays in Honour of Raymond Klibansky*, 165–74. Ottawa: Carleton University Press, 1991.

Thurner, Martin. "Raymond Klibansky: A Medievalist Keeping His Finger on the Pulse of the Century." *American Cusanus Newsletter* 21, no. 2 (2004): 17–32. Bibliography, pp. 23–32.

Tomm, Jillian. "The Imprint of the Scholar: An Analysis of the Printed Books of McGill University's Raymond Klibansky Collection." PhD diss. McGill University, School of Information Studies, 2012.

Whalley, Michael J., and Désirée Park. "Bibliography of Raymond Klibansky." In "Méthode et Philosophie de l'histoire." Special issue, *Revue internationale de philosophie* 111–12 (1975): 167–74.

INDEX

Abelard, Peter, 30
Abu Ma'shar, 64
Academic Assistance Council, 27, 107–9, 113
Addison, Joseph, 148
Adjukiewicz, Kazimierz, 199
Adorno, Theodor W., 26, 210–12
Advice to a Desolate France (Castellio), 189
Agrippa, Cornelius, 26
Alexander VIII (Pietro Ottoboni), Pope, 175
All Souls College, 112
Ambrosio, Vittorio, 155
amor heroicus, 144
Anatomy of Melancholy, The (Burton), 24, 146–7
Anscombe, Elizabeth, 210
Apel, Karl-Otto, 210, 228
Apuleius, 92; epoch of, 175. See also *Golden Ass, The*
Aquin, Hubert, 161
Aquinas, Thomas, 14, 97, 183
Arendt, Hannah, 8, 56
Aristotle, 11, 24, 142, 202, 230
Arminianism, 185
Arnaldus de Villa Nova, 144
Arnim, Achim von, 76
Arnim, Bettina von, 70
Asoka, 34, 181
Aspidistra transmitter, 133
atheism, 186–8
Athenaeum (magazine), 76
atomic bomb, 119–23, 126–9
Auchinleck, Claude, 136
Augustine of Hippo, 94, 183, 205
Austin, J.L., 66, 210
Authoritarian Personality, The (Adorno et al.), 210
Avicenna (Ibn Sina), 144, 184
Ayer, A.J., 66
Ayer, Alfred, 209
Azzolino, Decio, 175

Baader, Franz von, 96
Babington Smith, Constance, 121
Bacon, Francis, 29
Bacon, Roger, 173
Battle of Monte Casino, 135
Baudelaire, Charles, 37, 82, 149
Baum, Marie, 73
Bayer, Raymond, 196
Bayle, Pierre, 188
Being and Time (Heidegger), 6
Benjamin, Walter, 26, 37–8, 228
Benoist-Méchin, Jacques, 109
Berdyaev, Nikolai, 115
Bergen-Belsen, 153
Bernard of Chartres, 16–17, 29, 91, 173–4
Bérubé, Camille, 161
Bessarion, 11, 75
Beth, Evert Willem, 197
Bethe, Hans, 42

Beveridge, Sir William, 113
Bibliography of Philosophy (International Institute of Philosophy), 33, 196, 214, 227
Biblionomia (Fournival), 175
Biblioteca Marciana, 11, 75
Bing, Gertrud, 18
Bingen, Hildegard von, 143
Binswanger, Ludwig, 140
Bitbol, Michel, xi
Black, Max, 33, 208–9
Blätter für die Kunst (journal), 59, 82
Bloch, Ernst, 212
Bloudy Tenent of Persecution for Cause of Conscience, The (Williams), 185
Blumenthal, Albrecht von, 84
Boccaccio, Giovanni, 144, 193
Bodelschwingh, Friedrich von, 152–3
Boehme, Jakob, 89
Bohr, Niels, 122, 129, 197
Boisson, Pierre, 138
Bölte, Felix, 42–3
Bonhoeffer, Dietrich, 117
Book of the Wise. See *Liber de sapiente*
Born, Max, 125
Bovelles, Charles de, 10, 19, 174
Bracken, Harry, 161
Braque, Georges, 43
Bréhier, Émile, 21, 195
Brentano, Clemens, 76
Brentano, Franz, 70
Brentano, Lujo, 70
Brethren of the Common Life, 96
Brethren of the Free Spirit, 99
Brouwer, L.E.J., 197
Bruno, Giordano, 12, 90, 172
Brunschvicg, Léon, 67
Buber, Martin, 202
Bunge, Mario, 161
Burckhardt, Jacob, 11, 101
Burton, Robert, 24, 146–7
Bussi, Giovanni Andrea, 92
Cachin, Marcel, 108
Calogero, Guido, 33, 209
Canadian Society for the History and Philosophy of Science, 162–4
Canguilhem, Georges, 207
Casimir III, 40
Cassel, Gustav, 78
Cassirer, Anne Elisabeth, 68
Cassirer, Antonelle (Toni) Bondy, 61, 66, 68
Cassirer, Ernst, 5, 9–14, 17–23, 26–7, 44, 93; hosting Klibansky, 60–2; later career of, 66–8; volume dedicated to, 163; and Warburg Library, 63
Cassirer, Eva, 62
Cassirer, Heinrich (Heinz), 9, 60, 68, 74
Cassirer, Max, 44
Castelli, Enrico, 201
Castellio, Sebastian, 189
Celan, Paul, 38
Celtes, Conrad, 25
Chagall, Marc, 40
Chalcidius, 173
Chamberlain, Austen, Sir, 113
Chamberlain, Neville, 113
Charter 77, 4, 32, 223
Chaucer, Geoffrey, 144
Choiseul, Charles de, Duke of Praslin, 167
Christina, Queen of Sweden, 175
Cicero, 75, 167, 173, 229
Civilization of the Renaissance in Italy, The (Burckhardt), 11
Coblenz, Ida, 83, 85
Cohen, Hermann, 14, 50, 90
Collège philosophique, 207
Collins, Anthony, 190
Comenius, John Amos, 217, 222
Commentary on Plato's "Parmenides" (Proclus), 91, 172
Community and Society (Tönnies), 57
Concerning Heretics: Whether They Are to Be Persecuted (Castellio), 189
Conférences Albert-le-Grand, 157

Confucius, 183
Contemporary Philosophy (ed. Klibansky), 197, 200, 202–3
Continuity of the Platonic Tradition, The (Klibansky), 29, 139, 169
Conversations with the Devil (Kołakowski), 205
Copernicus, Nicolaus, 174
Corbin, Henry, 109, 114, 184
Corpus Platonicum Medii Aevi, 4, 15, 27, 75, 139, 169
Council for Abolishing War, 123
Council of Ferrara, 75
Council of Florence, 191
Countess of Boufflers, 165–6
Cousin, Victor, 171
Cranach, Lucas, 148
Crisis of European Sciences, The (Husserl), 220
Croce, Benedetto, 67, 133
Crossman, Richard, 132
cuius regio, eius religio, 187, 189
Curtius, Ernst Robert, 69, 108
Curtius, Ludwig, 50–1, 69
Cusanus, Nicolas, 8–17, 35, 88–96, 104–5, 154, 171–2, 174–5; and pacifism, 190–2
Cusanusstift, 94, 96, 104, 154, 170–1

da Vinci, Leonardo, 12, 95
Dante Alighieri, 144
Dattatreya: The Way and the Goal (Wadiyar), 199
Debray, Régis, 207
Décarie, Vianney, 4, 223
Decline of the West, The (Spengler), 7, 55
De docta ignorantia (Cusanus), 9, 12, 15
de Gaulle, Charles, 137–8
Dehmel, Richard, 83
Dejean, Maurice, 137
Delmer, Denis Sefton, 133
De ludo globi (Cusanus), 95
Democritus, 146
De Mundo (Apuleius), 175
denazification, 104
Denburg, Chaim, 29
De occulta philosophia (Agrippa), 26
De pace fidei (Cusanus), 31–2, 35, 190
"Der Chef," 133
Descartes Congress of 1937, 195. *See also* World Congress of Philosophy
Descartes, René, 66, 200
Deschamps, Eustache, 149
Despoix, Philippe, xii
Deutschland deine Denker (Koesters), 155
De visione dei (Cusanus), 94
Déziel, Jean-Charles, xi
Dialectic of Enlightenment (Horkheimer and Adorno), 210
Dialogue avec André Gide, Le (Du Bos), 108
Diary of Otto Braun, The, 44
Diderot, Denis, 181
Die Ethik des Panaitios (Labowsky), 75
Die Probleme der Geschichtsphilosophie (Rickert), 103
Diels, Hermann, 43
Dilthey, Wilhelm, 54, 117
Divagations (Mallarmé), 82
Doctor Faustus (Mann), 210
d'Orléans, Charles, 150
Dresden, Max, 129
Dreyfus, Alfred, 125
Du Bos, Charles, 108
Duméry, Henry, 209
Duplessis, Maurice, 161
Durand, Georges-Mathieu de, 29
Dürer, Albrecht, 18–19, 22–6, 37, 62, 141–2, 230

Eckhart, Meister, 8–9, 16–17, 88–90, 96–9, 104–5; Nazi views on, 27
École d'Humanité, 45
Economy and Society (Weber), 70
Écrits *pour l'art, Les* (journal), 82
Edict of Nantes, 187
Einstein, Albert, 27, 113, 119, 121, 123–6, 163
Elisabeth of Bavaria, 123
Endemann, Friedrich, 101

Engels, Friedrich, 58
Episcopius, 185
Essay on Human Understanding (Locke), 180
Exhibition of the Fascist Revolution, 104
Existenzerhellung, 8, 53

"*Fabula mundi* and Cleopatra's Nose" (Kołakowski), 205
Faust, August, 101
Fehrle, Eugen, 101
Feng Youlan, 197, 203
Fermi, Enrico, 122
Fichte, Johann Gottlieb, 47
Ficino, Marsilio, 23, 25, 144–5, 148, 175
First Battle of El Alamein, 136
Fischer, Kuno, 180
Flasch, Kurt, 16
Foucault, Michel, 157
Fournival, Richard de, 175
Franck, Sebastian, 89
Frankfurter Zeitung (newspaper), 124
Frankfurt School, 25, 150, 210–12
Freud, Sigmund, 37, 149
Frisch, Otto, 122
Fritz, Kurt von, 117
Frombork, cathedral of, 174
Fuchs, Klaus, 118
Führerschicht, 57
Funck-Brentano, Frantz, 70
Furly, Benjamin, 188
Fürtwangler, Wilhelm, 73, 151–2

Gadamer, Hans-Georg, 33–4, 208, 216, 228
Gaselee, Sir Stephen, 156
Geheeb, Edith (née Cassirer), 44
Geheeb, Paul, 5, 44–5
Gemeinschaft, 57–8
General Consultation on an Improvement of All Things Human (Comenius), 222
General Psychopathology (Jaspers), 53
Gentile, Giovanni, 21, 67, 133, 135
George, Stefan, 5–6, 22, 59, 79–86, 108
Gérard of Abbeville, 175
Gide, André, 69, 71, 108
Gilson, Étienne, 21, 67, 108
Giraud, Henri, 138
Gleichschaltung, 102, 105
God Owes Us Nothing (Kołakowski), 205
Goebbels, Joseph, 77, 151
Goering, Hermann, 199
Goethe, Johann Wolfgang von, 5, 45–6, 148
Golden Ass, The (Apuleius), 175
Goldschmidt, Lazarus, 40
Göller, Thomas, 26
Gombrich, Ernst, 64–5
Gomułka, Władysław, 204
Gonseth, Ferdinand, 197
Grese, Irma, 153
Gris, Juan, 43
Groethuysen, Bernard, 21, 117
Groffier, Ethel, xi–xii
Groves, Leslie, 122
Guevara, Ernesto "Che," 207
Gumbel, Emil Julius, 77–8
Gundolf, Friedrich, 5, 21, 26, 76–80, 83, 85–6, 107
Gustav III, King of Sweden, 166

Habermas, Jürgen, 210
Hadamard, Jacques, 125
Hahn, Otto, 122
Halmer, Nikolaus, xi
Hamann, Johann Georg, 17, 90
Harris, Arthur, 155
Hasidism, 202
Havel, Václav, 227
Hegel, Georg Wilhelm Friedrich, 15, 20, 29, 89–90, 96, 180; Neoplatonist influence on, 171
Heidegger, Martin, 6–8, 52, 56, 61, 103–4, 184; Patočka's critique of, 221–2
Hellingrath, Norbert von, 82
Heraclitus, 146
Herder, Johann Gottfried von, 46
Heretical Essays in the Philosophy of History (Patočka), 35, 221

Herrschaft und Dienst (Wolters), 84
Hersch, Jeanne, 8, 56, 209
Herzog August Library, 193
Hildebrandt, Kurt, 84
Hintikka, Jaakko, 204
Historical and Critical Dictionary (Bayle), 188
History of the German Army (Benoist-Méchin), 110
Hitler, Adolf, 26–7, 58, 70, 84–6, 101, 112–13, 120, 131; attitude toward atomic bomb, 127; opposition to, 85, 117–18; relations with Mussolini, 136–7
Hobbes, Thomas, 58
Hoffmann, Ernst, 9–10, 13–15, 17, 37, 67, 91
Hoffmann, Peter, 85
Hofmannsthal, Christiane von, 76
Hölderlin, Friedrich, 5, 38, 46, 50, 82
Horkheimer, Max, 210
Hübner, Walter, 117
Huch, Ricarda, 73
Huddleston, (Ernest Urban) Trevor, 68
Huguenots, 187
Huizinga, Johann, 21
Humboldt, William von, 29, 47–8, 56, 103
Hume, David, 32, 164–8
Hungarian Academy of Sciences, 190, 211
Hunt, Richard William, 28, 134, 139
Husserl, Edmund, 7, 117, 219–21
Hyppolite, Jean, 207

Idées sans frontières (Klibansky), 32
IG Farben, 154
Imamichi, Tomonobu, 203
Imperial Iranian Academy of Philosophy, 199
In Search of Lost Time (Proust), 69
Individual and the Cosmos in Renaissance Philosophy, The (Cassirer), 9–10, 19, 88
Ingarden, Roman, 199
Institut d'études médiévales, 28–9, 157
Institute for Social Research, 210
International Congress of Philosophy. *See* World Congress of Philosophy
International Dictionary of Philosophy, 213–14
International Institute of Philosophy, 4, 32–3, 181, 195–215
Introduction to the Philosophy of History (Hegel), 180
Introduction to the Sociology of Music (Adorno), 210
Is Germany Finished? (Viénot), 71
Ismert, François, xi–xii
Iwasaki, Chikatsugu, 202
Izutsu, Toshihiko, 202–3

Jaffé, Edgar, 73
Jakobson, Roman, 67
Janicaud, Dominique, 198
Jansen, Cornelius, 205
Jaspers, Karl, 6–8, 17, 50, 52–4, 56–7, 104, 117
Jayachamarajendra Wadiyar, Maharaja of Mysore, 199
Jeunes Filles, Les (Montherlant), 115
Jolivet, Jean, 29
Journal of the Warburg Institute, 107
Juan de Segovia, 191–2

Kabir, Humayun, 199
Kaiser Wilhelm Institute, 119
Kemal, Yaşar, 206
Kant, Immanuel, 54, 61, 89–90, 148–9, 165
Kantorowicz, Ernst, 83–4
Kessler, Harry, 58, 108
Khosrow I, King of Persia, 200
Kierkegaard, Søren, 8, 54, 149
Kleist, Heinrich von, 46
Klibansky, Erich, 116
Klibansky, Hermann, 5, 39, 106–7
Klibansky, Pinkus, 42
Klossowska, Baladine, 108
Klossowski, Balthus, 108
Klossowski, Pierre, 108
Kojève, Alexandre, 109
Kołakowski, Leszek, 33, 161–2, 204–5

Kommerell, Max, 84–5
"Königinhofer-Codex," 219
Konstantinov, Fyodor, 212
Kosik, Karel, 218
Kotarbiński, Tadeusz, 198–9, 207
Koyré, Alexandre, 108–9, 184, 207–8
Kramers, H.A., 129
Kreuger, Ivar, 78
Krońska, Irena, 189–90
Kultur, 70

Labowsky, Lotte, 5, 28, 61, 75
Labrousse, Élisabeth, 188
Lacretelle, Jacques de, 115
Lacroix, Benoît, 31, 176
Landerziehungsheime (school movement), 44
Landmann, Edith, 83–5
Language of the Pentateuch, The (Yahuda), 124
Laurencin, Marie, 43
"Law for the Restoration of the Professional Civil Service," 105
Lawrence, Frieda (von Richthofen), 73
Lebenswelt, 220–1
Lechter, Melchior, 85
Le Doeuff, Michèle, xi
Leibniz, Gottfried Wilhelm, 20, 66–7, 180
Lenard, Philipp, 100–1, 125, 128
Leopardi, Giacomo, 149
Lepsius, Sabine, 83
Lessing, Gotthold Ephraim, 46, 192–3
Letter Concerning Toleration, A (Locke), 32, 181, 184–7, 191
Levi-Civita, Tullio, 125
Levinas, Emmanuel, 34, 40, 228
Lévi-Strauss, Claude, 206
Lévy-Bruhl, Lucien, 67
Liber de intellectu (Bovelles), 174
Liber de sapiente (Bovelles), 10, 13, 88
Litt, Theodore, 67, 117
Llull, Ramon, 30
Locke, John, 4, 32, 180–1, 184–91
Löwith, Karl, 104, 208
Lukacs, Georg, 211
Luther, Martin, 65, 148, 179

Macrobius, 91
Magnes, Judah Leon, 125
Mailloux, Noël, 161
Maimonides, 16, 97–8, 229
Main Currents of Marxism (Kołakowski), 205
Mallarmé, Stéphane, 82
Manardo, Giovanni, 145
Mann, Golo, 74
Mann, Thomas, 5, 44, 70, 210
Mannheim, Karl, 21, 71
Mantle of Caesar, The (Gundolf), 76
Marcel, Gabriel, 207
Marcus, Ruth Barcan, 210
Marcuse, Herbert, 160
Margarita Philosophica (Reisch), 25
Margerie, Jenny de, 114–15
Margerie, Roland de, 114
Marrou, Henri-Irénée, 161
Marvell, Andrew, 185
Marx, Karl, 58
Marxism, 197–8, 205
Masaryk, Thomas, 219–20
Mashhad, 200
Maugeri, Franco, 136
Maximin, 83
Mayer, Gertrud, 8
Méchoulan, Éric, xii
Medieval and Renaissance Studies (journal), 28, 139
Mehmed the Conqueror, 190, 192
Meiner, Felix, 13, 15
Mein Leben mit Ernst Cassirer (T. Cassirer), 61
Meitner, Lise, 122
melancholy, 23–6, 37–8, 141–50, 230–2
Melanchthon, Philip, 65
Melencolia I (Dürer), 18–19, 25–6, 62, 141, 230
Meno (Plato), 28, 92, 172–3
Merleau-Ponty, Maurice, 207

Merrill, Stuart, 82
Metaphysical Horror (Kołakowski), 205
Metaphysics (Aristotle), 202
Michelstaedter, Carlo, 150
Milton, John, 185–6
Mirabeau, Honoré Gabriel Riqueti, Conte de, 181
Moerbeke, William of, 14
Montgomery, Bernard, 126, 151
Montherlant, Henry de, 115
Morwitz, Ernst, 84
Moses ben Kalonymos, 86
Mossner, Ernest, 165
Murray, Gilbert, 75
Mürren (Switzerland), 78–9
Mussolini, Benito, 112–13, 136–7
Myth of the Twentieth Century, The (Rosenberg), 16

Nabokov, Nicolas, 151–2
Nagy, Imre, 211
Naipaul, V.S., 206
Nathan the Wise (Lessing), 192–3
Nazism, 84–6, 108–9, 112–13, 129
negative thinking, 9, 15, 35, 88, 93
Nehru, Jawaharlal, 45
Neo-Kantianism, 8, 11, 14, 20, 52, 90
Neoplatonism, 9, 15, 19, 21, 24–5, 75, 90–3, 150, 169–77
Nestroy, Johann, 149
Newton, Sir Isaac, 174
Nicholas V, Pope, 191
Nietzsche, Friedrich, 8, 95, 136
Nonino, Giannola, 206; Nonino Prize, 205–6
Norton, David, 167–8
Novum Organum (Bacon), 29

O'Connor, R. Eric, 158
Odenwald School, 5, 44–9, 56, 60, 108, 118
Oduber Quirós, Daniel, 158–60
Ohe, Seizo, 202–3
Oizerman, Teodor, 216
Oliphant, Mark, 122
On the Peace of Faith. See *De pace fidei*
Opera omnia (Cusanus), 9, 12, 14
Operation Barbarossa, 137
Operation Husky, 135
Operation Sea Lion, 126–7
Orientierung, 8
Ortega y Gasset, José, 67
Osler Library of the History of Medicine, 31, 37, 164
Otto II, Emperor, 86
Oxford Book of Medieval Latin Verse (Gaselee), 156

Pahlavi, Farah, Empress of Iran, 200
Paine, Thomas, 181
Palazzo Schifanoia, 64
Panaetius, 75
Panikkar, Raimon, 201
Panofsky, Erwin, 18, 21–2, 25, 62, 140–2
Panorthosia (Comenius), 222–3
Paradis, Michel, xii, 188
Park, Désirée, xi
Parmenides (Plato), 14, 28, 170
Patočka, Jan, 4, 32, 35–6, 201, 216–23, 227
Paton, H.J., 21
Pausanias, 51
Pears, David, 33, 198
Peenemünde Raid, 121
Pelzer, Auguste, 86
Perelman, Chaim, 209, 216
Peter the Venerable, 30
Petrarch, 11, 144, 175
Petzäll, Åke, 196
Phaedo (Plato), 92, 172
Phaedrus (Plato), 92, 103, 143
Philo, 229
"Philosophical Character of History, The," 163
Philosophical Commentary on These Words of the Gospel, Luke 14:23, A (Bayle), 188
Philosophie de la religion (Duméry), 209

Philosophie en Europe, La (Klibansky and Pears), 33, 198
Philosophy (Jaspers), 53
Philosophy and History (ed. Klibansky), 67, 163
Philosophy and World Community series, 33, 181, 189–90, 217
Philosophy in the Mid-Century (ed. Klibansky), 197, 199, 202
Philosophy of Modern Music (Adorno), 210
Physics (Aristotle), 29
Picasso, Pablo, 43
Pico della Mirandola, Giovanni, 12, 145, 192, 227
Piłsudski, Józef, 199
Pindar, 44
Pirenne, Henri, 107
Pirenne, Jacques, 107
Plato, 15, 23–5, 31, 92, 142–3, 169–70, 177, 204, 230
"Platonism and the Middle Ages," 13
Plotinus, 4, 29, 92, 200
Plutarch, 60
Poincaré, Raymond, 41
Polish Spring, 198
Political Warfare Executive, 27–8, 115
Pope Eugene, 75
Popper, Karl, 216
Popple, William, 184–5
Pos, Henrik, 67
Prince de Conti, 165–6
Principle of Hope, The (Bloch), 212
Problema XXX.1 (Pseudo-Aristotle), 22–4, 142–3
Proclus, 14–15, 17, 28, 88, 90–2, 170
propaganda, 130–3
Proust, Marcel, 69
Pseudo-Aristotle, 22–3
Psychologie der Weltanschauungen (Jaspers), 53
Puech, Henri-Charles, 109
Pugwash Conferences, 123

Qu'est-ce que la phénoménologie? (Patočka), 218–19
Quine, Willard Van Orman, 204

Raabe, Paul, 193
Radbruch, Gustav, 71
Radhakrishnan, Sarvepalli, 199
Raid on Lorient, 166–7
Rare Books and Special Collections Department (McLennan Library, McGill University), 166
Rathenau, Walther, 100
rationality, 224–9
Raymond Klibansky and the Warburg Library Network (Despoix and Tomm), xii
Recherches philosophiques (journal), 184
Reflections of a Nonpolitical Man (Mann), 70
Reflections on History (Burckhardt), 101
Regenbogen, Otto, 43
Reinhardt, Karl, 117
Reisch, Gregor, 25
Rhodes, Richard, 122
Richthofen, Else von, 73
Richthofen, Manfred von, 73
Rickert, Heinrich, 6, 14, 52, 102–3
Ricoeur, Paul, xi, 33, 204
Rilke, Rainer Maria, 62, 108, 115
Robin, Léon, 195
Rochefoucauld, Edmée de la, 115
Röhm, Ernst, 133
Rolland, Romain, 70
Romanticism, 22, 37, 50, 58, 76, 108
Rommel, Erwin, 136
Rorty, Richard, 224
Rosenberg, Alfred, 16, 97
Rosenzweig, Franz, 202, 229
Rousseau, Henri, 43
Rousseau, Jean-Jacques, 165–6
Rufus of Ephesus, 143
Rust, Bernhard, 127
Rutherford, Ernest, 113

Sainte-Beuve, Charles-Augustin, 165–6
Saint-Paul, Albert, 82
Santacroce, Girolamo da, 24
Santa Sabina, 104
Saturn, representations of, 19, 24–6, 140, 144–5
Saturn and Melancholy (Klibansky and Panofsky), xii, 18–19, 22–4, 62, 139–41
Saxe-Meiningen, duchy of, 44
Saxl, Fritz, 18, 21–2, 25, 27, 62–3, 107, 140–1
Schelling, Friedrich Wilhelm Joseph von, 38
Schiller, Friedrich, 45–6
Schlegel, Friedrich, 76–7
Schnabel, Arthur, 61
Scholem, Gershom, 202
"Science as a Vocation," 54
Searle, John, 210
Second Battle of El Alamein, 133
Seeberg, Erich, 16
Segonds, Alain-Philippe, xii
Seminaren, 51
Semi-Pelagianism, 205
Senghor, Léopold, 206
Shakespeare und der deutsche Geist (Gundolf), 76
Simmons, John Simon Gabriel, 126–7
Simon, Francis, 119–20, 128
Society for the Protection of Science and Learning. *See* Academic Assistance Council
Socinianism, 189
Soldatensender Calais (radio program), 133
Solf, Sabine, 193
solidarity, 35, 221–2
Solmitz, Walter, 5, 21, 46, 74
Sorrows of Young Werther, The (Goethe), 148
Soul and Form (Lukacs), 211
Sources of the Self (Taylor), 228
Southwest German school of Neo-Kantianism, 52
Speer, Albert, 127
Spengler, Oswald, 7, 55
Spinoza, Baruch, 50, 181
Spirit of Utopia, The (Bloch), 212
Spranger, Eduard, 103
Stalingrad, Battle of, 120
Star of the Covenant, The (George), 79
Stauffenberg, Claus von, 85
St Clair, James, 167
Steele, Richard, 148
Steel Helmets, 102
Stefan George und die Blätter für die Kunst (Wolters), 84
Strassman, Fritz, 122
Summa Theologica (Aquinas), 183
Świadomość *religijna i więź kościelna* (Kołakowski), 205
Symposium (Plato), 23
Szilard, Leo, 118–19, 122–3, 125

Tagore, Rabindranath, 44
Tantzen, Theodor, 56
Tatarkiewicz, Władysław, 199
Taylor, Charles, 4, 223, 228
Teller, Edward, 123
Theodorakopoulos, Ioannis, 50, 207–8
Theophrastus, 142–3
Theory of the Novel, The (Lukacs), 211
Théry, Gabriel, 30
Thierry of Chartres, 16–17, 29, 91
Thomas More Institute, 158
thought, weak, 203
Timaeus (Plato), 4, 17, 29, 31, 37, 173–7
tolerance, 182–94, 227–8
Tomm, Jillian, xii
Tönnies, Ferdinand, 5, 57–9
Tougas, Anne-Marie, 30
Tradition antique et tolérance modern (Klibansky), xii
"Transcending of Time in History, The" (Gentile), 133
"trésor de Kandahar, Le" (Klibansky), 34
Trouillard, Jean, 92
Truman, Harry, 123
Türkenbriefe, 190

Uhde, Wilhelm, 43, 108, 151
Universal Declaration of Human Rights, 214
Université de Montréal, 157–8, 161
Usener, Hermann, 42
Üxküll-Gyllenband, Woldemar Graf, 84

van der Weyden, Rogier, 93
Various Thoughts on the Occasion of a Comet (Bayle), 188
Vattimo, Gianni, 203
Verlaine, Paul, 82, 149
Verwey, Albert, 81
Vesco, Robert Lee, 160
Viénot, Pierre, 71
Vignaux, Paul, 161
Villiers de l'Isle-Adam, Auguste, 82
Vilna Gaon, the, 39
Voltaire, 180
von Braun, Werner, 128
Vorlesungen, 51

Wahl, Jean, 204, 206–7
Wahrhaftigkeit, 231–2
Waldberg, Baron von, 77
Walpole, Horace, 166
Wannsee Conference, 116
Warburg, Aby, 14, 17–19, 23, 62–6, 140
Warburg, Max, 107
Warburg Institute, 107, 114
Weber, Alfred, 70
Weber, Marianne, 6, 69–71, 152, 155, 211
Weber, Max, 6, 50, 54–5, 59, 70–1, 211
Wedekind, Franz, 44
Weigel, Valentin, 89
Weimar Republic, 21–2, 26, 58, 101–2
Werner, Heisenberg, 127–9
Wertphilosophie, 52
White Rose, 116–17
Wickersdorf School, 44
Wiehl, Reiner, 198
Wigner, Eugene, 123
Wilamowitz-Moellendorf, Ulrich von, 43, 59–60
Wildhagen, Kurt, 50
William of Conches, 174
Williams, Roger, 185
Willim, Petra, xii
Wind, Edgar, 21, 66, 107
Windelband, Wilhelm, 52
Wittkower, Rudolph, 107
Woburn Abbey, 115
Wolff, Emil, 153
Wolfskehl, Karl, 5, 26, 79, 86–7
Wolfson College, 168
Wolters, Friedrich, 84
Woodward, Sir Llewellyn, 156
World Congress of Philosophy, 160, 189, 195, 197, 199, 205, 210, 215–17
Wright, Georg Henrik von, 209
Wyneken, Gustav, 44

Yahuda, A.S., 123–4
Yawning Heights (Zinoviev), 200
Yça Gidelli, 191
Year of the Soul, The (George), 79

Zimmer, Heinrich, 75
Zinoviev, Alexander, 200
Zivilisation, 70